# Ocean Cruising Countdown

# OCEAN
# CRUISING
## COUNTDOWN

A practical guide to long term cruising –
turning the dream into reality

GEOFF PACK

**David & Charles**
Newton Abbot London
North Pomfret (Vt)

# Dedication

*For Lou Lou*

whose trust and willingness has always
been an inspiration to me

Illustrations by Mike Collins

**British Library Cataloguing in Publication Data**

Pack, Geoff
  Ocean cruising countdown: long term
  cruising —— turning the dream into
  reality: a practical guide.
  1. Sailing
  I. Title
  797.1′24          GV811

  ISBN 0–7153–8992–0

Phototypeset by ABM Typographics Ltd, Hull
Printed in Great Britain by
Butler & Tanner, Frome
for David & Charles Publishers plc
Brunel House   Newton Abbot   Devon

Published in the United States of America
by David & Charles Inc
North Pomfret  Vermont 05053  USA

# Contents

# Sailing to Freedom – An Introduction

Like all aspects of yachting in the last 30 years, ocean cruising has seen enormous changes. Not only have boats been revolutionised with the introduction of materials like glassfibre, aluminium and polyester, but enormous social changes during this period have meant that far more people are able to go ocean cruising, and they are different types of people these days too. In the 1950s there were a small number of adventurers who sailed their largely unwieldy craft across the empty wastes of the world's oceans, bumping into each other from time to time in port, but on the whole sailing into anchorages empty but for the local working craft. On the islands they visited these yachtsmen were instant celebrities, bathed in garlands, introduced to all the local dignatories, showered with gifts and never allowed to eat aboard their own boats.

These pioneers of ocean cruising fell into a number of groups. There were the genuine adventurers and blue water vagabonds like Bernard Moitessier, Paul Johnson and Henry Wakelam whose little boats and lifestyles were kept afloat by a combination of zest, enthusiasm and hard work ashore, whenever they could find it, to replenish the kitty. Next came the writers, yachtsmen like Anne and Peter Pye, Edward Allcard and Susan and Eric Hiscock, who supported their travels by magazine articles, lecture tours and books, because in those days crossing the Atlantic in a small yacht was sufficient to justify a book. Eric and Susan Hiscock's professionalism in both the voyaging itself and their subsequent writings and presentations earned them the deep (and continuing) respect of the yachting world and what is more, dispelled much of the 'sea-gypsy' image that ocean voyagers had. If anyone deserves the title of 'Father of Ocean Cruising', it is Eric Hiscock.

The last group in those early days were the yachtsmen and families who with modest incomes or service pensions, were able to cruise without the need for working. They realised that one of the joys of cruising, approached in the right way, is that it costs very little and although they may not have been able to live on their incomes ashore, once afloat their needs were small.

All these groups still exist, but today there are a thousand times more yachts and people doing it because social attitudes and economic circumstances have changed.

Early retirement is much more common, and also many in their mid-forties are finding themselves unemployed, with a redundancy payment in their pocket sufficient to buy a yacht. Unemployment, or the prospect of it, means that the younger generation too are going cruising, either as crew hopping from boat to boat, or buying a basic little craft, to put off the time they have to start looking for a job and laying down the roots of a career after college or university. For those still working, sabbatical leave is easier to arrange now, particularly in strongly unionised jobs where an employer is unable to cut back on staffing. A year's unpaid leave cuts down the company's overheads, but allows the employee to make an ocean cruise like the Atlantic Circuit and be assured his old job when he returns. The outdated concept of yachting as the domain of only the reasonably wealthy is quickly dispelled by seeing the varied collection of yacht crews in one of the 'crossroad' ports such as Gibraltar, Antigua, Papeete or Durban.

In the old days, the sort of yachts thought best for long–distance cruising were heavy for their size, and the major criterion was massive gear and construction. This was for good reason, because the materials used were not particularly durable. Sails blew out, ropes parted, wooden hulls could be strained and portholes smashed in heavy going. In an odd way, their heavy displacement worked against them because not only did that sheer weight require so much more strength to support it, but the inevitable slow passages tired crews and sapped moral which in turn could lead to mistakes and accidents. A brief encounter with a reef in an old wooden boat can often result in her loss, whereas a lighter fibreglass boat, or even better steel, stands a chance of bouncing off damaged but intact. Looking through an anchorage in a distant port you'll still see the occasional Colin Archer types, crewed by men influenced by those ocean cruising pioneers like Erling Tambs (whose dog, by the way, he named Spare Provisions!), but you will see many more standard production craft which sail very well over long distances and have been adapted by their owners for sailing long distances and living aboard.

Another major contributor to ocean cruising has been the revolution in gear and equipment. Not only have modern materials made equipment durable, reliable and largely free of decay but the advent of self-steering, reliable auxiliary motors, sophisticated radio communications and micro-chip navigation aids such as SatNav, have made the yachtsman's lot one hundred per cent safer and easier.

What is more, as the numbers of people ocean cruising increases, no longer do you have to regard yourself as a Slocum or Chichester to cross an ocean. Most of us involved in pleasure boating know of *someone* from the yacht club or moored in the same stretch of river who's planning to head off. The undertaking of a major ocean voyage should never, under any circumstances, be underestimated but it is nevertheless considerably easier these days in a reasonably modern boat than it was thirty years ago in a homely, if bulletproof, Colin Archer.

Because so much has changed in the last ten years a new book such as this was required to give those embarking on an ocean voyage guidance on choosing the best of what is new and leaving behind some of the modern marine products that are unnecessary. Even more importantly, it deals with the human element.

Many projects never get afloat and in nine cases out of ten it is for a human reason. It may be inability to get away from a business or job, the inevitable reticence to throw to the wind a home, belongings and status that has taken years to achieve, or perhaps a lack of confidence in the abilities to cope on a limited income, live in a tiny space or deal with the sort of emergencies that crop up on a yacht at sea. So this book is not only about looking at boats and equipment, but also about examining your own suitability before you take the big step.

Of those who actually get under way, there are unfortunately a large proportion who within a year give it all up and return to civilization. Examining these cases, it is very rare that the boat is the cause of the problem. Oddly enough it is often the immaculately kept and painstakingly prepared boats that are heading home. Invariably the reason boils down to the human element. Plain fear of sailing, boredom, and the inability to adapt and be flexible accounts for many. Crew friction is another big factor, and many couples married for a long time in a normal working society find it difficult to get on with each other in a small boat for twenty-four hours of every day.

The right attitude to cruising, being able to adapt and having a broad idea of what to expect without expecting too much (other than those palm-fringed lagoons you read about in yachting magazines) also strongly influence your choice of boat and how she is equipped. I believe that here are three broad aspects to successful ocean cruising – the right attitude, the right boat (these two are strongly inter-related) and the right preparation. With these three, the world is your oyster and I hope *Ocean Cruising Countdown* will clarify for you whether or not you feel you are 'cut out' for an ocean cruising lifestyle, and if you are, set you on the road for what can be a superb way of life.

# Part One
# THE HUMAN ELEMENT

# 1
# Fresh Outlooks

To cast aside the shackles of a conventional working existence and replace them with freedom, time and a yacht to visit faraway places is the passionate dream of many. What makes it so pleasant is that it is an attainable goal for most people with good health, an adventurous spirit and the ability to make sacrifices and changes. Visit a port like Falmouth, Cornwall in mid-summer and amongst the normal yachts you'll see craft with the familiar hallmarks of windvane gears, baggy-wrinkle in the rigging and a boot-top line long since lost under the water. All are heading for faraway places, their crews with a blue water glint in their eyes.

However, for every craft that gets away there are probably fifty which don't make it. Of those that do get away about half will give up, sell their boats where they are, or sail them home to put them on the market. In order to understand what makes for successful ocean cruising we must first look at why others have failed in fulfilling what seems at the outset to be the purest form of hedonism. It may seem cynical, but among those ex-patriates who live in the West Indies is an expression 'another rotten day in paradise' (I've substituted rotten for the vernacular!).

Too many prospective ocean cruising people throw themselves into the project concentrating wholly on the suitability and preparation of their yacht. They don't consider long enough whether they personally are either suitable or prepared for the enormous changes in their life. The first section of the book examines some of the more common worries, difficulties to be overcome, and changes in attitude to contend with. In most cases there are no easy remedies offered because we are all different and must come to terms with the problems in our own way.

## The Psychological Break

It is said about ocean cruising that when it's good, it's really good, when bad it's awful. For the majority of us living in a conventional way in western society, the margins of both our enjoyment and unhappiness are drawn for us. Barring genuine disasters, there is invariably a buffer of some sort to stop us getting really low, whether it's the support of a family, a doctor to ease our pains, a mechanic to repair our car or supplementary benefit to keep the wolf from the door. Alternatively, neither does 'the rat race' offer very much in the way of pure joy, supreme challenge and fantastic excitement or experience. There are exceptions of course, events like childbirth, marriage, professional achievement, running a marathon and so on, but on the whole life is a lot of gradual uphill cycling before a brief steep hill to freewheel down.

In going ocean cruising you are widening those margins of joy and misery by leaving behind the sheltered existence most of us experience. When you've got a toothache 1,000 miles from land, need to repair the engine starter motor when anchored at a deserted atoll, or come into contact with a corrupt police force, you very quickly realise that it's easy to take for granted the advantages of boring everyday life in a democratic society. When you're thousands of miles from home you'll have no one to turn to but yourself to solve difficulties. You will need to be adaptable, resourceful and a jack of all trades.

As age sets us in our ways it also makes learning new skills harder. So one must strive to remain flexible and acknowledge the self-sufficiency concept wholly. Before you set sail and during your cruise you may have to learn skills that passed you by in normal society and they may be the ability to recognise the symptoms of the more common diseases and first aid, the capability to complete a sound fibreglass repair below the waterline, or diplomacy in dealing carefully with a bureaucratic port official. Acquiring such knowledge may be straightforward, but you have to ask yourself if you have the inclination to adapt and learn much that may be new to you.

Self-sufficiency at sea cannot be over-emphasised and although it doesn't matter if many of the conveniences carried aboard yachts today break down, their breakdown can start a chain reaction that puts the yacht and her crew into danger.

An obvious example is the failure of the electrics, a common enough occurance not usually serious. A few years ago, my wife Lou Lou and I, employing five other crew, took on the delivery of a 40-ton luxury ketch from the West Indies to Bermuda. She was a complicated vessel, as is necessary when designers try to incorporate all the comforts and conveniences of domestic life aboard a yacht. She had no generator and relied on the engine to charge the batteries and keep the fridges and freezers cold. Seven crew consume a lot of food and as her galley was designed to be used in harbour and not at sea, much of the provisioning took the form of frozen convenience foods which could be prepared in the microwave.

Half way through the delivery the engine went badly wrong and with it in pieces, requiring spares we didn't have aboard, we lost our ability to charge the batteries. We had no navigation lights, no log, no compass light to steer by at night, no RDF, and no VHF to seek help with. We couldn't even get water out of the tanks except by scooping it in cups from the inspection hatches. Being in the tropics, the freezer's contents very quickly went bad, instantly putting us on to basic rations because it was flat calm and we had no idea how long we might be out there. It was May, when the sun's declination was very close to our latitude, therefore right overhead at noon making a latitude fix questionable, and giving pretty nearly north/south position lines any other times during the day. As my course was northwards towards Bermuda, with its dangerous outlying reefs, I needed my latitude urgently (there were no sight reduction tables for star sights aboard) and without the log I could not judge dead reckoning with any accuracy. What had one day been a very comfortable if not luxurious cruise on a £¼m yacht turned overnight into a nightmare. We completed the trip successfully, and subsequently sailed on to the USA, but I took more risks than I care to think about. Other than the fact the boat was unsuitable, despite her size, for long offshore passages, I was to blame for relying too heavily on her services and not considering the implications of a minor problem (the lack of a spare head gasket and torque wrench) causing a chain of events that left us ill-nourished with attendant low morale, and with little more than a vague idea of our position when making a difficult landfall.

A similar situation could arise on a modern cruising boat, if for instance a fan belt had broken and you discovered that you had every description of belt aboard but the appropriate one. Or perhaps a deck leak had put out the alternator. Unless you have some other form of charging (solar panel, windmill or shaft alternator) you only ever discover the problem when the batteries are low and you come to charge them. By then, you haven't much power left to conserve, and the voltage will quickly dip below the minimum 11½ V required by most SatNavs. It's surprising the number of ocean-bound yachtsmen who fit something like SatNav and never get around to learning astronavigation, or who learned years ago, but have become dangerously rusty since relying on electronics.

Today we rely on micro-processor technology heavily and on the whole its reliability is excellent. Even if something goes wrong, a technician can easily identify the Printed Circuit Board (PCB) giving the problem and swap it for a good one. The salesman will tell you the reliability of such marine products is exemplary, but always remember that he won't be there to argue with in the middle of the Pacific and neither will the technician.

It would be naive and against the purpose of this book to say that modern electrical equipment is unsuitable on ocean cruising boats. Some is good and some is superfluous, but never be totally reliant on it. Always regard gadgets as an aid and be sure you can operate quite normally, if inconveniently, without them. In this way, never install a Weatherfax if you don't know basic meteorology. Even simple electrical equipment like a speed/distance instrument must be backed up by a mechanical trailing log. I doubt you'll ever find an experienced deep water yachtsman who wholly relied offshore on *anything* that required electricity.

### Doing Without Consumer Society

In the past 25 years consumerism has become a dominant aspect of our modern society and economy. The 'throwaway' concept which it embraces started in ball-point pens and has spread widely, from cars with in-built obsolescence and even buildings constructed cheaply in

Consumerism pervades boat shows but when you're trying to find spares or maintain that glistening exterior in a jungle rain forest anchorage, Earls Court seems a long way away    *(Yachting Monthly)*

the certain knowledge that they only need to last 20 years before being pulled down and replaced. This is fine to live with so long as the consumer is able to buy the next ball-point pen, or replace a piece of equipment now worn-out or superseded by something better, but in the majority of places that ocean cruising yachts go, very often the most basic spares and supplies are difficult to get hold of. Therefore the consumer attitude that is easy to adopt when living in England, Europe or America, doesn't work well when cruising because you simply can't go out and buy a part or replacement and in any event you probably won't have sufficient income to support a consumer lifestyle.

A by-product of consumerism is the whittling-down of standards and quality. The wheels of modern industry rely on frequent replacement. You are leaving this contemporary thinking behind. Your yacht and all her equipment must be reliable and durable. If it starts to wear out, break down or cause problems it will be difficult and often impossible to rectify in a distant port and will undermine your confidence in the vessel at sea in rough conditions when every component is being pushed to the limit.

## Quality, not Quantity

It is a false economy to fit out with anything less than high quality equipment for a long distance cruise. The item designed for occasional weekend use will probably let you down after constant use. The cost of having spares or a replacement sent out to you (not to mention the hassle, time, telexes, telephone calls and customs hold-ups of having it shipped) by far outweigh the extra cost of good quality from the outset. Most ocean cruising projects are working to a strict budget and advice about buying the best can be irritating but I cannot over-emphasise that in the long run your money is far better spent on a limited number of products of known quality than on a wide range of cheaper goodies. Good examples are sails where you'll get better service out of a high quality working suit than a full wardrobe bought for a 'special deal', or electronics where it can be tempting to buy a complete set of economy wind instruments for the price of one really decent speedlog.

This philosophy also goes for the boat itself. The Far East has long manufactured products of a much lower price than Western countries and is now building yachts. Places like Taiwan have produced some fabulous craft, but a fair proportion are constructed of poor quality materials (despite outwardly attractive local teak finish) and they are built by people who have never been aboard a yacht at sea in their lives. The same caution is necessary with amateur-built yachts, especially after the rash of big boats spawning in back gardens during

The ocean cruiser must at times put up with terrible punishment like pounding to windward for days or even weeks on end; at times like this the quality of her equipment will seem worth paying for    *(Geoff Pack)*

the '70s when ferrocement construction seemed the ideal way to obtain a lot of boat at low cost. It can be a difficult decision when you are confronted with the spaciousness of a cheaply-built 44-footer for a similar price to a named quality 38-footer. Needless to say, look very carefully and if you're in the least uncertain, get in a surveyor. However, don't immediately write-off a yacht with an 'amateur' tag attached to it for some home builders have high standards and it will almost certainly have much more love, care and attention in it.

Most yachts sit in marinas or at moorings unused for nine out of ten days of the year. They are the equivalent of a saloon car parked in the garage with a low mileage accumulated on short trips around town. But your ocean cruiser will be your yacht, your home, your car and the tool of your trade. Like a workman's tools, it will be used every day. It won't be sailing every day, but long and often arduous ocean passages will be interspersed with time in port when the pumps for fresh water, shower or heads are used all the time, when the dinghy is a workhorse carrying crew, water containers and provisions around, the varnish is forever being walked over, door latches used, light fittings switched on and off, hatches open and closed and so on. To withstand that constant use without giving trouble, quality and not quantity must be the watchword throughout.

Consumerism and its disregard for quality has little place aboard the ocean cruiser for other reasons too. Consumerism relies on turnover being generated by high consumption which in turn requires money as its lifeblood, and most cruising yachtsmen of necessity must be fairly thrifty. The consumer tinkering with his car on a Sunday afternoon might use half a roll of paper kitchen towel to wipe up grease. Tissues and paper towel are forever useful on a long distance cruiser, but the wily ocean going yachtsman would probably use rags (washed out afterwards) for his engine cleaning and a tiny amount of paper towel for other jobs because he knows it is precious. He won't be near a shop selling it for a few months yet and such luxuries in poor island communities are three or four times as expensive as in a high street shop at home.

Another by-product of modern consumerism is a lack of pride of ownership. Because so many items are here today, gone tomorrow, you don't develop any attachment to them. The average family car, in the 1950s was loved, given a name, cherished, and polished every week. Nowadays there are so many cars, they depreciate so quickly and we are encouraged to change them regularly, so they are regarded only as a utility. The ocean cruising yachtsman must rely heavily on nearly all the equipment he has and in some cases his life may depend on it. There should be little on board that is superfluous and what gear he chooses to take with him he soon gets to know quite well, whether it is the trailing log he dismantles on a quiet morning watch to lubricate, the sail he has put countless stitches in, the echo sounder whose every rogue flicker is familiar as it alerts him passing over many a reef, or the steady thrum of the diesel he knows and trusts.

Everyday life has changed so much that most normal households have many 'conveniences' – the paraphenalia of modern living from washing machines and tumble dryers to TV sets and videos. When you go sailing, pretty much all of this must go and whilst you occasionally find a boat fitted out with much of this equipment (as often as not by a husband trying to persuade a reticent wife) very few of them get far because that attitude doesn't normally mix with the simple life of ocean cruising. Alternatively, they find they grow out of wanting those sort of items on board, and the sunset with a glass of West Indian rum in your hand becomes far more attractive than watching the video.

If losing those conveniences seems hard to swallow, remember that many of them came about to save the time spent on household chores and the one thing you will have in abundance is time. Some of the appliances become redundant anyway when you are living aboard in the tropics wearing swimsuits, tee-shirts or pareos (fabric wrap-around dress/skirts) which dry in no time in the warm breezes. At home the ability to cook a baked potato in the microwave in minutes may seem alluring, but it's not half the fun of cooking them with breadfruit thrown in at an impromptu beach barbecue with friends from nearby boats. Having time to spare puts a completely different complexion on things, and it doesn't matter if a cocktail takes a quarter of an hour to make because you haven't got the blender. A car is another thing you think you'll miss sometimes. We've occasionally hired one to do a lot of provisioning or go sight-seeing with friends. For the rest of the time walking keeps you fit and you don't begrudge the time it takes because you have plenty. And as every port you stop is different even a trip ashore to find the post office is a new adventure.

Successful ocean cruising is more than anything else an attitude of mind. You won't miss all those consumer and disposable goods, but you may need time to adjust.

# 2
# *The Awkward Decisions*

If going cruising was easy, many more people would be doing it. There's no turning away from the fact that some very uncomfortable decisions and heartfelt sacrifices need to be made before you can consider yourself ready to sell up and sail away. It is invariably these decisions that are the insurmountable hurdles rather than a boat not quite ready, bank account not quite big enough, or the countless other excuses dreamers come up with to avoid making the break.

## *Insurance*

Unless a rich old aunt has died, most of those going cruising will have worked hard and sacrificed a lot over the years in order to get into the position to own a boat, equip it, and head off. Those that build their boats themselves make a massive investment in time and effort. Others may have bought a boat through long hours in overtime or putting every hour into their own businesses. Wives go back to work when they would really prefer to be at home with children, or perhaps the boat was achieved by renovating your house to improve its market value. Some couples deliberately don't start a family so that their plans and efforts are unimpeded. When the boat finally materialises, the idea of risking those years of sacrifice by sailing away with it uninsured is abhorrent to most people, and yet even the most basic insurance is almost impossible to arrange for long-term shorthanded ocean cruising, and if possible, prohibitively expensive. Are you prepared to take this calculated risk?

Eric and Susan Hiscock never insured in all the years they cruised, and believed that proper precautions, good seamanship and a well maintained yacht make up for all that an insurance broker can offer. There are no two ways about it, cruising without insurance hones one's skills and seamanship, just as being insured can develop a false sense of security. Sailing without it means you don't take risks entering harbours at night, you choose your anchorage very carefully and never fail to be within close reach of a hurricane hole during the hurricane season. The knowledge that a broken mast might easily wipe out your cruising funds means that you don't press the boat as hard as you might have done on weekend thrashes when you were working and the yacht was fully insured. In short, being uninsured is

The ultimate horror of coming back to your uninsured boat and home to find she has dragged ashore; this is the Roth's *Whisper* which was wrecked, although eventually repaired, in Patagonia

the best teacher of good seamanship and may prove paradoxically to be an advantage.

There are compromises which can ease you into the world of being totally uninsured. If you're sailing from Northern Europe, it is usually possible to get insurance cover for the Mediterannean, often out as far as the Canaries, and very occasionally across the Atlantic (although at the time of going to press, an obligatory requirement was three experienced adult crewmembers aboard and this was in the process of being increased to four). If you plan to stay in the Caribbean for any length of time, you can obtain insurance for this, as you can if you intend cruising up the Eastern seaboard of the States. However, if you've crossed over without insurance it will be necessary to get the yacht surveyed again before even your old company will re-insure (they've had to pay out for items broken or lost during the uninsured period). This sort of insurance is not cheap, organising it from far away is not easy and it usually only covers total loss and third party risks.

The problems increase when you venture further afield and head down to Brazil or perhaps the coasts of Venezuela, Columbia and thence into the Pacific. Some people obtain cover, at great expense, for just total loss but by far the majority spend the money buying equipment which they feel substitutes for insurance, like extra anchors, better fire extinguishers, more charts, bigger fenders, or perhaps a SatNav to assist them in the poorly-charted areas of the Pacific where tides and currents are unpredictable.

Six months insurance for an average 35-footer will buy a SatNav, whilst a year's insurance will buy that plus some heavy ground tackle and a good quality windlass to haul it up with. It is a personal decision, but my view is that this equipment will look after you and the boat much better than an insurance policy.

Insurance is one of the protective buffers of modern life that you are losing by going away and which becomes less significant the longer you are away. When you have been cruising for a few years in out of the way places, you quite accept the risk of sailing un-insured in your stride, and yet travelling on a bus seems terribly fast and dangerous and crossing the street you do with great caution.

The other way of looking at the insurance problem is planning from the outset not to put all your eggs in one basket. If the boat is absolutely *everything* you own, and losing it would be a catastrophe, you could buy a smaller boat and invest the rest of your capital in a house, which you could rent out to pay the remaining mortgage fees. Then if disaster struck you would at least have something to go back to. Another alternative, and one becoming increasingly popular, is to have a steel boat. They are not indestructable, but will often survive a fire, are less susceptible to serious damage in a collision and will withstand a moderate stranding that would write-off a vessel built in any other material.

## What About the Children?

It is fine for father and mother to have great ambitions to sail across the oceans and live in different places around the world but it's unreasonable to expect your children's education and future prospects to suffer as a result. Not working and a simple life cruising in the Pacific may be pure heaven for you, but your son or daughter's greatest ambition may be to become an accountant, living in a city, buying a new car every year and having 2.4 children. How much would you jeopardise their future by taking them away from the conventional pattern of education? Anybody with children of dependant age obviously has some heartsearching to do.

Cruising with children can produce some great benefits. Parents we have spoken to say how children give them instant introduction to locals ashore that they'd never normally get to know. They also seem oblivious to bad weather and while mother and father are worried on deck, life carries on as normal down below. Initially, the big plus factor you have in your favour with children is their adaptability. Adults may take time to accept the confines of a boat after a lifetime in houses. Children may moan at first, but soon forget as new challenges and activities absorb them. A dinghy with oars, or better, a sail that they are put in charge of soon helps them to forget the bike they left behind.

When you have children, the influence they have on the choice of a suitable boat is important. It will require a certain amount of customisation, such as handholds low down throughout the boat, and netting around the guardrails. If you are fitting out or modifying a boat with children in mind there are several significant features you can incorporate to make a relatively child proof vessel. Avoid sharp corners wherever possible down below, especially around the companionway area where a child can fall from some height. Make certain that all the instruments, switches and controls are beyond the reach of tiny fingers. Ideally children should have their own cabin, a well-lit and ventilated area that they can set up their toys in, and the installation of a cheap stereo in here will help no end. The cockpit must be well-protected and preferably deep.

Children's safety is a major consideration. The ability for a child to be able to swim is absolutely imperative as no child will put up with the shackles of a permanent lifejacket or harness. As well as an ability to swim, parents must work diligently and patiently to insure that the child is confident in the water and not scared of it – fear of water is something we are taught, it is not instinctive. This confidence could spell the difference between fun and disaster if a child were to fall in whilst playing on deck, in the dinghy or from a quayside.

Most parents agree that infants afloat are the easiest to cope with. A French yacht we met in the Canaries had two children aboard under the age of 18 months, although judging by the number of nappies always drying on the guardrails (they had a huge water capacity, 200 gallons [900 lit] on their 37-footer, and washed nappies in a mixture of half fresh/half salt water) it must have been hard work. Under the age of four months infants are so vulnerable to infections and temperature, it seems an unreasonable risk to live permanently aboard, although breast-fed babies are believed to be more immune to such problems. As soon as babies start to crawl problems increase because then they need constant supervision, which on occasions when both parents are needed on deck, conning through a reef passage, or shortening canvas quickly with the approach of a squall, can be very difficult. Richard and Diane Steele aboard *Gub-Gub* deal with this one by keeping their toddler Joanna in the cockpit on such occasions and she always knows that anywhere outside the cockpit is firmly out of bounds.

The primary years of education are something most cruising parents reckon they can cope with themselves, arguing that two hours or so of individual tuition a day will teach them as much as they would learn all day in a class of thirty at school. The wise ones embrace the rudiments of teaching as part of their preparation before leaving and work to a proper timetable and scheme. However, physically sitting down and doing that teaching when you are cruising requires a great deal of discipline by both parents and children. There are so many more interesting distractions for both and after the first few months the teaching schedule slides into obscurity. Another disadvantage is that you do not have the educational aids and equipment which are an everyday part of modern schools, especially for computer training which starts at a very tender age. On the other hand showing children the world and a different lifestyle is often a reason for wanting to go in the first place and is seen as an educational advantage in itself.

There is no easier way to learn a foreign language than by being in that country and making friends. Geography is more interesting when you have been to the places and seen different rock formations or the special crops of a country growing in the fields. The concensus of opinion among cruising parents is that their children very quickly settle down when they go back to school and rarely if ever have to go into a class lower than that for their age in order to catch up. There are a wide variety of well-established teaching schemes specifically designed for children being taught by parents overseas and the Parents National Education Union and Worldwide Education Service at Strode House, 44-50 Osnaburgh Street, London NW1 3NW is the starting point to find the best for your children and circumstances.

Most parents consider that by the age of 11 or 12 a child must begin formal education, and that signals the end of their wandering life, unless they can send them to boarding school and go off again. Many children have continued cruising into their teens, but it is taking a big risk with examination results that may be badly wanted for university entry or a future career.

Education apart there can be problems in keeping children happily occupied and it is important to see that they meet plenty of others of their age. Decisions about where to go may often be determined by the plans of other yachts with children aboard who will be company. Cruising often dispels shyness in a child because of the need to make new friends all the time, but a single child on a boat among grown-up company all the time can become prematurely adult and withdrawn. In such a case it may be wise to slow up your itinery to allow longer stops in places where your child can attend the local school for a while.

## What About Home?

It may be that the only way of getting enough money together to buy a suitable boat and get going is to sell your house. However keen you may be to rid yourself of material possessions and adopt the more philosophic cruising lifestyle, getting rid of the roof over your head, the very symbol of all you have worked and saved for all these years, is a harsh decision. It may also be very difficult to reverse unless you are sure of having the finance to buy a property if you should wish to stop voyaging in a few years' time.

Leasing your house is preferable if you don't need the capital but being a long distance landlord is not easy. It only requires one flight back from a faraway place to sort out problems to whittle away the rent. The ideal is to pay a trusted and competent friend, neighbour or relative to manage the letting of the house. It is not an exceptionally demanding job but does take away problems that could be very difficult for you to solve from several thousand miles away, so it is a good insurance to pay them well.

Without such a person to manage the property the obvious answer is to go to a property or estate agent. Impersonal attitudes are the root of nearly all house-letting problems – the tenant not having respect for the property or its contents, and in turn the agent not really caring a great deal either, letting it run down then employing anyone to do the maintenance regardless of their standards or prices. If there is any way of renting the house to friends or family even at half the normal rent it might be better. Otherwise try to deal through agents you know and trust.

Unless you have a very small or non-existent mortgage, or have an exceptionally desirable property which can command high rent it is unlikely you'll make much money by letting. Agents' fees, income tax on the rent (payable even if you are ex-patriot status), rates, insurance and essential maintenance will eat up the gross proceeds. At best, the property should at least pay for itself and keep abreast of market values. And it will be there if you decide to return, but do have a watertight tenancy agreement and check up with your lawyer what the legal position is should you wish to re-possess. Some middle-aged couples who were not especially needing the extra income have asked their grown-up offspring to live in the house for them while they were away and they have been only too glad to oblige.

Even if things go smoothly renting your furnished house to strangers with all its sentimental attachments can be difficult. An alternative may be to sell your own house (which if needs be will free some funds for the boat and cruising life) and buy a house or flat in a holiday resort and earn money from short lets. In this way, you avoid any emotions, and have somewhere to come back to, albeit during the off-season, if you make a brief visit home. Again, financially, the gain is not high because you will need an agent to manage it and have to pay cleaner's bills among others. Summer rents are high, but the season may be a short one so compare the probable results with those of a long lease.

The final choice is to sell up and put the money in an offshore investment account. If you do, the hardest thing to resist is drawing on the capital. In fact if you want to maintain parity with property values against your return to dry land living you should plough the annual interest back into the capital.

The single largest influence on what to do with the house is the rate property values are rising annually. This book is written in 1987 and in Britain house prices have been galloping for the last 15 years to an extent that it is difficult to go wrong financially by keeping a property. However, that may change and many wonder when the property bubble will burst. If the property price race slowed down, I would not hesitate advising you to invest the money where you will receive only Statement of Acounts from time to time, rather than urgent telexes informing you the roof has blown off or the windowsills gone rotten.

### Family Ties

Leaving family behind can be the hardest part of going away cruising and comes high on the list of reasons people give backing out of cruising plans. Few people feel easy about or are capable of disappearing over the horizon away from an ageing or ailing parent for instance, but on the other hand it could be very frustrating to be otherwise ready and prepared and then watch the best years of your life slipping by because you feel tied.

The problem can often be eased by frequent contact. Letters every week, telephone calls wherever it's possible and even ham radio (this is dealt with in Chapter 13) allows family to know exactly where you are and what you're up to. Elderly parents who are still active may be pleased to be asked to handle your affairs while you are away provided they're not too taxing (more detailed suggestions for this are dealt with in Chapter 21) which is a practical method of involving them and keeping them in contact. And if they are still fit they may be delighted at the prospect of flying out to join you somewhere for a couple of weeks, perhaps taking accommodation ashore.

Your grown offspring are not often a problem because they will be too busy leading their own lives to worry about you, but you will want to keep up in touch with them. An annual trip back home by plane for a month or two will make a big difference.

Grandchildren are also missed but the solution is easier. Many cruising people pay for them to be sent out during school holidays. This is often a superb experience for all concerned. For the kids, delivered by parents on to the plane and met by grandparents at the other end, it's the experience of a lifetime; grandparents get to see them for a few weeks (children can easily enough sleep in the saloon for the period); and the parents have a couple of weeks 'off', perhaps to have a rare holiday together. The cost of a couple of flight tickets is a small price to pay, all things considered.

# 3
# *Is This the Life for Me?*

## *Removing the Safety Nets*

So far we have dealt with the problems posed by the things you are leaving behind – house, family, modern amenities and so forth. Now it is time to look at what lies head in your new life and ask yourself whether you can cope and if it is really what you want. Are you prepared to abandon the safety nets of civilised society and rely on your own resources?

There are some limited crutches to help you out of awkward situations overseas, but overall you are on your own. The ocean cruising community invariably help each other out. When my wife Lou Lou's hand was crushed by a barge hitting our yacht in Funchal, Madeira, a well-known cruising yachtsman, Dr. Ronnie Andrews put his departure back long enough to not only make sure the hand was alright, but see Lou Lou through her convalescence. We were lucky that there was a qualified medic, but there is invariably someone in an anchorage who'll be able to help out another 'yachtie' who doesn't know much about a particular problem, perhaps a faulty alternator, a VHF that doesn't work or a refrigerator playing up. Payment is rarely expected, but it is a goodwill fund that must be contributed to.

If you run into legal difficulties in a foreign port, it is unlikely you'll find a shore-based lawyer to help you out even assuming there is not an insurmountable language barrier. The fair and impartial justice we take for granted does not extend to all countries and your national consulate can often provide only limited assistance.

My friend Roger Brake took the law into his own hands the morning that a fishing boat put a 4sq ft hole in the side of his trimaran, again in Madeira. It was six o'clock in the morning, and after being so abruptly awoken, Roger had the presence of mind to chase the offending fishing boat in his outboard-powered inflatable, eventually catching up, boarding it and physically forcing them back into harbour. It was only this sort of determination, and the help of the American consulate, that meant he was finally able to make them pay up for the damage, but his is a rare success story.

Another friend had his inflatable dinghy and outboard stolen from the back of the boat as he slept in a West Indian port. He woke up minutes later and saw the thieves, who were only interested in getting the outboard, slashing his dinghy to shreds on the foreshore before disappearing with the outboard. He reported the incident to the police immediately but they took no interest whatsoever. A few days later he was surprised to see his outboard being used on the back of a local fishing dug-out. He knew it was his because he'd only days earlier painted the upper half of the drive casing a distinctive colour. When the dug-out returned that night he discreetly followed the fishermen home, recognising them as the two who'd stolen the outboard and dinghy. Even when he returned to the police station and gave them the thieves' address they took no action. Finally, he was reduced to 'stealing' his outboard back one night before leaving for the next island. This is not untypical.

The popular yachting areas see many yachts come and go, and in many of the third world countries the yacht is worth more than a native will earn in a lifetime so the temptation is great. Also, because of their transient nature, yachts provide ripe pickings for thieves. Even if they're caught the culprits are often released, because skippers do not want to stay long enough to press charges and go through lengthy court procedures. Not all the yachtsmen are angelic either, some leaving without paying bills for example so unfortunately in certain places yachtsmen are not as welcome as they were a few years ago.

The only answer is to avoid trouble at all costs, locking your dinghy when you are ashore and taking a lot of trouble to make the boat as

When seriously damaged by a poorly-handled fishing boat in Madeira despite it clearly not being his fault, American Roger Brake had no help but his own initiative to sort the problem out financially and physically   *(Geoff Pack)*

anti-thief proof as possible, so it at least deters the more amateur criminals (suggestions for doing this are in Chapter 19 of the book). The reverse of the coin is to make sure you sail with a 'clean wake', pay your dues, don't leave rubbish on the quaysides, and don't throw your weight around ashore. If there are any local projects going on that you can help with, such as being spectator boat for a swimming race, or loaning a rope for a tug-of-war, bend over backwards to oblige. In this way the ocean cruising fraternity will enhance their reputation.

### Realistic Expectations

You will be unusual if you have not already read half a dozen narrative books by ocean cruising authors. Probably what you remember of them are only the beautiful anchorages, the 160-mile days, the friendly customs officials and so on. Force yourself to realise it isn't always like that. If it were Nirvana, there'd be more people doing it. There are rainy days, the boredom of prolonged calms, fruitless searches for spare parts you desperately need, or signs of osmosis, gribble or electrolysis when you haul out and times when the budget is tight.

Don't assume all your dreams will come true as soon as the boat is ready and you depart. Go to any port along the tradewind route and you will nearly always find a broken dream. Money is rarely the root of the problem. People with little money who have a will to cruise invariably find work before it runs out altogether. Inexperience is also rarely the cause unless the crew have lost all faith in the skipper. More often, broken dreams are caused by disillusionment resulting from high expectations at the start and not anticipating the occasional miseries, fear and hardships one must put up with living in a small boat in harbour and at sea.

Relationships can be severely strained by living in close quarters and an essential aspect of deciding to go must be your confidence in getting on with your companion for 24 hours a day, even if you've been married to him or her for 15 years. Having the responsibility of being skipper can often manifest an aspect of someone's character you never knew before. The Captain Bligh image is common and often tolerated with amusement on a two week holiday cruise but the prospect of living with it indefinitely could be unbearable.

Crew harmony, especially when there are only two or three aboard, is made no easier by the fact that at sea you can't pour your heart out on the phone to Mum or a close friend and even in harbour it's not always possible to confide in a new-found aquaintance.

If you have been working hard for years, wrestling with business or professional problems in a society you feel has you trapped by its bureaucracy and materialism, you may well feel that nothing can put you off becoming an ocean vagabond. But stop and try to visualise the

Palm tree surrounded lagoons abound in tropic regions, but don't forget the filthy commercial harbours one is sometimes obliged to use   (Geoff Pack)

bad times. If you can sail with a balanced vision of your new life it will be the best way of ensuring you don't turn back in bitter and expensive disappointment.

### Have I Enough Sailing Experience?

It is difficult to know when you are ready and capable to command a small yacht to sail across oceans, but there's a first time for everything and if it makes you feel better, there isn't an ocean cruising yachtsman alive who hasn't faced the same question.

A trap many people fall into is to worry about how little physical sailing experience they've had, and put off the decision to go until they have had a few more seasons' sailing. In short, you'll learn more after a month's intensive full-time cruising (taking in a longish passage or two) than ever you pick up in years of sporadic weekends and occasional week-long trips. However, that comment must be qualified by saying that you must always be cautious, understand the weather and know where you are. Good knowledge and confidence in those three factors are the basic and essential requirements before heading off.

Unfortunately, for those leaving Northern European countries

Just how much know-how is needed to keep watch? In fact very little as long as the skipper has the knowledge and experience to deal with emergencies and awkward situations   *(Yachting Monthly)*

there is a natural barrier for the inexperienced – the Bay of Biscay. This could well be the most demanding sailing you are likely to experience for years, and although Biscay isn't forever bad, it has a tradition of sorting the men from the boys, and has turned back a large number of potential ocean cruising projects even with experienced crews over the years.

The best answer to gauging whether or not you have the knowledge and experience to go long distance sailing is to ship aboard a delivery passage as crew. Very often made under pressure of time and season, a delivery trip with an experienced skipper offers the greatest likelihood of meeting bad weather in an unknown boat which may give you the chance to test your mettle.

## The Best Age?

One rarely meets anyone who thought they had left too early to go cruising. In my experience nearly everyone over the age of 28 or 30 wish they had started sooner, particularly those over 55 who see that a time will come over the horizon when they have to trim their cruising activities out of age rather than choice. Some we have met felt that age was more valuable than money, there being little point in striving for the perfect retirement boat if every extra year you spend working towards it means less time cruising. For younger couples children will be the most important influence and the best time to go cruising is probably before you have children or after they are off your hands.

From making hundreds of cruising friends over the years, and seeing quite a few people who had cruised for too long, I firmly believe that one must consider cruising as a way of life for a limited number of years at a time. Ten seems to be about the maximum before one yearns for a break. The ocean-cruising yachtsman invariably returns to the lifestyle again later, but that is another matter. This aspect must be considered when making long-term plans. A couple who burn bridges to retire early in their late-40s should not lose sight of the fact that they will probably find they'll want a break after a few years. If by retiring early they were only able to set themselves up with a modest income for cruising, it may not support a return to shoreside living they might then prefer and at this age it may be difficult to start finding new work.

On the other hand, a young married couple in their mid- twenties who plan to start a family at some point are best to get away as soon as they can, even if it means a less-than-perfect boat. A baby born 'en voyage', even if you are careful to be in a port with modern medical facilities, will nearly always halt a cruise either for the necessity of a bigger yacht or for more funds. A couple who have young children already will have to work out timing in relation to their education as we have already discussed.

Career planning can be another important factor. A few years' break after university is often the only choice for those intending to follow a professional career and this is a time when very few people without independent means are in a position to buy a boat. For them there are only two serious options. The first is to 'ocean hitch-hike' aboard other people's yachts, stopping ashore to work when necssary. The second is to 'slave and save' long enough to buy something like a Folkboat, which with adaption and alteration is capable of making long offshore passages. Although they may not be particularly comfortable, some of the most ambitious and successful cruises have been carried out in smallish yachts like these with shoestring budgets (witness boats like *Eric the Red, Shrimpy, Trekka* to name but a few of the well-known ones) so don't immediately disregard this option.

## Health

Cruising is a very healthy way of life, you are living in unpolluted sea air, eating more natural foods (in harbour, anyway), swimming regularly, and walking a lot if only to do the shopping.

Apart from this your body quickly tones up with all the physical aspects of running a boat whether it's transporting water containers

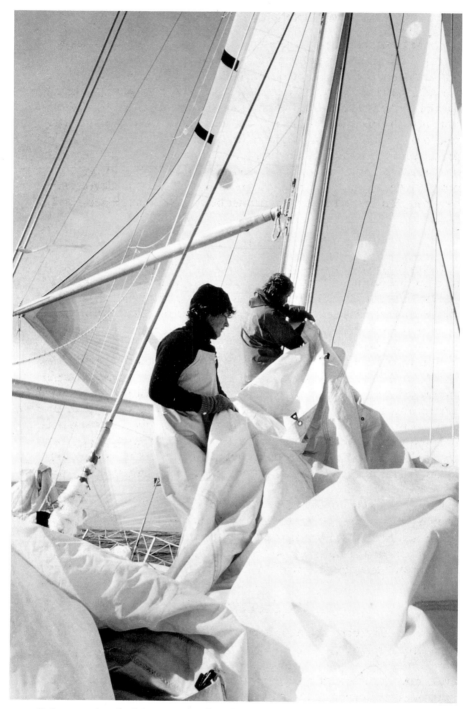

Labour-saving devices are to be found aboard most modern yachts but ultimately sailing is a very physical activity and the size of boat and gear should never be underestimated by a weak or perhaps ageing crew from tap to boat (a 5-gallon jug weighs 50lbs, and you soon get used to carrying one in each hand), rowing the dinghy, raising the anchor or the invisible constant effort of bracing yourself on a boat moving at sea. This, combined with a rich tan and sun-bleached hair can make a formerly palid middle-aged commuter look like Charles Atlas after a few months of tropic cruising. So even if in your present daily routines, with not enough opportunity to keep fit, causes you health problems in our damp cold winters, don't assume that they will necessarily accompany you. Cruising is recuperative and the average non-athletic person will find they have never been so fit. Nevertheless a thorough medical check up is a must before you make a decision.

## Leaving Behind Society

It is very easy when working toward an ocean cruising project to begin to convince yourself that you can't wait to leave behind aspects of modern day society. The average '80s person is quite complex and we all absorb and thrive on many aspects of modern society that are easy to take for granted when you have them but can be missed when they're unavailable.

You may not read a daily newspaper avidly or take it particularly seriously, but when you haven't seen one for a few months you begin to realise how much you appreciated it subconsciously. When you've been cruising for a few months you devour and savour every last word in a woman's or yachting magazine that you might have flicked through in earlier days. The TV set is symbolically something many people long to escape from although in reality they can easily enough do so by simply not having one in the house – but rarely do you find them doing this . . .

Cinema, libraries, the local pub, art galleries, evening classes, browsing through bookshops, car boot sales, dressing up for special social functions, window-shopping, craft fairs and even fish and chips are just a few examples of the fabric of modern life that one all but abandons when going off cruising. Don't assume you won't miss them.

## The Litmus Cruise

After years of dreaming about warm tradewinds, freedom, and living away from the ratrace, you may still hesitate at the finality of giving everything up, or your partner, husband, wife or children may have grave doubts. The ideal solution is a 'litmus cruise' where you spend a year away but keep the homefires burning in your absence. It is said that if God created the West Indies, he must have been a sailor – a 450-mile string of islands running north-south served by a fairly reliable Force 4 easterly tradewind has to be near perfection. However he also

The Atlantic circuit litmus cruise offers an ideal way to get a taste of tropic sailing and the lifestyle before committing yourself and boat for a long period *(Geoff Pack)*

created the surroundings for a perfect mini-ocean cruise for all aspiring ocean voyagers living in Europe or America – the Atlantic circuit.

To take a year off is not always easy to arrange, but an increasing number of employers these days will consider it and may regard it a convenient economy. A mid-life change of career, perhaps accompanied by a redundancy compensation is also much more common and may provide an opportunity to try out the cruising life for a year before picking up the threads of normal life again, without having burned your boats entirely. In these circumstances you have very little to lose by making an Atlantic circuit litmus cruise.

In simple terms, the winds and currents of the North Atlantic flow in a constant broad circular clockwise direction. The westerly wind prevails across its top edge as the Gulf Stream pushes its way from America across to Europe. Off the coasts of the Iberian peninsula blow the so-called 'Portuguese trades', fairly reliable northwesterly winds with an offshoot of the Gulf Stream flowing southwards. Down towards the latitude of Madeira and the Canaries blow the first vestiges of the famous northeasterly tradewinds as the current starts to build in a southwesterly and then westerly direction, aided the further one goes south by the increasingly constant tradewind. This wind and current continue on to the West Indies. Between the West Indies and Bermuda are the horse latitudes where the wind doesn't really have any particular characteristics, but once north of Bermuda one can pick up the westerlies and Gulf Stream again.

This makes a very convenient circuit for the yachtsman to sail from the English Channel down to Spain and Portugal, the Canaries, West Indies, then back via Bermuda or USA and the Azores. Not only this, but on the basis of a one-year schedule he follows the correct seasons all the way round and has just about the right amount of time in each of the very different cruising grounds it takes him through. Leaving during the English summer, the first test is the Bay of Biscay, a passage which can be as pleasant and placid as often as it is vicious and dangerous. The carrot at the end of this trip is the fabulous cruising and scenery in the beautiful mountainous rias of northwest Spain. A few weeks can be spent exploring here before heading south through the unspoilt fishing ports of Portugal and striking out for Madeira or the Canaries. Most transatlantic yachts gather in the dry and touristy Canary Islands until late October/early November by which time the tradewinds are usually beginning to establish themselves. While the Canaries-West Indies run has been dubbed 'the milk run' in the past, it can nevertheless be quite a taxing 2,700 mile voyage. The blasé few describe it as 'setting the twin jibs and self-steering, then sunbathing and book-reading till Barbados comes over the horizon ahead' but it can at times be frustrating for lack of wind (particularly early in the winter) or conversely be a wild roller-coaster of a ride downwind with the crew very happy to stop at the other side.

Some people prefer to sample a Christmas spent at sea, but otherwise there are always a series of parties on the congregating yachts in the principal West Indian anchorages which make up for a Christmas away from home and family. One has between December and the end of April to cruise the Caribbean chain of islands and archipelagos before heading north again on your passage homewards. Many yachts stop in Bermuda, itself a lovely place on the route whilst others prefer to press on direct for the Azores. One can easily spend a month or two in these superb islands before the beginning of August, a prudent time to consider the final 1,200-mile leg back to the English Channel.

The Atlantic circuit litmus cruise takes around a year to complete and its beauty is the fact that it gives a good all-round idea of what ocean cruising is likely to be like. There's a good chance of heavy weather on the early and late passages but you also sample tradewinds, tropical heat, the calms of the Sargasso Sea and the occasional frustrations of Biscay. A year is quite enough to decide whether or not you would be happy about the life on a more permanent basis. A lot of yachtsmen find that it fulfils their urge to make long passages, while for others it only fuels their thirst for more.

The other major advantage of an Atlantic circuit litmus cruise is the ability to gauge what you really require in an ocean cruising boat. The best boat to make the cruise in is a standard production boat at the upper end of the quality scale, which you buy (or maybe already own?) on the basis she will be resold at the end of the voyage. A popular production boat like a Westerly, Rival or Nicholson is usually a good bet in resale terms and what is more one doesn't need to make huge changes (and therefore spend alot of money you won't recoup on resale) to such a boat to make an Atlantic circuit cruise. A thorough overhaul and refit, and probably a re-appraisal of the sail wardrobe combined with the addition of a self-steering gear, and a collection of spares (most of which you can take with you to the next boat) will in many cases be all that is required to take such a boat long distances.

This boat won't necessarily be your eventual ocean cruiser, but she will be a vital yardstick when it comes to deciding what for you constitutes the best boat. If you're very lucky it could be she is broadly right and only needs slight modifications and additions to be suitable for the big cruise. What is more likely is that you will discover that your next boat needs berths to be a little wider, doesn't need as big an engine, the cockpit must be more comfortable and you need a bit more accessible stowage and perhaps a shower. The list is endless (and make sure you compile it as you approach the English Channel on the final leg) but a highly important ingredient to the success of the big project – assuming you still want to carry that through.

The litmus cruise has dozens of advantages especially for those who have twinges of doubt (or plain fear!) about many aspects of the ocean cruising lifestyle. For the businessman it gives him the ability to see if his company can function without him and will teach the householder some of the ins and outs of leaving the home behind. Finally, the best thing about the idea of an Atlantic circuit litmus cruise is that learning has never been so much fun . . .

# Part Two
# CHOICE OF CRAFT AND GEAR

# 4
## The Efficient Ocean Cruiser

The process of designing, building or buying a yacht (in most cases the future ocean cruising yachtsman is confronted by a blend of all three), is a fascinating but at times frustrating juggle of hundreds of requirements and features, balancing one against the other, which must always result in a compromise of sorts. We are no closer to the perfect boat than we are to perpetual motion and the sooner the yachtsman realises this the quicker he'll reach the goal of organising the best boat for his purposes.

The choice of a new or secondhand long-distance cruising yacht is normally determined by her principal design features; size, mono- or multi-hull, keel configuration, construction, deck layout, self-steering qualities, rig and accommodation plan. However, it's very easy to fall into the trap, having found a boat with the major points you want, of disregarding as trivial a number of other details which, in sum, could lead to the boat being as unsuitable as if you'd bought a junk schooner when you really wanted a bermudian sloop.

This is when the Atlantic circuit litmus cruise pays huge dividends in terms of preparation for the 'big off'. The key to shrewd choice of an ocean cruiser lies in appreciating and anticipating what she will have to achieve over and above the straightforward weekend and holiday cruising boat. Obviously, the difference between the two is chiefly the extent to which they are used. This can be broken into two broad divisions which, allowed for and understood, should improve the quality of your choice.

The first relates to the everyday functions and routines of living aboard. Daily living and sailing has got to be smooth, easy and efficient. While ultimate seaworthiness is important, this shouldn't interfere with the in-port suitability and comfort. Even the most active ocean cruisers spend an average of five days in port for every one at sea. Even when they're at sea, assuming they're not sailing to the

Poles or circumnavigating south of the three Great Capes, the proportion of time they spend in weather that justifies tiny or non-existent ports, tight squeeze-through companionways, back-breakingly heavy gear or decked-over cockpits simply doesn't warrant the discomfort and inconvenience these features cause the rest of the time. In this way the sturdiest Colin Archer, traditionally thought of as a long distance boat, can be the worst possible ocean cruiser. Therefore the balance between ultimate seaworthiness, comfort and efficiency has to be weighed carefully in the light of your intended cruising parameters.

Consider what you will be doing each day, from getting up in the morning and washing to decanting water containers into the tanks, cooking, reading, navigating, writing letters and then imagine yourself doing those things in your chosen boat. That neat little washbasin in the heads looked fine in the brochure, but you probably weren't aware that you have to crouch under the sidedeck with legs twisted around the toilet to try and shave over it. The saloon table might have an uncomfortably high fiddle round it, which makes letter writing difficult or the largest galley locker may be directly behind the cooker, so the cook risks being burned reaching it.

Details that we can all put up with in an ordinary cruising boat like underbunk water fillers, fiddly locker catches and gas-bottle turn off switches situated just beyond arm's reach will soon drive an otherwise content and happy crew member crazy. It's surprising how, when living aboard, simple omissions like a convenient place to put a rubbish bin in the galley can be a continual, if petty, irritant.

The second major consideration of continual use of a vessel is related to maintenance. An ocean cruiser needs a lot of work and attention paid to her to keep in trim. Checks and maintenance are a normal and vital part of a cruising lifestyle and the routine needs keeping up not only for the sake of the ship, but for your own temper. Excuse the dreadful adulteration of the proverb, but procrastination is the thief of efficiency. If something is easy to do, you'll do it. If it's difficult or awkward you'll put it off until perhaps it's too late.

Of the many criteria to be checking a potential boat for, one of the highest on the priority list should be this element of ease and therefore efficiency. A battery hidden in the darkest corner of the engine compartment will be a constant annoyance for the person who has to check the acid levels or take hydrometer readings so they will probably do the job less often. The same goes for the engine dipstick, the accessibility of the water tanks for cleaning, the layout of the ground tackle (if it's difficult to get the anchor up you'll take a risk and stay where you are rather than move to shelter), and even the reefing arrangements. A simple winch that is easy to dismantle will get greased far more regularly than one whose springs and pawls fly in all

So often Oriental-built boats bristle with ornate and attractive woodwork but suffer from stupid design errors such as this which cause an owner constant problems from day one   *(Geoff Pack)*

directions the moment the drum is released.

It is easy to see how the maintenance factor is multiplied by the constant usage when you consider that the heads unit that is used once or twice every other weekend on an ordinary cruiser usually works for years without giving trouble or showing signs of wear, but one used every day of the year by two or three crew will need attention and replacements regularly. If you choose a boat whose heads and attendant machinery and plumbing are artistically concealed between interlocking GRP mouldings or joinery it will probably take longer to dismantle the toilet compartment than it will to replace the work-worn gasket. Ask anyone who owns a boat with numerous or even one-piece interior mouldings if they've ever tried to track down a wiring short-circuit!

When you are looking over that potential ocean cruiser, inspect her equipment, fittings and machinery with an eye to having to work on them offshore or, just as bad, in a place where spare parts and chandlers are unheard of. Will that smart and sophisticated dual switchover double-action bilge pump take your improvised rubber plunger, scissor-hewn from an old sailing boot? Will a locker of tools, modest supply of sheet copper, rubber, wood, fastenings and sealants, as well as a bosun's bag of old adaptable sailing fittings cover most eventualities? Although over-simplification isn't necessarily a virtue, there's nothing more frustrating than carting around a boat full of superfluous broken gadgets and equipment. My earlier story of the luxury-equipped yacht with inoperative electric water pumps and no other way of getting at her full tanks is a typical example.

Many boats these days are built to the throwaway ball-point pen concept. With features like glassed-over keelbolts and all deck fitting fastenings concealed under a permanently sealed deckhead liner, they are impossible to inspect and maintain, and if something does go wrong, butchery is required to get at it. Look at the design of your boat's hull and deck joint (if she's GRP). Consider if after many thousands of ocean miles combined with tropical heat it might leak. Would it be possible for you to trace and repair it?

There are a number of other points which, in a normal yacht, are useful features, but in ocean cruisers have no place. A good example is the trend by some builders (particularly those in the Far East) to mould imitation planking seams into GRP hulls. This undoubtedly gives a certain character to a bland GRP hull, but it is very difficult to clean thick harbour oil from it and virtually impossible to match evenly if the hull has to be repaired.

Apart from the wear of full time use, ocean cruisers are also subject to a higher rate of damage. We have found that 90 per cent of this is caused by other craft and people, usually in circumstances over which

Efficiency is multi-facetted and a feature such as ventilated drawers will make life that much more pleasant in a hot and humid climate   *(Yachting Monthly)*

you have little or no control. Every boat in its lifetime can expect the occasional quayside knock or brush with another boat, but it is a rare occurance if it is kept in a marina week in, week out. An ocean cruiser visiting a host of different ports and anchorages doesn't have this home-base security and is vulnerable to any number of dangers. Various boats of ours have been damaged over the years and we don't know of many others which haven't suffered to a greater or lesser degree. Consequently, the 'maintainability' of gunwhales, stanchions, rails and other appendages is imperative. Look at your chosen boat and make sure stanchion bolts aren't all glassed over, or if the pulpit gets torn off it won't take the foredeck with it.

It is better to have a boat whose hull you can repair anywhere in the world. Steel, wood and ferro and to a lesser extent GRP can be repaired almost anywhere, but damaged aluminium is both difficult and expensive to weld in most places. Exotic materials (including special core materials) and unconventional construction techniques have no place on an ocean cruising yacht. Replacements abroad may be unobtainable or sub standard and expertise lacking.

Finally, Robin Lee-Graham, the youngest ever circumnavigator and inspiration for hundreds of ocean cruising yachtsmen, once said going cruising was a matter of learning how little you needed, not how much. There's a great deal in this philosophy. The majority of new ocean cruising yachtsmen are guilty of taking *everything* with them down to the kitchen sink, their boats way down on their marks, lockers stuffed and decks cluttered with gear they'll hardly ever use. Try not to fall into the same trap and learn from the experienced men who often carry little but the bare essentials of living.

The life of the average ocean cruising boat is one full of variety. One month she may be put through the punishment of thrashing to windward for days or even weeks on end. The next month she could be nestled like an egg in a sack of potatoes in a commercial ship harbour, while the next she may be floating in transparent suspension tied to the palms of a deserted lagoon. All the time she is working, moving, functioning. She must be a smooth run home, and an efficient workhorse, at the same time as being capable of weathering *any* storm. To select the basic design features of your ocean cruiser is obviously very important indeed. However, it is the easy part and probably only constitutes 20 per cent of the total process. It is the other 80 per cent, which is so easy to overlook, that leads to a suitable, efficient and therefore successful ocean cruiser.

# 5
# Construction Materials

The choice of construction material for your ocean cruiser can be a perplexing one. Very often it is decided for you when a boat which is suitable in most other respects turns up. Nowadays with excellent coatings to prevent rust and taking the difficulty of insuring against damage into consideration steel takes a lot of beating as a material for long distance yachts. This is especially so if you are prepared to build or have one built, but buying secondhand in steel can be quite dicey. Other construction materials – GRP, wood, aluminium and ferro-cement have their different advantages and disadvantages.

The ocean cruising yachtsman's priorities are first strength, then maintainability and durability. Cost is an inevitable parameter, and the yacht must also be capable of being repaired comparatively easily anywhere in the world.

The strength of a yacht takes a much bigger testing in ports, anchorages and near the shore than ever it does in the open sea in gale conditions. Most properly rigged modern yachts can safely stand up to wild weather at sea. The real strength is needed in withstanding running on a reef, a severe grounding entering a shallow port, or damage by other craft dragging on to you. It is for this reason that heavy displacement yachts have often been favoured for long distance sailing. It is more realistic to bear these sort of hazards in mind than the ravages that a gale at sea can inflict on a yacht. In proportion to the numbers of ocean cruising yachts serious mishaps are not that common, but accidents will happen and any experienced ocean cruising yachtsman knows of half a dozen friends who've either lost or come very close to losing their boats. For that reason, even if it seems a rather pessimistic outlook, each material is now examined in the context of extreme circumstances.

## GRP

Glass reinforced plastic turned the yachtbuilding world on its head within a few short years in the 60s and 70s. Its construction and maintenance advantages are too well known to need repetition here. From an ocean cruising point of view, the suitability of GRP is unquestioned and illustrated by the fact that approximately four out of ten of all ocean cruisers are built with it.

GRP construction has, inevitably, changed over the years as the technology and experience have developed. Early fibreglass boats, those built until around 1970-72, were often massively built (for example, the early Nicholson 32s were fully framed as well as stringered), because no-one was quite certain how strong they needed to be and the oil-based resins were then cheap. Naturally enough, boats from this era have proved very durable, and as long as other features are right, their construction makes them very suitable for ocean cruising. The mid-70s oil crisis changed things and as oil prices rocketted, so the GRP scantlings came down to a more realistic standard.

For a weekend cruising boat, GRP's lack of maintenance is absolutely ideal, but strange as it may seem, this can be a problem for the long distance cruising boat. She will be taking many more knocks, bumps and scrapes that can be difficult to repair cosmetically. A wild night moored alongside a little fisherman's stone quay in the Azores with a raft of boats moored outside you can leave permanent scars on a GRP boat's beautiful topsides. Though it may seem a chore that wood or steel needs complete repainting from time to time the result seems to be a generally better turned out boat.

The maintenance of our GRP Rival 34 became a worry after a while because in many ways she was too nice to take into places where we knew she would emerge covered in thick oil which for months afterwards left an immovable yellow stain, or where we knew the harbour was busy and we might receive a bump. The hazards might be minor but they are numerous. In the West Indies for example 'boat boys' come alongside selling their wares. Their dinghies are heavy, wooden and the fender-less capping rail has often long since broken off leaving the nails sticking out. You generally know of their arrival by the bump as they come alongside . . . It broke our hearts to let the yacht deteriorate, so in the end we avoided the risky (and likely as not, more interesting and deserted) places and became slaves to keeping the boat looking nice. It changed the character of our cruising lifestyle and we learned the valuable lesson, that unless you can come to terms with the shine and corners being rubbed of your newish or immaculate boat, it is better to invest in a rather older, tattier craft.

One of GRP's huge advantages over wood is its immunity to rot and marine borers like teredo worm. However, osmosis is more prevalent in warm tropic waters, so if you're scanning the secondhand market, a boat which has been appropriately treated and protected definitely scores high. If you're starting with a new boat, make sure she is two-part epoxy coated before she even leaves the building shed. For several years there was much unjustified scare-mongering about osmosis and now it seems that yachtsmen have come to terms with the fact it is not a serious problem if nipped in the bud. All the same, it is something to be avoided by preventive maintenance. Not only can it be an unplanned drain on financial resources but if discovered while slipped in some far off location the chances of finding suitable products to rectify it are slim indeed. Procrastinating about its treatment could be a very expensive mistake.

If you're looking at GRP boats, avoid those with dark coloured gelcoats. Not only do they show up every scratch and knock but in warm climates the dark colours fade and chalk, so repainting will be required that much sooner. A dark colour also absorbs the heat so the cabin temperatures will be higher.

GRP sandwich construction has enjoyed much success over the years, especially where a high strength:weight ratio is necessary (ie in light displacement craft and multihulls). If you hit a harbour wall its impact resistance is very good indeed and it is very stiff. However, having such thin GRP skins on each side of the core material, its abrasion resistance is not nearly as good as conventional laminated GRP and this puts its suitability for long distance cruising into question. Were you to ground on a sharp and unyielding coral reef the boat could quickly be quite badly damaged or even lost. If the boat were damaged and repairs attempted in a distant location, finding a suitable core material such as sheet end-grain balsa or Airex foam would be almost impossible.

### Timber

Until a few years ago everyone thought timber was on the way out as a boatbuilding material. Most of us still enjoy the aesthetic pleasures of a wooden boat, but, the lack of suitable seasoned timber and the many advantages of modern materials combined to eclipse them. However, the development of modern epoxy resins and techniques such as the Gougeon Brothers' Wood Epoxy Saturation Technique (WEST) has given timber a new lease of life and makes it a very strong and light method of construction for custom boatbuilding. As well as being strong the WEST-built yacht has the advantage of being impervious to both rot *and* osmosis.

Although traditional wood construction has many good advantages such as the ability to be repaired almost anywhere, it also has drawbacks, of which the initial building cost compared to alternatives is often one. Proneness to rot is another and good protection against wood borers is vital for sailing wooden hulls in warm waters. A protection system can be used but it is important to make sure it isn't breached by nudging a coral head or going aground. Copper sheathing is a traditional protection which blunts teredo teeth and also acts as an antifoulant for much of its life. This is a major expense, although if you plan to keep the boat for a long time, the costings work out well in the long run.

Fibreglass or Cascover sheathing is only a long term success if it is applied when the boat is new, or when she has been hauled out long enough to be tinder-dry. Thereafter it is an effective protection for five to ten years, before it tends to blister and lift off. It then becomes a regular maintenance routine to grind the affected areas off and re-fibreglass over them.

A good barrier of antifouling paint has worked to deter borers on countless wooden yachts but it is taking quite a gamble and teredo will quite often get a hold in the crevices round the rudder trunking, the base of the keel or deadwood, where the antifouling brush hasn't reached.

It is essential that a wooden boat is hauled out at least twice a year to be checked over and re-antifouled. As hauling out isn't cheap and you can rarely do an adequate job by careening the price advantages of having a wooden boat become eroded the longer you cruise and always lingering in the background is the possibility of uncovering rot or worm.

In a situation where a yacht goes ashore or is badly stranded, all things being equal wood will deteriorate and the yacht break up faster than GRP, ferro or metal. And of course the longer a boat remains intact the more time you have to leave it safely, or to do something about saving it.

There will always be those for whom the appeal of a wooden vessel is strong. If you are one of their number you should be aware that there are considerably better materials for the hull of an ocean cruising boat before you reach a decision.

## Ferrocement

Coming on the scene in a big way in the late '60s and early '70s, ferro was regarded by many as something of a wonder material. Not only did it lend itself to custom designs but it was comparatively simple for the inexperienced boatbuilder to construct and above all a very cheap way to build a hull and deck. The resultant construction, properly executed, created a very strong hull that was durable, impervious to rot, rust, borers and osmosis.

It all seemed too good to be true and the '70s saw hundreds of hulls being built in back gardens and yards around the country as dreams to sail off around the world were spawned. In a way, its inexpensiveness and simplicity killed it because for every smooth and sound hull produced there were three dippy and bumpy ones that had been built by complete novices, badly faired and plastered. Then came the more serious problem that tripped up so many builders. Because of its weight (and the early ones were very heavy with inexperienced builders ladelling on the cement) ferro lent itself to boats of 35ft and

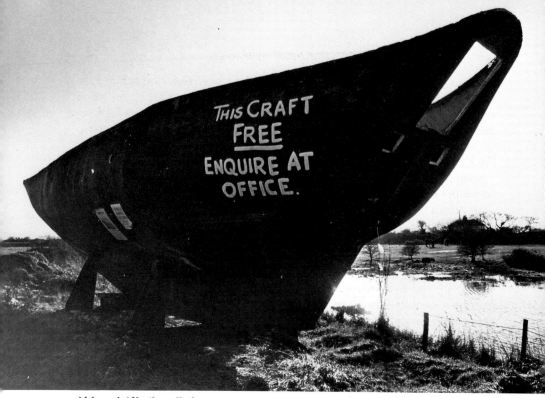

Although if built well, ferrocement is an excellent material for hulls, commercially it still suffers the stigma of the many failed projects of weird shapes, sizes and standards *(Yachting Monthly)*

over. You could build an enormous hull unbelievably cheaply and many people did, dreaming that they could earn their living from chartering their 50 or 60 footer when they got to the South Pacific. The hull might have been cheap but all the other elements of fitting out cost no less and big boats need a lot of proportionally expensive fitments from big engines to big spars and big sails. In another section I argue the case for fitting out simply, but to a high standard, a slightly bigger boat than you might otherwise build or buy. That can work as long as you have a reasonable amount of capital to start with and the boat isn't too big. Many inexperienced big ferro builders mistakenly thought that once the hull was done most of the work and spending was over. Dozens of their dreams went sour, and a lot of bare hulls, many built badly, went on the market. This flood had the effect of bringing prices down sharply. Others were finished, but they looked terrible and the overall result was that ferro got itself a bad name, despite the fact there were many good examples around. A stigma built up around ferro boats and even well-finished ones were not that easy to sell and prices were generally low. You may need to keep the eventual re-sale value of your ocean cruising yacht in mind so it is important to be aware of this history of ferrocement, regardless of the merits of the material.

Nowadays, very few new boats are built in ferrocement because of the commercial implications of their resale value. This doesn't detract from the fact that there are some excellent ferrocement boats afloat and normally their market price is lower than similar sized boats built in another material. Well built ferro, and I should emphasize that it must be well-built and finished, has many merits for long distance cruisers. As I have said, it is strong, durable and doesn't rot, or rust, or get eaten by borers or infected with osmotic blistering. As experience of using ferro progressed, hulls became steadily lighter and many medium-displacement designs were built and even raced with some success such as the Hartley RORC 39.

The adhesion of paint systems can be a problem with ferro boats. For many years one regularly saw them shedding their paint in sheets. Like steel, it is necessary to shotblast and use modern epoxy paint systems (especially tar-epoxy) to resolve the problem. Ferrocement is otherwise a very low maintenance material and one need only really think about cosmetics. Any chips knocked off through a graze with a quay are easily filled, sanded and overpainted.

Another minus point against ferro construction is the difficulty of dragging them off reefs in a stranding. If the yacht has pounded for any length of time and the cement has been pulverised out of the framing and mesh, the friction created by this exposed steelwork makes towing off very difficult indeed and many boats, far from mortally damaged, have had to be abandoned for this reason.

If you consider ferro you stand a good chance of getting a slightly larger boat for the available money and one with few problems, but balance this with the knowledge that in Europe ferro boats are notoriously difficult to sell and in America they are almost impossible. In Australia the attitude is different. Their resale value is good and they change hands quickly, although for the foreigner selling an alien boat there are enormous importation fees.

## Aluminium

Aluminium is regarded by some as being the very best building material for ocean cruising boats. It is about 65 percent as strong as steel but is only one third as heavy. It also has the great advantage that it doesn't rust although being low on the galvanic is subject to corrosion with dissimilar metals. You have to avoid, for example, mooring for any length of time alongside a steel boat or pilings without hanging plenty of zincs in the water around the boat.

The owner of an aluminium yacht must also be very very careful of electrolysis. Stupid errors can be disastrous, as was demonstrated by the owner of a 28ft British production built aluminium sloop in the '70s. Hoping to save himself some money, he had taken delivery and chose to do the commissioning of the yacht himself. A few months

This 30ft aluminium sloop went ashore in the Azores. Although she took a terrible pounding that would have obliterated wood, ferro or GRP construction, ultimately the aluminium split and holed. On a steel boat this is much less likely to happen (*Geoff Pack*)

after launching he was disappointed when he discovered she was leaking. He had her hauled out and traced the leak to a small pinprick, but was also horrified to discover that all the underwater hull plating was paper thin and that the leak was the first of hundreds about to happen. The problem was quickly diagnosed. He had antifouled the yacht with some cheap unlabelled paint which had turned out to be a strong copper-based antifouling. There was a similar story about the crewmember who lost his short change out of his trouser pockets into the bilge when getting undressed one night. Although he pulled up the floorboards and found most of it, the odd pennies he couldn't find gradually ate their way through the bilge plating.

In terms of raw material costs, aluminium is expensive at between 10-15 times the price of steel. However, it should be remembered that when a labour-intensive metal hull is built for you in a shipyard, raw materials rarely constitute more than 25 per cent of the price. Added to this, the actual hull and deck of a boat is only between 10-45 per cent of the total outlay dependent on the standard of finish and equipping. So in these terms, an aluminium boat needn't be exceptionally expensive. In comparison to steel which can be repaired in the most remote outpost, the welding of aluminium is a headache in many areas, although MIG welding equipment is gradually becoming more common in major centres.

French yachtsmen are particularly keen on aluminium and very often they don't paint the exterior but leave it bare. This might not be to everyone's taste, but on this basis it has to be the lowest maintenance material of all, including fibreglass which requires regular cleaning, polishing and after a while repainting or spraying.

When compared to wood, fibreglass and ferro, aluminium is incredibly strong if one is unfortunate enough to run into a reef or get stranded on a shore. It will take an incredible pounding, but it can split and hole which steel is unlikely to do. The photo opposite shows an aluminium boat we saw in the Azores which had run on to a rocky foreshore on the island of Faial. Her crew of five (none of whom had been on watch) had got ashore unscathed, and the yacht was later salvaged to be stripped of her gear. A wooden boat would have been matchwood in no time and a fibreglass yacht ground to pulp. However, the sight of those splits and tears in the hull was enough to tip my opinion in favour of steel as the best compromise material for long distance yachts.

## Steel

There is a steadily increasing trend for ocean cruisers to use this material and many skippers who go on to commision or build a second cruising boat choose steel – a telling statistic.

One of the more bizarre sights I've seen while ocean cruising was a French steel sloop lying in St. Barts in the French West Indies. She had a massive v-shaped indent into her topsides and deck amidships which extended about 3ft (1m) inboard from the line of her original gunwhale down to the waterline. She had been run down by a ship and survived it. Her owners didn't have enough money to have the repairs done, so until they'd saved enough were continuing cruising in her.

One of the reasons more people are turning to steel is the increasing difficulty of getting insurance for ocean voyaging, not to mention unreasonable premiums and restrictions. Steel's proven strength and durability is comforting for the uninsured yachtsman because there are dozens of accounts of steel boats going ashore and proving almost indestructable. A good proportion are hauled off and live to sail again.

Steel is well-suited for amateur fitting out because once the hull and deck structure are finished the interior joinery and bulkheads don't contribute to its strength. Unlike fibreglass then where the integrity of bulkheads and certain interior furniture is paramount, the worst an amateur can do is create a bad joinery finish. The hull itself is a different matter. Experienced welding techniques and correct welding sequences are essential to avoid unbalanced stresses being set up and

The secret with steel is keeping the paint undamaged; the stainless steel protection around the gunwhale and cheeks of this bow roller means that the vulnerable paint will hardly be touched by the ground tackle   *(Geoff Pack)*

the plating overheating, which results in it being stretched over the framing and giving a 'hungry dog' look. A steel hull *can* be built by the amateur and be very strong but unless filler is used, the skills required to produce a fair hull only come after much experience.

For many years the two major disadvantages of steel were rusting and weight. Of course it weighs the same today, but whereas once upon a time hulls had to be built with a reasonable thickness to give longevity against rust, now that the rust can be avoided (with good design and more particularly modern epoxy finishes) thinner scantlings can be used, so both disadvantages are significantly diminished in modern hulls. While modern steel hulled yachts don't ever have to be of especially heavy displacement as once was the case, it is nevertheless very difficult, on yachts less than 45 feet, to build to a design that is much less than moderate in displacement.

Rust nearly always attacks from the inside, so it is imperative that the interior treatment is the very best from the beginning. Once all the wiring, plumbing, insulation, and domestic fit-out is added, the interior of the hull is unlikely ever to be properly prepared and painted again. Mistakes can be made with the exterior, and although expensive it is quite possible to grit blast and re-coat, but not so with the inside. Again, modern insulation materials largely eliminate sweating in the hull which can be a problem in colder climates. It has probably been written a thousand times (and ignored almost as often) but it is vital that all areas of the hull are accessible for wire-brushing and proper painting. It should also be entirely self-draining so water can never collect. If an area, perhaps only one frame, is difficult to paint properly the chances are that it will not receive adequate treatment and the inevitable result will be rust. Therefore the interior design in this respect is just as important as the general design of the yacht. An experienced steel boat owner will be able to point out dozens of bad points to you, particularly in older yachts. Features like an angle-capped toerail with wooden capping is not only going to be a problem if moisture ever gets between the wood and steel, but also trying to chip, wire-brush and paint effectively on the underside of that capping piece will be difficult in the least.

In terms of maintenance, the modern steel ocean cruising yacht does not fare well against other materials and an older steel boat comes far and away at the bottom of the list and can be a constant maintenance problem. The name of the game is keeping the paint on the steel and this has three prongs. Firstly, water must never be allowed to collect or preferably even linger where there is painted steel. If possible, no external surface on a steel boat should be horizontal or nearly so, as water will remain here and seek out any flaws in the paint, ultimately undermining it. Secondly good design will avoid any sharp corners or edges that do not hold paint well. At construction stage, it will pay to look very closely at where radius can be used (either by employing rod, pipe or simply grinding off a curve) to help the paint stay intact. Thirdly, certain areas of a boat will receive hard treatment and more than a normal amount of knocks or abrasion. The most obvious are the cleats and fairleads, but there are plenty more, like the edges of the forehatch where sailbags are dragged in and out or the perimeter of the transom that gets a regular knock from the dinghy. Ideally, these should be capped with stainless steel. Even with these precautions, the cosmetic maintenance of a steel boat will be a constant occupation (some say thorn in the side) of the long distance cruising yachtsman.

If you've ever been aboard a yacht at sea during an electrical storm, you know the feeling of vulnerability of your mast being the only high metal object (ie lightning conductor) for miles around. Lightning strikes are far from uncommon. A minor one can wreck the yacht's electrics and electronics, a major one can easily start a fire and has been known to shatter topsides between chainplate and waterline to the extent that the yacht has foundered. Because it is the perfect conductor and due to the Faraday's Cage effect, a steel yacht is immune from serious damage during even bad lightning strikes. This has to be a major advantage in steel's favour.

Another plus in steel's favour is the ability to repair, alter or modify it almost anywhere in the world because even the tiniest inhabited islands have a welding kit somewhere.

It would be foolhardy to assume that steel is an ideal material because it is not – it only lends itself to certain designs and care and attention to detail of the original design and steelwork will reflect heavily on its subsequent maintenance and lifespan. Also against it is the fact that its maintenance-intensive characteristics make it less than desirable for the normal yachting market so there are few production steel boats to choose from. As a result, when buying you will nearly always be looking at a custom boat and the two extreme tendencies are highly expensive and individual custom yachts at one end, or cheap home-builts at the other. Hopefully there is a happy medium, but the choice is quite limited if you have clear ideas on what you want to buy.

# 6
# *The Hull*

## *The Right Size*

It is quite incorrect to assume that the size of the boat in which you plan to sail away will be in direct proportion to the extent of your finances. When a boat-buying budget is depressingly tight this may seem to be the case, but scratching below the surface, you'll find it isn't the only influencing factor to choosing size.

The clearest way to assess what is about the right size for you is to briefly imagine yourself in the highly desirable (and unfortunately rare) situation of having, within reason, unlimited funds to purchase the yacht. Don't let your imagination run away with the idea that you will have any more money than you presently budget for cruising costs once the boat is ready to go. Just stick at assuming enough money to buy and equip the boat. This will enable you to assess what would be ideal as a basis to work towards.

The number of permanent crew aboard is the principal influence. If they are a growing family, this gradual expansion is another factor to take into account. Alternatively, if they are teenagers about to leave the nest, you don't want to be left with a large and unmanageable yacht in their absence.

Much depends too on your outlook to the sailing lifestyle. This is underlined by a simple maxim in the cruising world. Smaller ocean cruising boats are sailed much more frequently than bigger yachts that are more complicated and more trouble to get under way. If you are an adventurous type who wants to explore every last little bay and islet in an archipelago and take your boat up close to the reefs to dive on them, beware of setting your sights on a biggish yacht.

A larger yacht will be considerably more time-consuming to maintain. They generally have more sophisticated equipment and this too will have a snowballing effect as her crew spend more time servicing or fixing items like the water pressure systems or the electric windlass. Sewing a ripped mainsail is a major job on a 48-footer, but relatively quick on a 33-footer. Sophistication also needs feeding from time to time with specialist spare parts, many of which the prudent yachtsman will carry but some he will not. Waiting in port for spares to arrive can spoil your pleasure no end.

Having spent two years skippering a 56-footer I was desperate to get into a small simple boat again and I was fortunate enough not to have been picking up the bills. Simple things like cleaning round the waterline or scrubbing the decks take so much longer. Keeping the topsides reasonably clean and occasionally polished seemed like a Forth Bridge operation (as soon as you've finished at one end, it's time to begin again at the other). I remember an occasion early one morning (before the sun became too hot) revarnishing the deckwork teak. Friends on a nearby 34-footer had been doing theirs too and we were commiserating. They had finished all theirs, taken a bus to view the nearby volcano and later gone off for a swim and windsurfing session before I'd wielded the last brushstroke.

What may also prevent you getting the most out of your cruising is physically getting a largish boat under way for a short passage, maybe out to a reef or a nearby coral atoll. With her capacious accommodation there is a lot more work involved in making her ship shape – more hatches and ports to close tight, more items to put away in safe places. The awning is not only a fairly big job to get down, but it then has to be folded up and put away (not to mention re-setting when you get to the next anchorage a few miles further on). Getting all the sail covers on and off is time-consuming and rarely much fun. Larger boats generally have bigger dinghies which usually need more powerful and heavier outboards, so that lot will have to be lifted up on deck and lashed down. A bigger boat might well have an electric windlass which makes raising the anchor easier (assuming the windlass is working and not waiting for a new solenoid to be sent out from home), but if that anchor hauls up a load of mud and weed (and big anchors hold a lot), it's going to need more than one or two swilled bucketfuls of water to clear it as that muck makes its way back aft, clogging up around the stanchion fittings etc. I am deliberately exaggerating to illustrate the point that there are drawbacks to large boats even if you can afford them. If you and your wife are ocean cruising to get away from hard work and don't have extra crew, you'll be jumping out of the frying pan and into the fire if you look at boats over 45ft (13.71m). With a crew of two or three willing teenagers (and they must be willing) it's a different matter altogether and a larger boat will give you some privacy.

The other important element of larger boats is cost of running. Running expenses do not rise in proportion to size – a 44-footer doesn't cost 20% more to run than a 36-footer because she is 20% longer (any more than she costs 20% extra to purchase initially). Remember that a medium sized boat (say 36ft [10.8m]), does *exactly* the same job as the 44-footer – they are probably equally seaworthy and equally capable of supporting a cruising lifestyle. When the two are motoring along a windless coastline together each doing five knots, the larger will not only be using 50-75% more fuel, but when her engine service period comes up she will probably require half as

Very nearly an ideal mainstream ocean cruiser for two people, with a good turn of speed, exceptionally spacious accommodation, easily handled rig and production-built by a reputable builder much oil again, and larger, more expensive filters. Yet they will both arrive at the same time at the same place. The only real difference is the interior volume and stowage capabilities of the larger and marginally more speed under sail, but you will pay a high price for these advantages so be sure you really want or need them.

In the last fifteen years, since ocean cruising has become so much more popular, the trend in the size of short-handed (two or three crew) long distance yachts has been concentrated in the 35–40ft (10.6 –12m) bracket, though three or four feet either side of is common also. There are also hundreds of smaller boats, less than 30ft (9.15m), crossing the oceans these days. Other than financial considerations, there are few real advantages to going below 30ft for extended cruising and most owners readily admit they would like something larger if they could afford it. However, a small, well designed, well built modern production yacht can be very seaworthy indeed (with good hatches and windows they are good examples of the 'well-corked bottle' theory of seaworthiness). They inevitably create certain discomforts and difficulties for their crews; they are easily and invariably overloaded and, with short waterline length, passage times can be long. All the same, one regularly sees boats like Vertues, Contessa 26s, Folkboats, Vancouver 27s, Twisters, Frances 26s and Great Dane 28s in far flung ports of the world.

At the beginning of this chapter I argued that you don't necessarily have to determine boat size by the extent of your bank account. It is straightforward enough to suggest to a wealthy man that he and his wife might be happier in a sensibly thought-out 40-footer, rather than the luxuriously appointed 55-footer he could afford. However it is also possible for the skipper with a limited budget looking let us say for an oldish Nicholson 32, to afford a more suitable 37-footer if the real needs are considered carefully. The fact is that it is the finish of boats that costs money, further compounded by the goodies added on. Mirror-finished topsides, shiny stainless steel, a big engine, solid and chunky varnished hardwoods and a navigation table surrounded by electronic wizardry are fine for people who can afford them. Frenchman Bernard Moitessier sailed his *Joshua* engineless for the first season whilst he worked her as a sailing school to raise money. His masts were telegraph poles he had hewn into shape and the rigging was rough galvanised steel. Instead of 'yachty' cowl ventilators, he had one quarter of a tyre inner tube fitted on the deck (which was flattened whenever a wave passed over it, thereby stopping the water getting below).

For some people this is too big a sacrifice and they are prepared to work and save for the standards they want before getting away. But if you have a tight budget and are enthusiastic to get going quickly, a yacht that is very simply fitted out is attainable at a very low price if

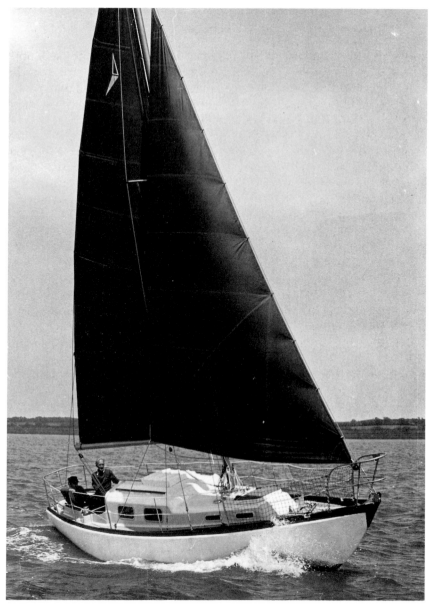

Beware of spending the best years of your life saving for an ideal boat; a yacht such as this Trintella 1, suitably strengthened and modified, is just as capable of long voyages as a boat half as big again, even though you will have to put up with smaller living space

you are prepared to finish and equip her yourself. She may not be perfect, but she'll get you afloat and sailing long distances.

Lou Lou and I started ocean cruising in this way. By selling our London flat we realised we could raise £5,000. In 1979 it seemed like a small fortune. In those days, £5,000 would have bought something like a Folkboat or Contessa 26 but with not much left over for essential equipment and savings to sail with. Although we were universally considered very foolhardy, we put the flat up for sale and it went immediately. I've always been well-built and reckoned that a small boat like a Folkboat, which with modifications is capable of ocean passages, could be a disaster to live on board for me. Instead we bought *Foreigner*, a secondhand Wharram catamaran, which at 35ft x 17ft seemed like a ship in comparison, and inspired by Moitessier refitted her *very* basically with 'nothing fancy', living aboard in London at the same time.

We learned from our mistakes (and we made plenty) and I'm sure many people laughed at our rather *infra dig* sailing machine with her rough appearance, but it nevertheless enabled us to be away ocean cruising without any financial help by the time we were 22 years old. Her outboard engine was hopelessly unreliable and expensive to run so for most of the time she was handled under sail and in the end we became quite proficient at it. I always looked forward to the day I could afford a boat with a diesel, but we, like thousands before us, managed quite happily without. After a couple of years cruising, including an Atlantic crossing and visiting most of the Windward and Leeward Islands, we sold our much loved *Foreigner* in the West Indies. She had been far from ideal at times, but had got us cruising on the tiniest budget and taught us an enormous amount that we could incorporate in the next boat.

Another ocean sailor Nick Skeates, lost his *Wylo* on a Pacific reef and arrived in New Zealand a few months later, almost penniless and with only some gear salvaged from the wreck. Within two years he had designed and built the 32ft *Wylo II* from scratch and was off again, subsequently completing a circumnavigation in her. This was in 1979, so prices are a little different, but she was built and equipped complete for less than $5,000 US. I met Nick and went on board the yacht in the West Indies and if she didn't have the glitter and finish of a Boat Show exhibit (he boasted that she didn't have a single piece of stainless steel on her), she had nevertheless been sailed half way around the world.

Ocean cruising folk's second or third boats are invariably more representative and telling than their first, which is exceptionally difficult to get right without experience of your personal requirements. So it is interesting to look at a few well-known ocean cruising yachtsmen's boats and see how they progressed in terms of size.

**Eric and Susan Hiscock** I have huge respect for these two because they were prepared to experiment, go along with the times and if necessary change their published ideas in the cause of progression. For many years Hiscock advocated paraffin for cooking and heating but as circumstances changed, paraffin's quality diminished and its availability thinned, he changed to gas (he wrote an article explaining why and how he'd done it) and never looked back. He started ocean cruising in the 24ft (7.31m) *Wanderer 11* and later progressed to the 30ft (9.15m) heavy displacement sloop *Wanderer 111*. He was later to say that she was his favourite with her simplicity and easy handling, if she was a little slow. They then decided to sell their Isle of Wight home and made a big step up to the 49ft (14.9m) Jongert ketch *Wanderer IV*. They owned this very comfortable yacht for some 15 years before finally opting for the wooden 39ft (11.8m) *Wanderer V* which was something of a compromise between *Wanderers III and IV*.

**Eric Moitessier** Progressed from a tubby home-built 28ft (8.53m) ketch to the 39ft (11.8m) *Joshua,* a heavily constructed steel ketch. In her he made some remarkable passages (including twice around Cape Horn) and she was his home for 17 years. When she was lost on a Mexican beach he replaced her with *Tamata*, a 36ft (11m) steel sloop.

**Lin and Larry Pardey** Although they passionately argued the cause of small ocean cruisers, when the time came to replace their 23ft (7m) *Serrafyn* the new boat was quite a jump bigger at 30ft (9.15m). Maybe their next boat will be around 37ft (11.27m)?!

## Hull Design

While the ocean cruising yachtsman looking for the suitable boat need not know too much about naval architecture, the basic concepts discussed here will help in the choice of a hull and displacement within limits. The finer points of hull design are a complex subject, well documented in a number of books for those who want to go into it more deeply.

The characteristics of a hull's design are closely related to displacement, so when considering a suitable boat the two go hand in hand. The merits of heavy versus light or moderate displacement have kept yacht club bars alive with lively conversation for years past. Simplifying matters as far as possible, a heavy displacement boat is built strongly and her design allows her to sail with not only this weight, but considerable amount of stores as well without being adversely affected. On the face of it, this makes her well-suited for long voyages and nearly all early ocean cruisers were heavy displacement wooden vessels built to withstand the rigours of the sea. In simple terms, the heavier a boat is, the stronger she needs to be built to withstand her own weight being thrown at and off seas. This requirement for strength adds to the weight which in turn requires heavier sails and gear, stronger hatches, and stouter spars. The result is that she is only likely to sail well in stronger breezes and slop the wind out of

The bulletproof Colin Archer still makes a good ocean cruiser but, benefitting from the last 90 years of design and development, the modern yacht is much more likely to make a better long-distance liveaboard cruising boat

her sails in lighter going, giving her a poor general performance. Her ability to carry a large crew and stores will also be at the cost of extra scantlings in her construction or extra lead required for her keel. She will also be expensive to equip, requiring larger sized gear, ropes and so on, which also means she will be more costly to maintain.

At the other end of the scale (and I'm deliberately stating extremes to illustrate the point) a light displacement boat is built with trimmed down scantlings, but is just as seaworthy because the mass being thrown at seas is so much less. Imagine her as a ping pong ball tossed in the waves compared to a golf ball. She also needs less power to drive her so the rig can be smaller and lighter which makes her easier to sail and usually faster. Similarly she will have a smaller engine using less fuel and lighter, less-expensive ground tackle which needs no heavy windlass. However, the light displacement boat has the disadvantage that her load-carrying capability is limited because stores constitute a much larger proportion of her total weight in comparison to the same stores on the heavy boat. And people on light displacement boats don't eat any less! The result is that she will go down on her marks, and the more that is loaded into her the less capable her structure will become to withstand the greater mass as she pounds away at sea. The result will be not only bad sailing performance, but *in extremis* the danger of breaking up.

Looking at the two extremes then it becomes clear that somewhere between the two will be the best answer. Displacement is generally regarded and simply calculated as a ratio of displacement/waterline length. The table below illustrates the displacement/length ratio of several designs to give you some idea.

| | | | |
|---|---|---|---|
| Moody 36 | 205 | Rival 34 | 345 |
| Sadler 32 | 255 | Salar 40 | 350 |
| Sunbird 32 | 255 | Nicholson 35 | 365 |
| Pioneer 10 | 260 | Giles 38 | 365 |
| Rival 38 | 300 | Rustler 31 | 400 |
| Warrior 35 | 300 | Nicholson 32 | 440 |
| Vancouver 32 | 310 | Bowman 36 | 440 |
| Bowman 46 | 325 | Endurance 35 | 470 |
| Vancouver 27 | 330 | Tradewind 33 | 500 |

These figures are computed by dividing the displacement in tons by the $(LWL \times .01)^3$. Making sure you have accurate displacement figures

Of necessity, cruiser/racers are built very strongly and even hard weekend racing is unlikely to tire them; many of the less extreme and un-twitchy ones, such as this UFO 34, can be re-arranged for short crew and make superb long distance boats

The Rival 34 is an evergreen ocean boat which set the standard as an ideal compromise between the advantages of the traditional long keel and the more efficient fin and keg configuration

you can easily make the same calculation on your chosen craft. As a rough guide, expect an average ocean cruiser capable of carrying sufficient loads with a reasonable turn of speed to come between 250 and 350. This doesn't necessarily imply that craft outside these figures are unsuitable. It simply means you must anticipate the penalties of limited load carrying at one end of the scale or alternatively high cost and poorer performance at the other.

## Waterline Length

Waterline length is the next most important aspect of hull design to consider. For an ocean cruiser the longer it is the better. Not only does a good waterline length mean greater speed, but also much more usable accommodation or storage space for a given overall length. Our Rival 34 *Euge* always drew admiring comments wherever she went with her very pretty overhangs, fabulous sheerline and counter stern. But although excellent in many respects, her waterline length was only 24ft 10in (7.56m) for her 34ft (10.36m) hull length. As a result her accommodation was small compared to others of similar LOA. She was also sensitive to having weights, such as the ground tackle, in the ends and with a maximum speed of just over seven knots, we had to work that much harder sailing to keep up respectable daily averages. With a longer waterline we could have relaxed a bit and maintained similar speeds at 60 percent potential, instead of the 80 percent we had to keep up.

## Beam

Beam also affects how much boat you get for a given length. The contrast is enormous between a narrowish yacht with pleasing overhangs and a beamier, full-ended hull which can easily have twice the volume for the same overall length. Some of the popular French multichine steel designs such as the Group Finot Reve D'Antilles have superb accommodation for their length and with sensible professional design manage to maintain good sailing performance and seakeeping qualities too. Their increased beam and therefore form stability means they can trade a little ballast for load-carrying which within limits is a desirable feature for long distance sailing.

Generous beam has a lot of advantages for the ocean cruiser, such as increased deck space which makes for easier working and for stowing a lot of the gear a long distance boat needs, like running poles, extra ground tackle, liferaft and maybe a rigid dinghy. However there are snags in having generous beam. The wider a boat the harder she is to design properly, as heeled underwater shapes can distort badly and create inefficiencies. These not only slash performance but lead to questionable handling characteristics which sometimes don't manifest themselves until conditions are bad when you need predictability. Also, for a given displacement, a designer will be trading underwater depth as he increases the beam. The resulting wide shallow hull has high initial stability which will drop off the further she heels, which is not desirable in a boat likely to meet severe conditions. So generous beam can be a good feature, but be careful that it is not excessive, as has been the case in some production cruisers built in the last fifteen years.

## Freeboard

Freeboard is an aspect of design which naval architects have tended to relax over in the last few years. If freeboard is too low headroom will be limited, unless there's a high coachroof which is not good for heavy weather work. Also, low freeboard means a wetter (and I don't mean spray) boat, which raises a number of problems, such as safety of crew working on deck, and greater reliance on the integrity and watertight-ness of hatches, windows and ports. Cabin leaks combined with a regularly-drenched crew will quickly sap morale in sustained heavy going and it is then that mistakes will be made.

Conversely, while high freeboard will keep the decks and crew drier, it has the ill effect of raising the yacht's centre of gravity, especially if she's a heavily constructed boat with proportionally heavy equipment. The higher centre of gravity works against stability, particularly in extreme conditions, making the boat more susceptible to being rolled over and less ready to self-right. A higher centre of gravity also works against sail-carrying ability and so reduces sailing performance.

Increased windage is another drawback to high freeboard, although for a given interior headroom the windage difference between low freeboard/high coachroof and high freeboard/flush deck is not great. High freeboard can be a bit of a nuisance too when getting aboard from a dinghy, passing up heavy shopping or water containers and high freeboard does make it considerably more difficult to retrieve a man overboard.

## Stern Shape

The merits of different stern shapes were hotly argued for many years among yachtsmen. The round or canoe stern was often favoured because it gave the following sea an opportunity to break either side of it, but it was not particularly buoyant and cut out a lot of otherwise useful stowage space. It has largely vanished from modern design.

The counter stern is traditional, but has gradually blended in with the transom stern leaving us with the retrousse which gains the maximum waterline advantages of the former with the practicality and space of the latter. Ultimately, overall hull balance is more important than how the stern is finished off and a hull with the correct distribution of buoyancy fore or aft is likely to be the most seaworthy one. In my experience of running before severe conditions, when a rogue sea is big enough to seriously poop the yacht, the stern shape is irrelevant compared to the boat's ability to resist broaching through the good design of her overall hull shape.

## Draught

This really depends on the sort of cruising you wish to do. Some people, while keen to cross oceans, may want to explore places such as the Bahamas or areas of the Great Barrier Reef. The European canal system will require shallow draught and numerous Pacific atolls, especially in the Tuamotus for example, are opened up to a boat drawing little water. River cruising in locations such as the Nile or Amazon is also possible with shallow draught.

However, unless you're a shoal draught enthusiast, the depth of water required is rarely a problem until you need more than around 6ft 6in (1.97m) when you have to start looking carefully at whether or not an anchorage or bay will accommodate you. Draught between this figure and genuine shoal is arbitrary because anyone lacking the advantages of true shoal draft will tend to anchor or moor in similar places to the 6ft 6in (1.97m) man. In this case, why not go for slightly deeper draught and gain from its advantages such as low centre of gravity, better tankage, and quite likely better sail-carrying ability and consequent performance.

## The Importance of Performance

Boat speed and performance are not looked on as being particularly high on the ocean cruiser priority list when compared to seaworthiness or comfort. It is common to hear potential voyagers saying that speed or weatherliness are unimportant when crossing oceans. One can only assume these people have never experienced a passage of over 20 days, and base their opinion on short trips where speed difference is not as noticeable.

Compared to other forms of transport, a boat travels exceptionally slowly. In proportional terms a boat that makes five knots against another doing four knots is getting there 25% quicker, which may not seem much on a short trip. But see how that difference is amplified over high ocean mileages. A 3,000-mile passage will take the four knot boat 31 days and 6 hours, and the five knot boat only 25 days. Some people (not that many if they're honest) are like Bernard Moitessier and love to spend as much time at sea as possible. But most of us, after two or three weeks at sea are still enjoying it but greatly looking forward to getting in. If there were a way of shortening the trip by six days, nine out of ten would jump at the prospect of fresh food, plentiful water and a change in scenery and company. On the simple day to day routine of a yacht crossing an ocean, the daily position fix is something of a highpoint. An ocean is large and if those crosses only progress across the chart in tiny increments it can sap morale and crew happiness noticeably. A boat that is going well and making respectable daily runs will keep her crew smiling . . .

In this context it is worth remembering that respectable speed is as much a product of the skipper's philosophy as it is of the yacht's capabilities. A skipper who loads her right down on the marks may always be able to produce some special tool needed once in a blue moon, or a can of some favourite delicacy three years into the cruise, but if the sailing passages are tedium as a result, there is not much incentive to leave port and head for the next place. Of course you may be going in the first place to get away from the rush and hurry of modern living, but the performance philosophy still makes sense, because knowing you have the ability to get to places will widen your cruising range and general outlook. A 48-hour beat into a tradewind in a capable and weatherly ocean cruiser might well take you to an atoll that very few people ever visit. Efficient sailing has great rewards.

There is no single element in creating good boatspeed, performance philosophy is a combination of many factors. They include starting off with a good boat, not overloading it, making sure the underside is kept clean, the weight well distributed (preferably out of the ends and as low down as possible), and no unnecessary windage aloft. Then at sea she needs to be sailed consistently for twenty four hours out of twenty four.

## Keels and Ballast

Seamen are traditionally conservative because the man who goes to sea with or in something 'new-fangled' might be trusting his life to it. Not surprisingly therefore some new ideas take a long time to be accepted and among them the fin keel most of us today take for granted. The keel controversy raged for many years until the yachting boom of the 1970s pretty much established that the fin and skeg works was here to stay. That is not to say that the traditional long keel is unsuitable, but modern design and construction methods favour the fin and skeg configuration. Long keels still appear from time to time on 'new' designs, but more to be in keeping with a pseudo-traditional concept than for any practical reason.

The long keel evolved from the days of wooden sailing ships, when structurally it was the vessel's backbone. Smaller workboats such as the smacks and trawlers made it a little deeper for better windward performance. It was the yacht-like pilot cutters, whose competitive livelihood was dependent on their sailing performance that converted it into the wineglass-stem proportions of the classic long deep keel. It was soon realised that incorporating the ballast on the end of it instead of in the bilges made a significant difference and in due course the bolt-on external fin keel was tried. Post-war racing successes proved the better handiness and performance of the fin and skeg configuration and when monocoque fibreglass construction came along and did away with the need for a strong central backbone, the long keel's days were numbered.

For the early ocean cruisers, sailing before Blondie Haslar had pioneered the windvane self-steering gear, the long keel was good because it undoubtedly aided the yacht's ability to sail in a straight line. It made it easier for the helmsman and more reliable for sheet-to-tiller self-steering where steadiness counts. The other aspect that was, and still is, regarded as a great asset is that the long keel is an integral part of the hull structure so when a yacht is aground or stranded, it spreads the loads over a wider area – a comforting thought if you are starting to pound badly. Another merit is the ability to position the rudder on the after edge, a strong arrangement that protects the rudder enormously. Having the rudder like this, especially one externally mounted on the transom, is still one of the best and most practical arrangements for a long distance boat, and can simplify the installation and operation of windvane self-steering.

The long keel is gradually disappearing though as the fin and skeg (or even the fin and spade rudder) proves the better all-round arrangement. There are of course wide variations of fin keel. In the early '70s Peter Brett designed the Rival 31 (later to be stretched into the 32 and then re-modelled into the 34) which had a 'long fin' which was accepted as a good compromise between traditional long and modern fin. It maintained good directional stability with the handiness and better performance of fin and skeg. The concept of the long fin is still very good for the ocean cruiser for a number of reasons. First, the keel is mounted on the hull's underbelly over a greater length and in a stranding or heavy grounding the strains are better distributed. Secondly, the reasonable tracking a long fin gives allows the possibility of rigging a basic sheet to tiller self-steering if your self-steering packs up or is damaged. A sensitive narrow fin keeled boat whose helm you can't leave unattended for more than a moment is impossible to make self-steer on any point of sailing other than close-hauled and this will be a curse if Sod's Law decrees the self-steering gives up in mid-ocean.

The question of having encapsulated ballast (ie fitted within the hull or keel moulding) or an externally mounted casting is an interesting one. The yachtsman with encapsulated ballast doesn't have to think about corroded keel bolts (especially when the yacht is taking a pounding). However, the bottom of the keel will nearly always be the first part of a yacht to hit a reef or rock and stands a chance of being damaged. If the damage has cracked the laminate and seepage occurs, a cast iron keel will start rusting and there is nothing you can do about it. On the other hand, if you hit the bottom with an externally mounted keel the worst you will do is scratch the paint off the ballast, which can be wire-brushed and recoated at the next slipping.

If the grounding is a serious one, where the yacht has been pulled off but sustained quite serious damage to the keel foot, the encapsulated keel owner has the worry of the fibreglass being so badly damaged that the keel casting may drop out. You could also argue that an externally mounted keel's bolts would give up, or their attachment within the hull disintegrate, before you could get the yacht off the reef or shore. In a later section I describe a good way of building a sacrificial shoe for an encapsulated keeled yacht and with this fitted I think it tips the scales in favour of this ballast arrangement.

The design of bilge keels has improved by leaps and bounds over the last few years to the point where the performance difference between a yacht so fitted and an identical one with a fin keel is marginal. Assymetric aerofoil section and slight toe-ing in forward creates marginal lift to windward and helps to make up for the wetted-surface disadvantages. However, many of the older craft sporting bilge keels lost a great deal of windward performance. Many owners regard this as a reasonable price to pay for their ability to sit upright when dried out and it made them very popular, particularly in Britain, for coastal cruising. Many parts of the world have too little tidal range to take proper advantage of bilge keels, but they will nevertheless save their owner a great deal in slipping costs wherever the tide allows. Weighed against them is slightly diminished performance and the fact that when you dive and scrub off the underside at anchor, cleaning the inside face of the keels is a horrible job. Although in broad terms a fin keel is better suited to long distance cruising than bilge keels, if you have found a yacht which is otherwise well-suited to your needs you ought not to turn it down purely on the basis of her having bilge keels.

Centreboards deserve careful consideration. They have always been regarded as troublesome, partly because they can become jammed with mud, sand, shingle, or even barnacles but also because with older materials they were difficult to maintain, which in turn led to breakages. With a fibreglass case one need never worry about rot getting a hold inside, and with the strength of this material movement is minimal and leaks are rarely a problem. Nylon bushes control the board much better these days and modern engineering has made raising or lowering the board much easier.

If you are designing or building a new boat and have the ability to decide, the comparison between the centreplate and daggerboard is an interesting one. The fan-shaped hinging centreplate has always had a popular following with the advantage that it is possible to locate the board under the cabin sole, or fairly unobstrusively under the saloon table which it can support. The hinged board also acts as a primitive depth sounder which in reefy waters can be a big plus point. However, this type of board is still very difficult to maintain. Removing it to paint the inside of the box or the board itself is a fairly major operation and if it isn't easy to do, it's likely to be a job left until it causes problems.

The daggerboard is in many ways a better proposition if, and only if, you can organise the accommodation around it. With the box left open at the top (on deck), it should be possible to remove the board using a halyard and get it on deck to antifoul or patch up damage. If you also use a thick-sectioned chord and fit dinghy inspection hatches well above the waterline in the casing, with the board pulled out on deck it will be possible to get an arm inside the box to paint in there too.

The other advantages of a daggerboard are numerous. While a centreplate has always been regarded as useful as a depth sounder they will obligingly raise themselves as the vessel ploughs onwards on to the reef. Time is precious in such circumstances, and the extra few moments or even minutes it takes to wind up the board to get off the reef might be too long and result in the boat being driven inextricably shorewards with possibly disastrous consequences. On the other hand with a stout daggerboard fitted into a very strong box, the boat would be stopped very abruptly and would still be in water deep enough to give the crew time to sail or haul her off.

A strong daggerboard casing extending from hull to deck in the middle is also a desirable feature structurally, strengthening both hull and deck enormously and can also be arranged to take the mast compression loads.

A serious disadvantage of both centre- or daggerboard keel arrangements is that they raise the centre of gravity much more than conventional keels. There are ways to ease this, but they must be considered at design stage – building the board as heavy as possible, using lead instead of cast iron ballast, positioning the engine, tanks and batteries as low as possible and trimming down heavy top hamper. Wings fitted to the tip section would help a great deal too. The lifting keel for an ocean cruiser would also have to have an infallible method of holding the board in the lowered position just in case the yacht was rolled in severe conditions.

Accommodation can easily be worked around a centreboard case, but it is more difficult with a daggerboard which extends from keel to deckhead. Depending on the yacht's size and beam it is possible to site the saloon aft of the box, but with the case still within the cabin to some extent (as might be a keel-stepped mast). On a larger boat, 40ft and up, the saloon could be positioned to one side of the case. The French Kelt/Kirie 39 has twin forward cabins with a longitudinal central bulkhead dividing them, which solves the problem.

Most of us have no choice in the material used in the keel of our yachts because it is there already and certainly not worth changing. However, if you are starting from scratch and can choose, lead is far superior to cast iron, but much more expensive. The loading of an ocean cruiser inevitably raises the centre of gravity. By starting off with lead and therefore a lower initial centre of gravity you are effectively increasing the yacht's stability and safety. Lead also has a higher specific gravity, so requires less space and for the same weight therefore gives you spare room in the bilge for extra tankage or storage.

## Rudders

Although a rudder that is skeg-hung is less vulnerable to damage by hitting flotsam or whales, there are nevertheless thousands of yachts fitted with unsupported spade rudders who cruise the oceans without any problems. The spade rudder is generally more responsive than a conventional one because it is more efficient hydrodynamically. This type of rudder usually has a slightly balanced area forward of the stock axis which has the added bonus of easing the weight on the helm, which is a definite advantage when it comes to self-steering (unless it is over-done and the helm becomes too light which can throw some 'windvane gears).

Skegless spade rudders have been around for a long time, with designers like E G van de Stadt using them almost exclusively for the last 20 years on enduring production boats like the Pioneers, Excaliburs and Gallants. They have a very good safety record and the protection a skeg gives a rudder takes a lot of beating. For long distance cruising the rudder, whose operation is so vital, should have this protection and for me this outweighs the disadvantages of slightly less efficiency.

It is very easy to equip boats for ocean cruising with needlessly heavy gear. This is usually a sign of lack of confidence or experience, costs more money and cuts down on sailing performance. Nevertheless everybody who has experience agrees that rudder fittings (pintles and gudgeons) are one item that must be extra-extra strong. We've all seen articles about how to rig jury steering with floorboards lashed to the end of running booms and such like, but in reality it is very difficult indeed to make these lash-ups work even half efficiently without seriously sapping crew strength, a problem which is amplified for the ocean cruiser which by nature will have so much farther to sail to port.

Although twin rudders have been used from time to time before (for example 1980 OSTAR entry *Spaniel* used them) they have only recently become popular, developed largely by French naval architects. They were at first regarded as a passing fashion, but in use proved surprisingly effective and have a lot of advantages for the ocean cruiser. One of the reasons for their design was to create sufficient rudder area for centre- or daggerboard yachts which otherwise need a complicated lifting blade. Angling them so that the leeward rudder is more or less vertical when the boat is heeled improves the steering ability and sensitivity so greatly that several long-distance racing yachts (ie non-IOR) have fitted them, finding that the disadvantage of marginal increase in wetted surface is eclipsed by the better handling (when heeled the windward blade is clear of the water anyway). For an ocean cruising boat the linkage creates an extra complication, but it is re-assuring to know you have a second rudder if one is damaged. The only real disadvantage to the system, other than extra cost, is that close-quarters manoeuvrability under power is limited by not being able to use the prop-wash to kick the stern one way or another.

Finally rudder positioning needs consideration. A rudder situated right aft is undoubtedly best for long distance sailing. Not only does this make it easier to arrange a trim tab self steering (should finances be tight and you need to make your own gear) but also it makes trouble-shooting, particularly at sea, much easier. It is possible to dive down and free off a net or fish trap wrapped around the rudder at sea when the rudder is aft; it is impossible when the blade is tucked deep under a counter and the yacht is pitching. And if ever you need to rig basic emergency steering lines to the rudder blade the job is reasonably simple with the rudder right aft.

## Weight Distribution

We have touched on this in relation to other factors but the subject is important enough to need examining on its own. For many years racing boats have avoided at all costs having weight any distance fore or aft of the yacht's pitching centre, approximately amidships. Not only that, but all major weights are situated as low as is humanly possible. The performance difference is remarkable, not only in terms of speed, but also their ability to keep moving into large seas when the cruising monohull, with all the ground tackle in the bows and spare fuel, water and cruising necessities stuffed into the lazarette, is stopped, nodding to a standstill in the trough of one wave.

But what of practicalities? It's fine to say that weight should be kept out of the ends, but can it be done? Because the best living accommodation is in the middle of the boat it goes against the grain to use that centre area for stowage. However with a bit of thought and cunning it can be done. If you are in the lucky position of designing your dreamboat (or having it designed), the problem of weight distribution can be borne in mind from the outset. If you're working with an existing boat, similar principles can be applied which ease the problem. For a start, consider what are the major weights within a yacht; the ballast, the engine, water and fuel tanks, ground tackle, tools, stores and individual items of equipment like the liferaft, dinghy and outboard. Clearly, the ballast and engine cannot be moved, but the chances are that they are in the right place anyway. It is a much better idea in the long run to have ample water and fuel in the tanks than it is to carry extra in cannisters. The first priority on a new boat then is to design in as much water tankage as possible, and a minimum of 30-40 gallons (135-180 lit) of fuel, just enough to keep you going in cruising grounds where it's difficult to refuel, such as the Indian Ocean route from Australia to Suez. If you have an existing boat, make the increasing of tankage one of the high priorities of preparation. The lockerage under saloon berths is usually horrible to use and these spaces are a good place to start fitting flexible tanks.

Spare anchors should, if possible, be put in the bilge. If not, it is often possible to find a place for them in the engine compartment, especially aft of the gearbox where there's often free space on yachts. The working anchor can be taken off the foredeck and sat in chocks just aft of the mast (where it won't foul headsail sheets), and if you were able to organise it the main anchor chain locker could be stowed in the bilge in the mast area, stowed there through a hawse-hole on deck whose pipe leads down below next to the mast or its compression post. The liferaft can be positioned in its chocks just in front of the cockpit coamings or in the forward end of the cockpit. The rigid dinghy, if you have one, should also ideally be stowed aft of the mast on the coachroof or deck. Instead of fitting the dinghy's outboard on a bracket on the pushpit, consider arranging a stowage bracket for it in the forwardmost cockpit locker.

Most living possessions we carry around with us don't weigh very much and these can be put in the lockers forward and aft. Light sails like the spinnaker can happily live in the eyes of the focs'le with heavier ones nearer the centre of pitching if possible.

Correct distribution of weight is only a matter of discipline and a little thought, but the difference it makes to sailing performance, especially if you're about to confront a long windward thrash, makes it well worth the trouble involved.

### The Multi-hulled Ocean Cruiser

Throughout the spectrum of ocean cruising there are horses for courses in terms of yacht suitability. I'd happily take a reasonably standard production boat on a tradewind transatlantic passage, but it would be a questionable choice for cruising in high latitudes or for taking on the Southern Ocean passage. Multihulls are much the same.

Most writers on ocean cruising disregard multihulls but it would be foolish to ignore them as a possible choice for they have numerous advantages to offer. Without delving too deeply into the history of multihulls the point to remember is that these craft have had nothing like the time the monohulled yacht has to develop and evolve. They came on to the scene in the 1950s and in the first twenty years their designers, builders and sailors had an enormous amount of learning to do. Wild claims were made about their speed and capabilities, and whilst they were undoubtedly faster than conventional monohulls, none of the sailing establishment (who'd probably been overtaken by these strange and unnatural creations) were very sorry to see them come to grief fairly regularly in the learning process. Without much understanding of the structures or how to sail them, many broke up, a good few turned over and regrettably several lives of those pioneers were lost. Always happy to focus the spotlight on a controversial minority, the newspapers have to this day always catalogued every multihull mishap – a monohull sinking does not often make news but in terms of statistics is probably just as common.

By the early '70s multihulls had a firm footing and the learning curve was flattening out. Since then hundreds of multihulls have made successful ocean passages, James Wharram's designs proving the most popular and sometimes referred to as the Colin Archer of multihull sailing. Many notable passages have been made in the tiny 26ft Heavenly Twins class cats, including a singlehanded circumnavigation. Countless Catalacs have crossed the Atlantic and Prout Snowgoose cats have cruised all over the world and only one has ever capsized, being raced hard in a near-gale off the Isle of Wight.

It would be naive to suggest that every multihull is suitable for long distance cruising – there are good and bad. A serious cruising yachtsman wouldn't attempt a long-distance passage in a contempory half-tonner and he should no sooner try it in a multihulled equivalent. A catamaran or trimaran *can* capsize, but it is no more likely to happen than a monohull sinking. In both cases, it is a risk that all yachtsmen have to accept. Sailing a multihull one should consider the possibility of this happening and prepare for it in the same way a responsible monohuller would consider fitting emergency buoyancy bags.

One of the difficulties of opting for a multihull is the limited choice available. Very few companies have gone into the multihulls field with the result that there are only perhaps a dozen production classes, plus a wide variety of one-offs and amateur-built cats and tris built to stock plans. In strict investment terms it is a difficult decision. The well-known production boats command good resale prices and the one-offs and amateur-built boats are not so sought after, but this doesn't mean that all the home-built boats are not good. Many are better-constructed than those produced by the professionals, but the investment element must be carefully considered. The alternative, if you're especially keen to have a multihull and can't find what you want amongst the production boats, is to commit a smaller sum (with the rest invested) and buy a relatively cheap cat or tri that is suitable and, of course, sound on the assumption you're likely to lose a certain amount on resale, offset by the income from the invested difference.

Ocean cruising in multihulls is a completely different game and it is a common enough mistake to cruise them in exactly the same way as a monohull. They are very different craft (not necessarily better or worse) and they require a new philosophy to overcome their disadvantages and capitalise on their good points.

Weight, or more precisely load carrying, will always be a problem. A light multihull, and nine-tenths of them are light, cannot carry weight very well so the multihull sailor will have a constant battle with keeping loading to a minimum. He has certain advantages on his side though and with a bit of thought can make the best of them. Instead of carrying vast quantities of water, which is very heavy, the multihull (below) The Wharram family of catamarans is something akin to the Land-Rover of ocean sailing – seen all over the world, rugged, uncomfortable, basic but very capable (Geoff Pack) *(left)* Prout catamarans – the 31 or 33ft Quest or the 35 or 37ft Snow-goose – are probably the most popular production GRP multihulls used for ocean cruising and living aboard

sailor should convert areas of his large deck space into water-catchment surfaces and with a diverter valve and simple filtering system can direct this straight into his tanks. Another possibility is to have huge water tanks in the otherwise-empty outriggers. These would be filled in port so whilst you'd rarely see your waterline, there would be ample water for regular showers and fresh water laundry. They would be emptied before putting to sea.

That large deck space can also be used to advantage by fitting plenty of solar panels, thus saving on heavy batteries and diesel for charging. The marginally extra speed made by a correctly-loaded multihull will mean that the owner can also tap the charging potential of a propshaft alternator.

Changing anchoring techniques also gains many advantages over the deep keelers. The easiest option when entering an anchorage is to head for all the other boats and drop the hook there, whereupon the multihull makes itself unpopular by shearing around on a rope rode because they can't afford the weight disadvantage of all-chain cables. But, anchoring in very shallow water where other yachts can't reach has many advantages. Equipped with approximately 30ft (9.15m) of chain, this will be ample scope to lay in 3 or 4ft (1m) of water under

Sadly only a few multihull sailors really take advantage of their craft's unique advantages. Here the hull of a 60-footer is lifted (using levers) for antifouling in a quiet lagoon. When complete, the hull is lowered back down, the yacht turned around and the other hull prised up  *(Geoff Pack)*

chain only when she won't sheer as much. You won't have other boats dragging into you in the night and you'll be closer to the shore and won't need a heavy dinghy outboard and its fuel. If the crew has disappeared with the dinghy, you can walk or wade to the beach and put your clothes on there, and if you drop something over the side it will be easy to recover. It may raise some eyebrows, but if you're unhappy about the anchor holding, you have the option of walking out and digging a hole for it! In a hurricane anchorage situation, assuming there is no appreciable fetch, shallow water is by far the safest place for a multihull to lie, geographically protected as she is from deep keel vessels dragging on to her, for they will go aground long before they hit her.

The sensible multihull sailor will always be watching weight which can be a bore when you want to collect trinkets and souvenirs from your travels, but the way around it is to package them up from time to time and send them home. The weight problem also means that the multihull sailor can't have the luxury of stocking up for months in advance, so will have to provision in small batches with local foods.

The multihull's stable configuration can be taken advantage of in many ways. It shouldn't be necessary to have any more than a single inlet seacock in the entire boat, and with huge wingdecks one could install a couple of hatches *under* these. In this way, in port you could keep the hatches wide open and the accommodation sweet in the heaviest downpour while all the other boats in the anchorage are sweating out below with hatches dogged tight. Taking this a step further, if you're in a risky area for dinghy thefts, moor it overnight between the hulls. If the wire security painter is then taken from a strongpoint in the middle of the dinghy and up through this open hatch into the cabin the most determined dinghy thief will give up.

After food, the ocean cruiser's biggest outgoing is slipway and hoist charges. The multihull's light weight can obviate much of this because it is possible to drag it up a beach to antifoul, and also to go into a sheltered lagoon and lever one hull out of the water at a time on to props to work on it. A friend of ours had very strong stainless steel chainplates made so that his 46ft (13.8m) Wharram could be lifted out by a normal cargo crane costing half that of most Travelifts or commercial yacht yards. His next project is to make small removable axles and rubber wheels to fit at each end of both his stub keels so that using his mainsheet as a tackle, he can pull his cat up a beach unaided with his sheet winch. The cost of the axles and wheels will be about the equivalent of one commercial haul-out, but thereafter he was confident his hauling costs would be at the popular price.

The biggest 'if' about multihulls is the capsize question. This element of doubt puts off many people inexperienced with sailing multihulls from choosing this type of craft, which might otherwise be ideal for them. No multihull is incapable of capsizing any more than the *Titanic* was unsinkable. Given searoom, a monohull stands a good chance of emerging from survival conditions afloat, even if dismasted through rolling, having been left to its own devices. A multihull will always need looking after and the circumstances are rare when in a gale she can be left alone. I write from personal experience having sailed our 35ft (10.66m) catamaran through such conditions, and I believe that a sensibly-designed and well-built cruising multihull of 33ft and above can survive any conditions if she is sailed attentively and constantly. The crew must always remain alert to nurse her along, but they will have a better chance of cooking and sleeping comfortably when off-watch and so will be better nourished and rested than a monohull's crew.

It is essential for an ocean going multihull to have a comfortable and well-sheltered steering position to minimise fatigue and exposure in bad conditions and that the self-steering can quickly be over-ridden. Tyre drogues are the only feasible way of slowing the yacht to controllable speeds when running before survival conditions. Two tyres should be carried for such an eventuality (they can double up as storm fenders in port). They will need at least 400ft (120m) of warp so they are always trailing in the trough behind you. Pat Patterson is a multihull designer and sailor with a great deal of experience, including a circumnavigation at times in high latitudes. He is convinced that a catamaran laying beam on with a long drogue led to weather from bow to stern is almost impossible to capsize, even in the worst seas.

Multihulls are clearly here to stay and are chosen more and more for tropic passages. They are not everyone's ideal, but they warrant serious consideration as a solution to a number of cruising requirements.

# 7
# *Below Decks*

The accommodation area of a yacht has many demands on it, especially as at sea it must meet different priorities than in port. Accommodation on sailing boats has suffered from what Gary Hoyt describes as 'design constipation'. On boats less than 42ft (12.8m), nobody with the exception of the French, has dared to vary from the well-tried layouts that have lasted for generations. Broadly these follow a standard plan of a foc'sle with twin vee berths, heads and cupboard opposite, saloon with berth either side and divided by a table then aft under the main companionway, the galley to one side and chart table opposite, usually with a quarter berth as well. There are slight variations, such as the addition of an after cabin and in the last ten years, as yachts have sported fatter stern sections it has become more common to tuck these in the quarter sections of the yacht. Yards can hardly be blamed for not experimenting when the conventional layout, for all its faults, does actually work for the majority of the market. However there is no doubt that some features could be much better for those who will live aboard constantly, so we will consider what to look out for and how they can be improved slightly for ocean cruising.

## *Sleeping*

The standard layout works quite well for two people. Most couples use the vee-berth double in port so that they can have a bed made the whole time and there are no arguments about what time each prefers to go to bed or get up. This might sound like a minor point, but a saloon double can be irritating when you want to go to bed and your partner wants to stay up and read, especially as you have the chore of converting the saloon double and making up the bed last thing at night.

At sea, the forward berth is usually unusable, and generally the off-watch person sleeps on the lee side of the saloon. This arrangement is not so good because the off-watch person monopolises the best lounging seat in the boat and the crew on watch have to be very quiet and can't use the radio, stereo or VHF. So unless you don't mind sitting on the uphill seat throughout a watch, make sure the boat has a comfy place for the watchkeeper to sit, the most obvious being the chart table where he or she can update the log and position. A separate quarter cabin is more desirable. There the watch below can be

reasonably closetted but make sure it has curtains as a wedge of
sunlight from a porthole scything around a cabin is enough to keep
anyone awake during the day. The normal double berth may be better
divided into two. The snag with quarter berths is that they are
underneath the cockpit where there is a lot of noisy activity by those
working the ship. An alternative is a curtained-off pilot berth in the
wings of the saloon, which if made snug enough could be used on
either tack. If you have more than two people aboard, it goes without
saying that proper seaberths must be found for everyone not on
watch, and this may mean giving up the saloon as a living cabin which
is a nuisance.

While on the subject of seaberths, it is important to make sure they
can be used when the boat is rolling downwind. On *Euge* we found all
our berths untenable and just slightly too wide when gyrating down
the trades so we ended up sleeping on the saloon floor, wedged
between the table and berth front, and waking up four hours later with
something akin to *rigor mortis*.

Another point to look out for is the accessability of a berth. When
the time comes for 'all hands on deck' it's no good if the off duty watch
have been shoe-horned into berths a long way from the companionway.

Leecloths must be fitted to all seaberths. For constant use it is worth
spending some time making them easy to use with snaphooks instead
of knots to hold them up. We made ours with two pockets, a big one
to stuff the off-watch person's clothes into to pad the leecloth and a
small one higher up for things like spectacles.

### Saloon

As the main living space in what has become your home the saloon
must be as large as possible. It should be surrounded by accessible
locker space within reach to contain all the items you might need here
from letter-writing equipment and board games to books, cassettes,
drinks and glasses etc. Don't stow regularly-used items under the
saloon settees – for the person who's just got comfortable reading a
book it is irritating to be frequently moved.

Light and ventilation are essential and if you have a boat that has no
opening hatch over the saloon, make sure that fitting one is high up the
priority list – a single forehatch simply isn't enough for comfort in hot
climates. Ideally, there should be access forward to the heads through
the saloon without its occupants having to move to make way.
Saloons with an offset dinette area are usually OK in this way. If at all
possible, do not have a permanent sleeping berth in the saloon. It is a
constant source of aggravation to all, though of course it doesn't
matter for the occasional short-term guest.

For much of the time in hot weather crews like to live out in the

A seamanlike interior with 'captive' companionway steps (which give lateral footholds at sea), deep twin sinks and comfortably angled backrests. Pillars are essential to wrap an arm around whilst getting dressed at sea, although the overhead grabrails are no use when the yacht is heeled over   *(Yachting Monthly)*

cockpit, but the saloon must nevertheless be comfortable with well-angled seats and backrests so you can sit comfortably for a few hours reading. Fig 1 on page 91 gives some guide to dimensions to look out for. A standard boat whose seat angles are not so good can be improved with new contoured upholstery, a decision you might think extravagant before moving aboard, but one you will be unlikely to regret at a later stage. A couple of large bean bags can also be very useful for curling up in comfort. If your saloon upholstery is covered in vinyl sew up some light fabric covers (to be taken off in bad weather), otherwise bare flesh sticks to the vinyl with the salt atmosphere and constant dampness and this can cause sores on the backs of legs and bums.

The saloon table needs to be big so everyone can use a section of it without impinging on the next person. It must also be stout and about the only way of achieving this and maintaining the ability to fold out is to have a steel frame made for it, which is then firmly bolted in place. In my cruising experience in small boats I cannot remember having ever eaten a meal from plates on the saloon table in anything above a Force 2, so I think that fiddles should be dispensed with as they only get in the way. But a deep box (minimum 6in/15mm) should be fitted in the middle of the table to hold all the accoutrements of a meal – cutlery, condiments etc.

Some very experienced yachtsmen believe in gimballed saloon tables, and they certainly have a lot going for them. Our friends Francois and Pascal Grinberg on *Scherzo* have this arrangement and cunningly use the Reed's Sailmaker sewing machine as a counter weight. A gimballed table is only really suitable for two people facing each other fore and aft with their plates situated on the axis line.

## Galley

The design of a galley must be assessed with an eye to working there when the yacht is steeply heeled. Lockers with their doors facing fore and aft are hopeless because all the contents will come out at you when the locker is opened at sea. Better to have all the fore and aft facing area for the crockery in slide-opening bins, or have the locker opening six inches above the cupboard base, which effectively creates a very deep fiddle to hold bottles etc. Large lockers are little more than useless and are a nightmare when rolling because it is difficult to wedge all the contents in place. It is much better to have lots of small ones, with just one unit large enough for the few big items. Sliding locker fronts must only ever be sited on the fore and aft line. This may sound obvious, but some very well-known yacht builders still forget that a boat heels. They are better than hinged doors which may let out the entire contents when heeled over – with sliding doors you stand a chance of opening just a small section.

The sink should be as near the yacht's centre line as possible, otherwise as soon as you are heeled it will fill up with water (or need a hand pump to get rid of waste) and become useless on one tack. Twin sinks are quite useful, because at sea one inevitably becomes a dump for loose items like the detergent bottle. It is very useful to have different sizes, a large one capable of doing the laundry in port and a small deep one for washing up at sea. Both fresh and salt water must be arranged to serve both. Fit the salt water pump to the right of the fresh pump, so when hands are being washed or tea-cups rinsed, the immediate action is to go for the salt water faucet.

If a 'bum strap' is not fitted, try to envisage where one will go. The same applies for a crash bar across the cooker. In an ideal galley, the cook should be away from the main throughfare. Cooking is a thankless task at the best of times so if you change nothing else in the interior of your boat, consider changes to the galley to improve the cook's lot – after you've used it for a while to find its faults. Waste disposal for example is rarely ever thought out in galley design and yet it is a constantly irritating thing if the cook has nowhere to place rubbish other than a polythene bag which is falling over regularly.

An interesting traditional interior: opening portholes let in a bit of air, but not much light; high fiddles and plenty of varied locker space are good features; the single gimballed oil lamp is good for maintaining an economic dim light during night sailing and acts as back up in the event of electrical problems; buttoned upholstery looks lovely but keeps the crew busy cleaning out crumbs, dust and rubbish   *(Yachting Monthly)*

One idea incorporated into a charterboat we once ran was a drying up locker. It was a GRP-lined cabinet with drain and wire crockery baskets fitted inside. It was a huge success because it solved a common enough laziness problem – not drying after washing up.

Fiddles in the galley area must be high, but also consider fitting movable sea fiddles which break up a large work surface and make it usable under way.

### Heads and Ablutions

Some question the building of a commodious head in the best part of the boat when it is only used for a few minutes each day. Others feel that this essential place deserves some special attention. Many a long distance cruising yachtsman has ripped out the contraption altogether and used a bucket to simplify matters. Nobody would argue that facilities could get more basic than a bucket, although on Conny Van

Rietschoten's round-the-world race winner *Flyer* he had a rather classy little seat welded into the pushpit over the stern of the yacht and the crew used that winter and summer. It all boils down to personal preference, but do make sure that the ventilation is well dealt with – either a little solar-powered vent or better still a small aluminium-framed opening hatch.

I have lived with a wide variety of marine loos and only one stands head and shoulders above the rest – the Blake Lavac. Some people prefer Baby Blakes (and treat them with respect and love rather like old Morris Minors) but I've yet to find one that didn't leak slightly. If your boat is fitted with one of the cheap plastic-parted marine loos very common now on European production craft, change it immediately. They are designed for occasional weekend use, and simply don't stand up to prolonged living aboard.

Installations vary a lot, but try to ensure that yours is open all round, with all the pipes easily accessible for annual de-calcifying (taken out and hit repeatedly against a dock to clear constricting calcium build-up). If the pipes are tucked away in little lockers or uncleanable lining compartments, when they are removed the contents will pour away *somewhere*. The inlet and outlet seacocks should be at least two feet apart and ideally situated on opposite sides of the yacht. I guarantee that sooner or later your marine toilet will need work of some kind, generally as a result of an embarassing blockage. With this in mind, take it apart and familiarise yourself with all the parts before it needs to be done in anger, when the blockings will be turning your stomach and preventing clear thought. Some heads are easy to clear if you know how. Quite often the blockage is not in the unit, but at a turn in the exit seacock where quite considerable pressure can build up and the user must be told to stop pumping (many skippers subconsciously listen to guests pumping the loo – if the rhythm seems to slow or get harder the effect is electric!). To clear this requires going over the side with a short piece of hooked wire and the ability to swim very quickly afterwards . . .

Which leads us neatly on to showers. Like most ocean cruising people, I have showered in thousands of shore places and always longed to have a simple fitted shower on board. The ocean cruising yachtsman is independent by nature, yet still four out of five travel the world looking for showers . . . The need is less in places like the Caribbean and Pacific where you can dive overboard and wash in the sea, but in harbours as opposed to anchorages it is necessary to find a shower.

Many people feel that a shower adds complication to their boats with pressurized water, sump pumps and so on but this needn't be so. One of the best showers I ever saw was on a small trimaran. The focs'le was the heads and shower combined. A loo sat in solitary splendour in a large and otherwise empty glassfibre lined and watertight compartment with an opening hatch over, all painted white. Water (hot or cold) was supplied by a portable pressurized garden sprayer. After use the hull sides were wiped and the bilge area sponged dry. This arrangement was used daily with conspicuous success. An added benefit was that when it rained the forehatch could still be left open for fresh air to permeate below decks as the focs'le could be mopped up afterwards.

Unfortunately most boatbuilders insist on prissying up the loo/shower compartment with lockers, shelves and fiddly joinery. The result is that the showers are totally impractical to use and it takes a day for all the woodwork and contents to dry out and even then there are soap-laden puddles lingering. It becomes such a hassle to take a shower in such a boat that everyone searches for one ashore, so beware of being influenced to buy a boat on the basis of a fitted shower, unless it is a spacious and easily-drained GRP-lined module.

## Navigation Station

For the amount of use they get most chart tables take up an inordinate amount of prime space. Many skippers prefer to navigate on the saloon table, with a big fitted bookshelf behind them and charts rolled up under the deckhead. However a chart table and seat is most useful as a watchkeeper's position below, where he or she can sit and read, poking a head out of the hatch at each turn of the page and keeping out of the way of sleeping crew. Have one that is flat so that it can be used for other purposes, such as meal or drink preparation, in harbour. It is amazing how many essential books one accumulates, so aim to increase shelf space, allowing for large publications such as the Sight Reduction Tables. If the table has a seat it is better that it face fore and aft. And make sure that if the electric panel is situated by the watch-keeper's elbow or shoulder, as the majority are, that it has a clear perspex sheet protecting it for when the yacht is heeling that way. This also keeps off any spray flying about.

## General

A boat that is lived aboard should not be compartmentalised. Try to maintain an open plan arrangement by taking off doors and opening up bulkheads with large scallops (making sure they're not structural first).

One of the best accommodation plans I ever saw was on a Newick trimaran built by a friend of ours, Jan Ebbing, who had spent the previous 16 years cruising and covered 60,000 miles. Confronted with a bare hull (he'd built the boat himself) with one immovable structural bulkhead, he laid a sole at a fairly high level to give him plenty of storage low down in the bilge. Then he ran two bookshelves the length of the interior just under the hull/deck join. The floor, hull sides and deckhead were thickly carpeted throughout and the accommodation was completed by three or four big bean bags. That was it. The loo was a bucket (if you wanted privacy you went into the forward compartment or the cockpit) and the sink another different-coloured bucket. A simple propane cooker could be used anywhere and the bean bags made comfortable seating and sleeping. This may sound basic but it was one of the most functional boats I've ever seen, has made several long passages, and has been his home now for several years without modification.

Most accommodation plans can be subtly improved to make what was an awkward cabin into a comfortable home. A little thought on lighting (both natural and electric) always pays off, and judicious use of bright, light coloured paints instead of universal varnishwork can give an impression of space.

When considering stowage don't only look at just the extent of locker space, but consider its accessibility and convenience. Many boats have acres of storage under berths and seats, but this is nearly always inconvenient to use. People have to be moved, then perhaps bedding and the cushions, locker lids and so on. So these areas must be backed up by plenty of door-fronted lockers and drawers (opening, needless to say, on an athwartship's plane, not fore and aft). Big lockers should be split up, and it is a good idea to see if a framework cannot be incorporated in one of these to take stacked plastic bins which are very efficient stowage. A boat we once ran had these bins running on little wooden rails fore and aft in the bilges which utilized this otherwise unused space.

You will inevitably have several sets of clothes that need hanging up. A boat really must have a reasonable-sized hanging locker somewhere. A separate oilskin hanging locker situated right next to the companionway is also desirable, although one can live without it when there are just two people aboard. In the tropics in the daytime it's more practical to strip off your clothing if you're likely to get wet, rather than put more on and if you have a decent sprayhood that covers the forward part of the cockpit, the best place to dry oilskins is in the cockpit hanging up under that sprayhood, so that the dampness dissipates outside and not into the cabin.

All lockers must also be ventilated. This can be done in a couple of hours with a hole-cutter and fret-saw. The intention is to promote through flow so one hole will do nothing. Cut holes or slits low and high in a locker so that during the day, as the air warms up, it rises, escapes, and is replaced with fresh. This prevents musty clothes.

Finally a word on guests. If you have a boat less than 42ft (12.8m) and unless you regularly expect to receive extra crew, don't waste precious space by having a special guest cabin. Most people coming out to exotic locations to join you for a brief cruise will be only too happy to put up with a little inconvenience like sleeping in the saloon. Nobody could call you selfish for wanting to use every inch of the confined volume of a yacht that you have to live in for the rest of the year.

# 8
# On Deck

## Centre Cockpit Versus Aft

The choice between a centre or aft cockpit is an important one. I have met many yachtsmen who misjudged it and were regretting their choice.

When sailing, the centre cockpit is nearer the pitching point of the yacht and the motion is therefore easier. It is also closer to the mast which means a shorter time spent moving around on deck. The disadvantage is that being nearer the bows, a centre cockpit catches the waves and spray. This was a snag the Hiscocks disliked on their 49ft *Wanderer IV*. People who've sailed in extreme conditions with a centre cockpit also say that they offer a greater feeling of security by being planted in the heart of the boat. They also often comment they are safer with children board.

A centre cockpit normally commits you to having wheel steering and it is more difficult to rig windvane gear control lines in them.

The main reason for choosing a centre cockpit however is usually to divide up the accommodation and create a separate, more private after cabin. This is a desirable feature on a boat of 37 to 40ft and above, where it is possible to have a walkway connecting this cabin to the saloon. The size of this walkway will be the success or failure of the layout. Be suspicious of walkways on small boats though, because good headroom here will result in a high and exposed cockpit. If the boat doesn't have a walkway the desirability of the separate cabin is diminished. For example it will be necessary to clamber through the cockpit each time you want to use the loo in the night or brew up in the morning. This is alright in a tropic climate but no laughing matter if you live aboard in less balmy climes. More than one owner of a centre cockpit boat has turned over the crampt after cabin to stowage and ended up living in the considerably smaller forward accommodation quarters. Another point to bear in mind is that if the after cabin has a companionway and sliding hatch into the cockpit it will face forward and cannot be left open at sea and when sleeping there in port the washboards must be put in and hatch slid shut every time it rains. Few skippers sleep well when they are so far from the cockpit , so it is necessary to bunk in the saloon when at sea anyway. Therefore the time a centre cockpit with after cabin scores is when there are children aboard, because this cabin can be theirs to make as chaotic as they wish

The argument for a well protected centre cockpit is well demonstrated here. The aftercabin washboard will need to be in place for much of the time. This cockpit has several interesting features including a humped helmsman's seat and convenient cockpit table topped with a bin for holding handbearing compass/binoculars etc (*Yachting Monthly*)

without encroaching on the rest of the boat. Mum and Dad can sleep in the forward part of the boat and be just as private . . .

## Cockpit Features

It is absolutely essential that the cockpit of an ocean cruising yacht is comfortable, workable and generally liveable in. Ocean cruisers spend most of their time in harbour, in a warm climate. Combined with a well-designed awning, the cockpit is the coolest place aboard. It becomes a reading area, the workshop for tinkering with maintenance jobs, somewhere to sleep on hot muggy nights, a place to eat breakfast, survey the world going by or just somewhere to stretch out and relax. Unless it is comfortable you will be relegated to a hot saloon and not be able to look out and take in the surroundings you have just sailed thousands of miles to reach.

The design of a cockpit must also of course be efficient and safe at sea. The ability to self-drain is obvious, but it must empty the majority of the water quickly. Much has been written over the years about small cockpits for ocean cruisers, but the aspect most of these writers have overlooked is that it is the size of just the well itself that is critical, not necessarily the whole cockpit as long as it doesn't have very deep coamings. When your cockpit gets thoroughly filled, through being pooped or broaching, most of the water above the cockpit seats very quickly overspills the coamings and is gone. Normally, if the boat is heeled or rolling downwind all that is left is a well-full. If that well is small the extra weight of the water will not impede the yacht much and a long drainage time will be more inconvenient than dangerous. However, if the well is a largish size, an extra-big drain will need fitting. Some ocean cruisers, adapted from production craft, are fitted with a very large, up to 6in, pipe such as a plastic domestic waste glassed in from the back of the cockpit right through the lazarette locker to the transom which is effectively a storm drain. Located centrally, it won't drain the last dregs when heeled over (the normal fittings should do this anyway) but it will clear the large majority quickly. So when looking at cockpit size, try to imagine how much water will be actually contained on a bucking, heeling yacht, and judge the volume of the well before the whole cockpit.

Drainage when heeled is an aspect that most modern yacht designers have sorted out, especially as it is easy to arrange with GRP mouldings. However, make sure that the area between the seats and coamings can drain fully when heeled – half an inch of water here is quickly soaked up by the trousers of a crewmember coming into the cockpit and sitting down on the more comfortable lee side. Make sure this water can either drain out on to the sidedeck, or back into the cockpit well, not down into the cockpit lockers as is very often the case. Small seepage from rainwater while the boat is at rest is not a problem, but in bad weather when a lot of water is coming into the cockpit, you must make sure it is exiting out of the drains, not into the cockpit lockers and thence into the bilge. So irritated with this problem was double circumnavigator Leslie Powles that he ended up glassfibreing his cockpit locker lids permanently shut!

The sill of the companionway entrance must never be below the level of the cockpit seats on an ocean cruiser, because in heavy going there will nearly always be a few inches of water in the lee corner of the cockpit draining out and unless you have this high step a lot of water will creep into the cabin and possibly over the engine and electrics through the lower washboard. If you have a boat fitted with a low companionway, permanently screw the first washboard in place very thoroughly with plenty of silicone sealer around the edge to make it watertight.

Ideally a cockpit's seats and backrests should run more or less parallel to the yacht's centreline, otherwise with a particularly tapered cockpit (they often narrow toward the stern), when she is heeled over the tendency when sitting to leeward will be to slide you forward. The constant bracing to stay put can be enough to give you a stiff back after

a couple of hours on watch or at the helm. The forward ends of the
cockpit should really be tried out for comfort because they are usually
sheltered by the spray dodger and the most popular places to sit at sea.
The best is when the after cabin bulkhead is high enough to give
comfortable support to the back and also slopes forward slightly, as
many do.

The size, shape and angle of cockpit seats and backrests are critical if
you are going to enjoy being seated there for any length of time.
Before the early '70s yachtsmen had to put up with a narrow, hard
horizontal bench with a coaming at 90 degrees to it, whose edge
invariably hit you in the small of the back. Since then, GRP construction has allowed more comfortable shapes to be introduced. French
naval architects have always led the field in cockpit comfort. Fig 1
gives some idea of proportions that work well. If your cockpit seating
is uncomfortable it is not a difficult job to remodel it. If you have
simple plank coamings their height can be increased in port by having
extentions slot over the top. The shape of both the seats and the
backrests can be completely altered by cutting comfortable-profiled
'frames' then screwing slats to them park-bench style. When a wheel is
used for steering, a 'hump' on the athwartships seat can make a trick at

**Fig 1** The comfort of cockpit seats is imperative, bearing in mind the time you will be
spending there. These dimensions give an approximate guide to comfortable
proportions (**a**) 15in (38cm), (**b**) 105 degrees, (**c**) 20in (50cm), (**d**) 15in (38cm).

the helm much more comfortable and some classes have this as standard. It is very easy to make such a hump with two plywood contour frames and park-bench slatting and make it portable for use as an ordinary seat in harbour. If all else fails in terms of cockpit comfort, equip it with plenty of closed-cell foam cushions.

A cockpit should also remain clear of fittings as far as possible, because it always becomes the congregating place for crew or friends coming aboard. There is nothing worse than sitting on the coaming only to uncomfortably discover a cleat between the winches, then moving down into the cockpit, tripping over the tiller lines, knocking knees on the tiller itself, and getting yet another cleat or self-steering block neatly in the small of the back. A protruding mainsheet track with its stops and jamb cleat can mess up the forward end of the cockpit seat and the engine gear controls clutter it up astern . So many of these protuberances can be eliminated. Nothing can be done with winches, but there is no need for sheet cleats. A tugman's hitch (see photo on page 127) on the winch will do all that a cleat can; once accustomed to using them, you'll wonder why we ever had sheet cleats, because they are quicker to use than a turn on a cleat and tied properly don't jam up either. When cockpit cleats are needed (for the boom vang lead for example), they should be bolted to the outside of the coaming or on the deck alongside.

Engine controls (particularly the vulnerable key start) should be fitted in a moulded recess so that they are flush with the cockpit and cannot be kicked or have ropes caught around them. If yours are not flush, it is worth investigating the possibility of either moulding a little recess yourself or approaching the builder of any quality production yacht who will normally have a separate mould to make the recess in his yachts and persuading him to laminate an extra one for you. I once saw a boat whose engine control levers were just inside the cockpit locker. It meant the skipper always had to have that locker lid open when manoeuvring, but he argued that having the controls out of the way meant they didn't catch anything and, being away from wind and salt, stayed in better shape. Do remember though that you need engine controls and instrumentation where the watch-keeper can keep an eye on them while motoring for long periods. Malfunction alarms are often drowned by the sound of the engine, but situated in the cockpit you have a better chance of hearing them.

Tillers are best if they can be unshipped or folded up out of the way in harbour. Wheel steering can monopolise the cockpit and more than one voyager we've met removed it in port, having the boss nut welded with big wings for easy refitting.

The humble cockpit pramhood cover is one of the best yachting inventions for a long time. Well designed (some suggestions can be found in Fig 2), it makes drier sailing probable. A dry crew is a happier

**Fig 2** If well designed, a sprayhood is a godsend and ultimately, by contributing to crew and therefore cabin dryness, can maintain morale when conditions are bad. It should always attach to a coaming and the height of (**a**) should not restrict easy access in and out. The length of (**b**) should enable a crewmember to sit at the forward end of the cockpit and remain dry in rain. The section of fabric (**c**) *must* overlap the coaming and if this part is made without poppers and tensioned with bungy, the sprayhood will absorb seas breaking on it and not split so easily

and more efficient one and won't bring wet clothing into the cabin. The framework for the spray dodger should be very strong because it will inevitably be used as a grabrail.

If the sprayhood extends over part of the forward end of the cockpit, as it should, the watch-keeper can remain fairly dry and if the primary sheet winches are within easy reach the crew will be able to trim the sheets without getting too wet.

Another feature that more modern boats are starting to incorporate is the companionway 'trough' (photo overleaf) an eminently seaman-like design which not only improves accommodation greatly but also makes a very comfortable watch-keeper's position.

Sleeping in the cockpit is a great pleasure and absolute necessity in some climates, so the seats must be a minimum of 6ft 6in long and 20in wide and their bases angled outboard slightly to hold you in with the

A 'companionway trough' makes an ideal and protected watchkeeping position with all sail controls led aft and close to hand    *(Geoff Pack)*

boat rolling gently. A cockpit table is a great help when living aboard so find out whether it is possible to have one in your boat. It should be stout and easy to rig and stow. If it is too fiddly it will never get used. A cockpit becomes grubby in no time with a ghastly concoction of breadcrumbs, spilt coffee, jumper fluff, dried salt and short curly hairs and the common teak grating does little except act as an unhygienic matrix for this unholy mixture. Although a teak grating looks lovely when scrubbed and clean, it belongs to the days when gentlemen had crew to keep it looking like this. Have one on a lived-aboard cruising boat and you will become a slave to it. The best cockpit sole is one left reasonably clear of dirt-collecting slats and one that can be quickly cleaned by a sluiced bucket of salt-water followed by a once-over with the deck scrubber.

### Anchor Handling

One of the differences between the standard boat and the ocean cruiser is that anchoring facilities are gradually diminishing on the normal cruiser, which spends less time at anchor and more alongside. A stroll along an average marina will show a crop of anchors on deck and in rollers that have hardly ever been used. Good ground tackle is most ocean cruisers' insurance policy and it must be complemented with good gear for handling it. When you are in a genuine storm at anchor you begin to realise the advantages of a well laid-out, easily worked and spacious anchor handling area.

The design and arrangement of the bow-roller fitting heads the list of priorities. Basically, the larger the diameter of the roller the easier it will be to haul up the anchor. If the existing roller is less than 2in diameter, seriously consider replacing the whole fitting. Another element is the angle a bow roller imposes on a cable between the person hauling and the anchor itself (see Figure 3). With this in mind, the lower the bow-roller is situated the better – good examples of this can be found on the Rival 41s and Southerly range of yachts whose bow rollers are actually situated in their foredeck anchor well. The second roller of a double bow fitting doesn't get a great deal of use, but it earns its keep when the conditions are bad and two anchors have to be handled, plus allowing that much more space for each cable's chafing gear. The rollers themselves should be made out of the same metal as the fitting (ie stainless, bronze, aluminium or galvanised). This is noisier, but rubber rollers don't last any time at all and plastic rollers (in particular tufnol and nylon) can split, spread or swell in the heat and seize up on the axle pin. The cheeks of the roller must be deep and have a pin to stop the cable jumping out. The cheeks should also splay out to reduce chafe when the yacht shears. Some production boats, particularly those from France, have started using cast aluminium bow-rollers which can be very harsh on the anchor rope.

**Fig 3** The more acute the angle a bow-roller imposes on an anchor chain (**a**), the harder it will be to haul up. Look for efficient features like the lowered roller in boat (**b**)

An hour or so of judicious work with a metal file will breach the anodising but improve the cheeks no end.

An anchor ought to be able to stow within the bow roller, at least temporarily whilst you approach an anchorage or shift to another. If it doesn't it is tempting to leave it hanging from the bow for a few moments where it stands a good chance of swinging and damaging the gelcoat or paintwork. If you have a roller-reefing headsail, make sure the drum is set sufficiently high off the deck (with a solid spacer) so the anchor can be lowered without the shank hitting the drum.

Whether you have a windlass must depend on a combination of boat size, bank balance and personal strength. Whichever you decide, it must be relatively easy to haul in your anchor otherwise you'll be tempted to stop in a potentially dangerous spot when you should move on. The arguments against a windlass are to keep things simple, cut down weight, and save money for something else. Our two ocean cruisers were both around 35ft and both equipped with 35lb CQRs and 180ft of five-sixteenths inch chain. It was the same specification ground tackle that Hiscock used in his *Wanderer 111* which didn't have a windlass. On the first boat, which was largely engineless, we nearly always sailed out the anchor which meant about five frenetic minutes of shortening the cable, hoisting sail and then with sails trimmed sailing over the anchor which then had to be hauled up and on deck quickly as by then we were hurtling through a crowded anchorage or harbour. When the anchor fouled, we hitched a line to it and led this aft to a sheet winch to haul up. A chain pawl is an old idea but considerably reduces the total effort required to raise an anchor by holding the chain for you whilst you grab another arm's length of chain, or simply rest for a moment. A grooved bow roller increases the efficiency of the chain pawl considerably, as does a length of shock cord as shown in Fig 4.

I was not disappointed when our second boat had a windlass already fitted. She also had a nice reliable diesel. In practice I found that the Simpson Lawrence windlass, highly popular and fitted on thousands of yachts, so slow and uncomfortable to use (you either had to bend awkwardly or use it on your knees) that I hardly ever used it. Instead, we would motor towards the cable which took all the work out of hauling, then when it was up and down put a turn on a cleat and break out the anchor with the motor running ahead. While Lou Lou kept the yacht on station with the engine I had all the time in the world to haul up the anchor. After those experiences I would avoid buying and fitting a windlass on a yacht less than 36ft (needing a 35lb bower anchor) unless it was absolutely necessary, and then make sure it was one of the fast action types. Having spent many hours and a lot of money repairing electric windlasses as the skipper of a charter boat I would also look at these suspiciously unless I could afford the very best

**Fig 4** If you have no windlass, a chain pawl will reduce the effort involved in hauling the anchor enormously. With a chain pawl, a 35lb (15kg) anchor and 30 fathoms (55m) of 5/16th in (5mm) chain can be handled without difficulty or need for a windlass

and a comprehensive selection of spare parts.

The foredeck of a serious ocean cruiser must have at least two king-size cleats and preferably three, for when conditions are bad you need to adjust each separate mooring or anchor warp independently. A lowered foredeck anchor well is useful because it allows you to stow all the cable and anchor in it temporarily while you wash off the inevitable collection of mud, sand, seaweed and kelp. All this muck goes out of the well scuppers rather than being spread all over the decks. However, such a well must have large drains to cope with lumps of seaweed and clear the water which will fill it as you punch into a head sea.

It is easy to forget that the boat will be moored by her stern from time to time, perhaps with the kedge anchor out to steady her in a rolly anchorage or to hold her off the shore while you are tied bows-on to a palm tree. So a stern roller is needed. It will also be useful if ever you have to tow a drogue or warps in bad weather. A good sized fairlead on the taffrail will do almost as well. It is important that there is a fair uninterrupted lead from this fitting to one of the sheet winches so the stern anchor can be hauled tight. This comes into its own if ever you go aground and try hauling the yacht off backwards.

### Deck Hatches

Until we have sailed in a hot climate, most of us tend not to pay too much attention to opening hatches on yachts. They are seen only as a

**Fig 5** If a hatch is mounted on a wooden or moulded plinth, when a green sea sweeps it the water is directed up and over the hatch thus keeping the direct flow of water away from the seal, cutting the chance of leaks

source of draughts and a danger to seaworthiness in heavy weather. That all soon changes in hot Mediterannean weather and muggy still tropic nights, when one cannot have enough opening hatches in hot climates. The aluminium-framed opening hatches fitted to most modern boats are very good, but if you've any choice in the matter it's worth fitting hatches which don't have fiddly thumbscrew-tightened support struts. In the tropics where rain-squalls are a common daily occurance, the hatches get opened and closed very regularly and those catches don't last long. And sooner or later someone will fall against or stand on your opened hatch and the inability to yield will quite likely distort the hatch and make it leak forever after. We have fitted Lewmar Superhatches and have nothing but praise for their simple operation and watertightness.

If you are building or refitting and can choose your hatches make sure that when positioned on a horizontal surface all the water can drain off entirely. If not they will soon leak.

### General Deck Layout

**Stowage** Ocean cruisers always seem to accumulate a fair amount of junk and equipment on deck, much of which is better stowed elsewhere. An accumulation of four or five full water or fuel containers, extra anchors, a couple of bicycles, spare gas bottles, and a few heavy drogue warps can have an adverse effect on the yacht's stability. Much of this equipment is little, if ever, used and every effort should be made to stow it low down in the bilge or at the bottom of cockpit lockers. Certain items are unavoidable and must be stowed on deck. The liferaft is best situated somewhere aft of amidships to keep it out of the way of solid water forward. When kept in the cockpit well, it serves the dual function of cutting down the cockpit's volume.

***The Dinghy*** This must have a home on deck and if you prefer to have a rigid tender, make sure it can be accommodated on deck without fouling any important working areas or gear. With ingenuity, dinghies can be adapted to fit on deck, by building a recess in the transom to fit round the mast (Fig 14) or a slit in the bows to snug up to the inner forestay. If the dinghy is stowed on the coachroof you might as well take advantage of its height by bolting handrails on its bottom panels so they can be grabbed when moving around on deck.

***Running Booms*** It has somehow become traditional among ocean cruisers to fit the running booms permanently aloft, either strapped to the mast or taken out to the shrouds. This undoubtedly makes them very easy to use, but has significant disadvantages. Windage is increased a great deal, as is the centre of gravity, but more important is their vulnerability in this position. The principal secondary use of running poles is to set up a jury rig if the mast is broken and if they are strung up in the rigging they're unlikely to survive a dismasting without being broken themselves. They are best stowed on deck as far forward as possible, so the crew can lift their after ends up and hook on to the mast fitting without fouling the lower shrouds. Running booms are by definition used when running downwind, when the boat will be

Beware of clutter; a combination of lower shrouds and mast 'toastrack' bars make it almost impossible to easily move this heavy bagged sail aft    *(Yachting Monthly)*

**Fig 6** Heeled ergonomics. The upright cabin and narrowish sidedecks of the yacht on the left make deckwork clumsy, inefficient and quite likely dangerous compared to the yacht on the right. In the light of the amount of seatime you will put in aboard your ocean cruiser, make sure the deck is easy to move around on at sea

rolling. If one person is trying to set up the boom it can be very difficult to keep 'one hand for yourself and one for the ship'. So it pays to spend some time establishing a routine and organising stowage for the booms so that only one end need be lifted. My own system uses a simple length of line permanently hanging between the after struts on either side of the pulpit. The front of the boom is disconnected from its deck chock, lifted and placed in this rope sling. Thus cradled, the after end can then be picked up and fitted to the mast, completing the operation.

*Miscellania* Keep the sidedecks completely clear of lashed down equipment and keep all miscellaneous gear like the boathook, scrubber, dinghy oars etc, within a centre area on a flush deck or on the coachroof. The less cluttered the deck, the less chance of accidents, foul-ups, or simply stubbed toes.

*Heeled Ergonomics* How good will your proposed deck layout (and in particular sidedecks) be in providing footholds when the yacht is well heeled over? Fig 6 shows how canted coachroof coamings can be a great advantage in this respect, and contrasts how bad a narrow-sidedecked boat with upright coamings is. Good stout handrails are as useful as footholds when working forward with the yacht heeled over.

# 9
# A Rig for Long Distances

For decades yachtsmen argued the merits of the sloop, cutter, ketch, yawl and schooner, but ultimately the arguments were settled, as are many things, out on the racing course. The 1970s saw a fierce leap in the level of racing competition, and considerably more money than ever before poured into the developments of rigs, sails and rigging systems. There was one clear winner, boring though it may seem in the eyes of lovers of tradition – the Bermudian sloop.

By the late '70s equipment and methods had developed to a stage where it was quite possible for one man to control a large sail area quickly and efficiently. There are, of course, big variations on the basic Bermudian-rigged sloop, from the positioning of the mast, proportions of each sail and the addition of an occasional cutter forestay making it an inelegant 'slutter'. The efficiency and practicality of this rig was clearly demonstrated in the 1986 BOC Singlehanded Around The World Race when every one of the 26 fleet (from 40-60ft [12.1-18.3m]) was Bermudian rigged and single masted.

For efficiency, practicality and speed, no modern yacht under 55ft (16.75m) needs more than one mast. However, other factors, even emotions, may determine the right rig for an individual. An older couple may well prefer the divided ketch rig with its smaller sails and many still prefer a gaff rig for the atmosphere and character it lends to their sailing.

The ketch has long been a firm favourite amongst ocean cruisers and will probably continue to be so. Its main advantages are that in squally weather you can quickly de-power the rig by lowering the main, and in heavy going you can sail under the snug and well-balanced sail plan of headsail and mizzen. Others are that if you lose one mast (especially the main) you remain with the basis of a jury rig, the facility to set a colourful mizzen staysail and the ability to leave the mizzen up at anchor, ensuring that the yacht lies head to wind.

Our first ocean cruiser was a ketch, and we subsequently went on to run two more, in total logging nearly 30,000 miles under the rig. Without doubt, in heavy or squally weather, with headsail and mizzen set the rig gave an air of confidence, but the disadvantages far outweighed this, especially as an ocean cruiser sailing within normal bounds and seasons shouldn't encounter heavy weather that often. Neither should we pre-suppose that other rigs are poor in heavy weather.

Against the ketch is sailing performance, especially to windward, plus the weight, windage and cost of that extra spar. There are also a handful of minor, but nevertheless significant points against it. It clutters the stern area of the yacht which is constricting physically (the mizzen boom for example nearly always needs to be ducked under), and makes setting a satisfactory awning difficult. The mizzen also often interferes with a self-steering vane and means an extra sail cover to be taken off and re-rigged.

The mizzen staysail has more value in romantic terms than as a working part of a cruising boat. It's the sort of sail that usually only gets set either when you're trying to get a portrait photo of your yacht or perhaps during a regatta. Otherwise, the narrow band of wind direction and strength that allows them to set combined with only very marginally better speed (which always has to be balanced by the increase in weather helm they normally introduce) means that their cost and the space they take up is better used on an ocean cruiser.

Where a ketch does score is if you own a simple, older boat over 40ft (12.1m) that doesn't benefit from material and equipment advances made in the last 30 years. With heavy wooden booms and weighty sails, maybe an old-fashioned reefing system, and smallish winches (by today's standards) the ketch is as suitable a rig as it ever was 25 years ago. Efficiency takes on a different context in these circumstances, but performance will be diminished and you will nevertheless have to put up with the disadvantages outlined above.

The yawl is a better proportioned rig than the ketch, because the mainmast and its sails are more or less the same size as a sloop's, so even ignoring the mizzen, you get almost as good a sailing performance as the single masted boat. The yawl scores when it comes to close quarters manoeuvring under sail, because the mizzen becomes a good handling aid to pull the yacht backwards, kick the stern from side to side and create balance for the headsail when sailing slowly without the main. At sea, the extra mast's contribution is insignificant and in port you get all the disadvantages of the ketch.

The maintainability of an ocean cruiser's rig is important. Masts, spars and rigging are vulnerable at sea and particularly in port. The ability to do running repairs or even replace a spar anywhere in the world must be considered. In just the same way as exotic materials are unsuitable for the hull of an ocean cruiser the same goes for the rig. The unstayed cat rig on boats like the Freedom and Nonsuch range is ideal for long distance cruising. It is easily handled, has virtually no

With modern materials and reefing developments, the ketch is starting to lose favour to the simpler, lighter sloop or cutter. All the same, a boat like this, the powerful Dutch Contest 42, is an excellent example of a well-built and fairly modern fast ocean cruiser   (*Theo Kampa*)

chafe and a much better safety record than conventional stayed rigs (borne out by the fact that insurance companies offer lower premiums to owners of such rigged craft). However, generally speaking the masts are either spun-tapered aluminium, carbon fibre or sophisticated construction of spruce and epoxy. While these rigs have shown themselves to be highly reliable under sail, there are too many potential accidents, particularly in port that could cause them to break and once broken there is a high chance they will be impossible to repair. Mast breakages don't necessarily happen at sea. A clumsy crane-driver in a commercial harbour can swipe a mast or you may be unfortunate enough to drag ashore where a mast can be vulnerable if there are any harbour walls. When circumnavigating in *Les Quatres-Vents* Marcel Bardiaux had a lorry drive over the end of his aluminium mast which was laying on the quayside ready to be stepped . . . The chances are thankfully rare, but nevertheless exist. Personal woodworking abilities aside, to find, shape and taper a suitable tree for a mast might be possible on a junk-rigged boat designed to be fitted with one originally, but such a replacement spar would be unlikely to be suitable on a cat-rigged boat like a Freedom.

When our ketch was dismasted off Martinique we were able to locate an inexpensive secondhand wooden bermudan mast of approximately the right dimensions relatively easily as a hurricane had swept the island the year before and several yachts had been lost and their masts salvaged. If we had had a cat rig with carbon fibre spars we would have had a long wait and a high bill for a replacement to be sent out.

## General Sail Area

Modern materials and related technology mean that reefing sails with a small crew has become much easier. So many people are now of the opinion that a larger sail area is to be preferred to a conservatively rigged yacht which comes to a standstill in light airs.

For ocean cruising the ability to sail well in light conditions is much more important than with a weekend cruiser when you can always motor back home. From time to time an ocean cruiser must contemplate long passages in regions of light conditions such as the Doldrums, Horse latitudes, and the Gulf of Panama, where heavy undercanvassed yachts have been trapped for lengthy periods. Being becalmed for more than a day or so is no joke, either psychologically or physically because of the chafe on gear and rigging it imposes. As soon as the wind arrives you can always shorten down, but the frustration of wanting more sail area when your heavy canvas starts slatting around in light going is far from fun. Ocean cruising yachts tend to be on the heavy side (or at least over-loaded), which is immediately against them in lighter going and it is illogical to have a boat that only starts to move well in a Force 5 when so much satisfaction can be had from keeping her at near hull speed in the much more pleasant conditions of a Force 3. Bernard Moitessier has always been a keen advocate of having plenty of sail area, and it enabled him to drive his heavy-displacement steel ketch *Joshua* consistently over long distances. The disadvantages of a large rig are when you need to sail in high latitudes or in boisterous tradewinds such as the Indian Ocean crossing but this can be overcome by having a small, heavier, mainsail bent on during these periods.

Many experienced skippers prefer to have a battenless mainsail. There are good arguments for this in that batten pockets are the most common area for damage or re-stitching on a mainsail, plus the fact that the battens themselves can break or be lost quite easily. Another good point in favour of the battenless main is the fact that you can haul the sail up and down when the wind is abaft the beam without any battens getting caught in the standing rigging. Against the battenless mainsail is quite simply sail efficiency and therefore boat speed. A 'hooked' or J-shaped leech saps speed and causes more leeway. Battens help avoid this and keep the wind flowing off the sail smoothly. With no battens the leech becomes scalloped slightly and you can expect to lose up to 10 percent effective sail area and therefore a noticeable drop in speed.

## To Lead Aft or not to Lead Aft

The 1960s and '70s saw the great re-emergence of the Chinese or junk rig which using modern materials is still very popular with cruising yachtsmen. The great plus is the ability to handle all the sail controls from one place, normally the companionway area. Junk rig sailors boasted about carpet slipper passages and not having to don oilskins and this idea of control from the cockpit converted many people to the rig.

Although the idea of leading one or two lines or halyards aft was far from new the development of efficient rope clutches and stoppers in the late '70s heralded an upsurge of interest in leading everything aft with Bermudan rigs. In fact, it is nearly impossible to lead absolutely everything aft. Certain sails like the spinnaker and cruising chute have to be rigged and set from on deck, although these aren't part of a normal working rig and are unlikely to be set or lowered by a short crew in bad conditions, or in the middle of the night (when the line-aft arrangement comes into its own).

The main disadvantage of having everything aft is the accumulation of ropes and lines that clog up the forward end of the cockpit. One has to buy more rope and if you are converting from conventional

Under the eminently practical Chinese rig, yachts have made countless ocean crossings. Nowadays, many of the rig's advantages have been incorporated into the standard Bermudan sloop with roller genoa, so the junk rig is less popular   *(Geoff Pack)*

controls at the mast you will need to completely re-new all the running rigging. Although one also needs more hardware like extra blocks at the foot of the mast, turning block sets and a handful of stoppers and/ or clutches, the cost of these is offset by the reduction in expensive winches needed. Another disadvantage is the increase in friction in all the lines being led aft.

On the other hand, assuming the boat is fitted with a roller jib, the principle advantage of leading lines aft, and one shouldn't under-estimate its implications, is that it is rarely necessary to go on deck for any sail handling. This is a major safety advantage, particularly if the crew are not particularly experienced at working on deck. A skipper's sleep and rest can be interrupted by many things, but the knowledge that most sail-handling can be done from the cockpit without needing to worry about someone risking going overboard each time the mainsail is reefed is a great comfort. When two people are cruising alone there should be a rule that when one is going on deck the other is always alerted. This is a good precaution, but it often means the off-watch partner loses some sleep. After long experience of this system, Lou Lou and I have decided that our next boat will have lines aft to cut down the number of forays on deck. Having lines aft also means that the chances of keeping reasonably dry are higher and this makes a big psychological difference on a long trip when salt-encrusted clothes and bodies never seem to dry properly and quickly absorb any moisture present.

The other aspect of lines-led-aft gets back to the old adage aboard yachts – 'if it's easy to do something, you'll get on with it'. The prospect of putting on oilskins and clambering over a pitching heeled deck to the mast to put in or shake out a reef, standing a good chance of a drenching on the way, will be enough to encourage a watch-keeper to procrastinate and hang on a bit longer with the yacht over-canvassed or under-canvassed and therefore straining and sailing inefficiently. If it is easy to reef from the companionway, you'll get on with the job as soon as it is needed. American Dodge Morgan completed a singlehanded circumnavigation in 1985/6 in his massively built 60ft (18.28m) sloop *American Promise*. She was equipped with every handling aid imaginable, including Hood Stoway mainsail reefing and when I spoke to him aboard the yacht in Maine, USA, after the voyage, Dodge reckoned that because sail handling was simple he hadn't had an incorrect amount of sail set for more than 15-minutes at a time in the entire 27,500 mile voyage. He sailed her efficiently and the rewards were that he not only halved the previous record time (he made the passage in 150 days, averaging 172 miles a day), but gear failures were minimal and he didn't have to put a single stitch in any of his sails.

Many of the disadvantages of a lines-aft system can be eased. Only

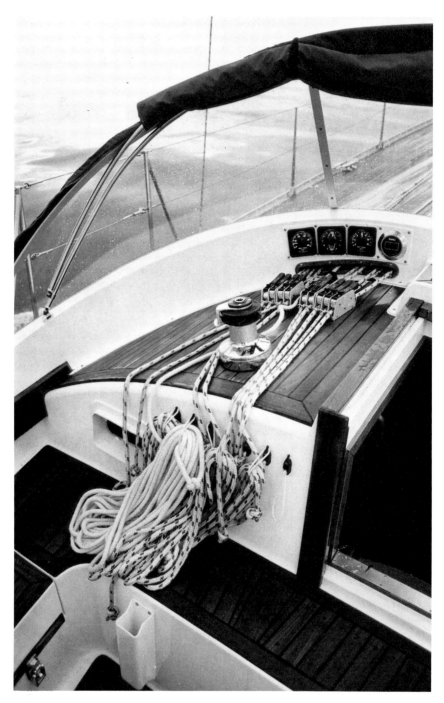

Properly arranged with good-quality hardware and rope stowage, leading lines aft to a single winch improves efficiency by taking the danger, wetness and hassle out of conventional reefing, therefore encouraging the crew to set exactly the right amount of canvas *(Yachting Monthly)*

high-quality equipment will solve the friction problem, although rope spaghetti can be tamed using canvas or acrylic pouches. Ideally the coachroof layout, forward cockpit coamings and work areas next to the companionway should be designed with a lines-aft system in mind, but seven out of ten boats can be adapted without too much inconvenience. Used in conjunction with well arranged lazyjacks (described on page 120) and a roller reefing headsail, the lines-aft system has to be the safest and most efficient rigging arrangement for the long distance cruiser. It has many of the advantages of the Chinese rig, without the windward sailing and speed disadvantage that the junk generally has.

## Rigging Details

Today the details of a yacht's rig, the gear used and the way it is laid out is far more pertinent than the number of masts she has. In discussing these details below it is assumed the yacht is Bermudian rigged, although many of the ideas can be adapted and used with gaff rig. They are modern ideas though which might go against the grain with some traditionalists.

### The Roller Reefing Headsail

The complication and potential unreliability of roller reefing headsail equipment has made ocean cruising yachtsmen slow to adopt this particular handling aid. Although far from a new idea, its re-emergence and staggering popularity for normal pleasure use has meant that the products have steadily improved and a number of very good models are now available. Again using the gruelling 1986 BOC Singlehanded Around-the-World Race as a yardstick, 20 out of 26 yachts were fitted with roller gears, most going for either Profurl or Hood.

The convenience of doing perhaps 80 percent of one's sailing without ever changing a jib on a bucking foredeck is obvious. There are incidental plus points too, including more space in the sail locker and keeping the sail clean by having it off the deck when the anchor is hauled in. The main advantage though, is the ability of a weaker crew, possibly a child or small woman, to reef down without assistance. The implications are numerous. The crew is safer by not needing to go forward and change sails (especially at night when chances of recovering a man overboard is slight), the off duty watch isn't called up to help, and the cabin stays drier through not having wet sail and people below. Also, it makes setting a running pole much easier by first furling the sail, clipping on the boom, then unfurling.

Against this are two major disadvantages which can both be eased,

When a roller-furling headsail is employed, the storm jib can be set up ready for use on a sloop's babystay. It is essential to strengthen attachment points on mast and deck and provide aft support for the mast at the hounds  *(Yachting Monthly)*

if not eradicated.

One is the possibility of a jam up, especially in mid-ocean. There are three ways to avoid the chances of this happening and they are the same as almost any mechanical item aboard – correct initial installation, subsequent preventive maintenance and correct usage. It is surprising the number of poorly installed roller reefing headsail gears on boats. The reefing drum being approximately double the diameter of the rolled sail means that the line has around half the strain on it that the sheet has. When you compare the sloppy arrangement and thickness of many headsail reefing lines to the careful alignment given to the headsail sheets, leading as they do through expensive sheet cars and turning blocks to two of the biggest winches on board, the contrast is remarkable.

Depending on which gear is used, another problem area for those with the halyard coming back down the mast rather than to the foot of the forestay drum, is the lead and tension of the headsail halyard. One of the few jobs it is worth paying to have done by a genuine professional specialist rigger is the initial installation of a roller-furling headstay.

The fact that most of these gears are constructed with a combination of stainless steel and aluminium and happen to be situated on the wettest part of the boat above the waterline means that unless the gears are completely stripped down, cleaned and greased regularly at six month intervals, electrolysis will freeze all the fittings and make dismantling almost impossible without heat. This regular strip-down will make sure the skipper is completely familiar with the gear and allow him to check the bearings and any other moving parts.

Using a roller reefing headsail efficiently requires a certain amount of technique, and one should be careful not to fall into the trap of simply letting go the sheet, hauling in some reefing line, then re-trimming the sheet. Similarly, when setting the sail be certain not to simply cast off the reefing line and haul on the sheet because the loose winding of the reefing line around the drum could lead to bunching and snarl-ups later when tension comes on to it. The reefing line should be led to its own winch and although the sheet must inevitably be eased, the sail should be rolled with just the right amount of tension

These marks, combined with predetermined corresponding numbers on the sheet tracks, take the hit and miss out of the correct sheet leads for a roller headsail (*Yachting Monthly*)

in it. The sheet lead changes as the sail is rolled, and if you wish to avoid leaving the cockpit altogether it is possible to rig up lines from the sheet car leading around a block at the front of the track and back to the cockpit. Putting pre-determined reefing marks on the foot of the sail and corresponding points on the sheet track makes the correct sheet lead easy to ascertain, particularly at night (see photo).

The second disadvantage of the roller reefing headsail is that when reefed beyond a certain point (normally about 65 percent of its area) the sail shape starts to go as the foot and leach roll tighter than the middle, resulting in a hollow bag which saps performance, particularly upwind. Sailmakers and gear manufacturers are constantly working to solve this thorny problem, but no one has yet come up with a really effective answer. As a result, some experienced owners fit a roller reefing headsail but regard it as something of a compromise and don't expect it to be a 100 per cent solution to headsails. Fitting a No 2 genoa to it, they have a good-all-round sail for normal conditions which they can reef by thirty per cent so it can be used up to a Force 5 or 6. For light airs they have a removable forestay (a spare wire foresail halyard can be used and set up with a halyard winch), which attaches just abaft the rolled sail. Onto this is hanked a light drifter. As soon as the wind goes above Force 6 and you need to go to windward the reefed genoa is rolled away altogether and replaced by a largish storm jib, set on an inner cutter forestay, or the babystay. If you have a generous budget, this storm jib is permanently set up on another roller gear, if not it can be hanked, but must have a row of reef points which take it down to hurricane size. This means that in heavy weather you have to leave the cockpit and set the storm jib. However, this is a reasonable compromise as you don't need to go right forward and the job is easier and quicker than changing down normally if the storm jib is left in its bag hanked to the inner forestay. This system obviates the roller reefing jib's other pitfall in that the headsail's centre of effort moves forward and upward as the sail is reefed which not only makes the yacht heel more, but can upset the yacht's balance and induces lee helm.

Rigged in this fashion, an ocean cruiser obviously doesn't have the flexibility of a comprehensive suit of five or six headsails, but it does save on stowage and expenditure.

Properly installed, regularly maintained and correctly used, there is no reason why a modern roller reefing gear should give any problems. What it gives in return is convenience, safety and the ability for one person to reef or unreef a large headsail unaided. The performance loss of having a thick leading edge and at times poor sail shape is balanced by the ability to make fine adjustments to the sail area and keep her going at her maximum with very little effort. Conversely, anyone who has sailed shorthanded with hanked-on headsails will have confronted many times the situation where you hang on just a bit longer (and a bit more . . .) to a wrong-sized headsail, either too big or too small, with all the sailing inefficiences and strains that imposes, waiting to see what the wind will do.

## Mainsail Reefing

Sail handling is the most common activity in the daily routine of a yacht on a long passage and the ability to easily shorten or increase sail area will not only lead to performance advantages, but will be much kinder on the sails themselves, which means you spend less time repairing them and less money in the long run having to replace them. One can often gauge a skipper's seamanship by the number of sails he moans about 'blowing out'. Modern sails are tough. Kept out of the sun as much as possible they last a long time but mis-use by not reefing in time or laziness over reefing or just not keeping an eye open for them chafing and they will quickly enough be damaged. Her mainsail is a yacht's workhorse. By nature it has considerably more use than any sail aboard and must be carefully looked after.

Mainsail reefing has come full circle over the last few years. All the old fore and aft rigged working boats used points reefing, a more complicated version of what the most up-to-date yacht uses today. There have been periods of popularity for mainsail roller-reefing, but the strength and durability of modern synthetic ropes has done away with the need and a very basic and beautifully simple version of the old points reefing called slab reefing, has emerged. With well-designed booms accommodating internal reefing lines spar- and sail-makers have developed this into a foolproof system that is difficult to fault. Practically the only problem is the likely chafe of the reefing pennant as it passes through the clew cringle. Certain small additions can improve the system. My personal preference is to lead all the controls aft to the cockpit, but if you keep them at the mast, a good idea is to construct a box around the foot which all the falls can flake into. This saves having to coil them and diminishes time spent on deck. The mast box can also be stowage for oddments like sail tiers, a shackle key, spare lashings etc. Marking the halyard with an indelible pen for the appropriate reefing positions will save a little time and rope colour coding makes a lot of sense.

If your main is fitted with slab reefing, never tie in the reef points! This may have old seamen turning in their graves, but a clew pennant takes an enormous strain and if anything fails, whether the rope, boom fitting, clew eye or perhaps even a rope clutch or stopper slipping, the flogging sail will be badly damaged as soon as the strain comes on to that first tied-in reef point. Having seen an otherwise healthy mainsail self-destruct in this manner before we could even get it down because

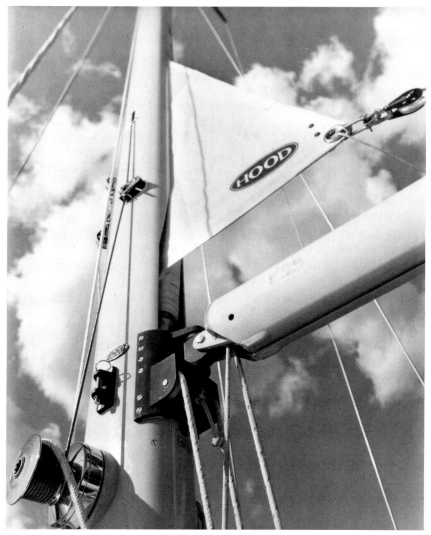

The Hood Stoway mainsail reefing system, and numerous of its contempories, have been very well proven and yet their sophistication has meant that their acceptance amongst the ocean cruising fraternity has been limited

the pennant rope parted, I will never tie in a reef however untidy it looks. Later in this chapter I will describe lazyjacks which automatically collect a reefed portion of sail. If you don't fit lazyjacks and don't like the reefed section flogging under the boom (in fact, it can be half-tucked on the windward side between the tight new foot and the boom) the best alternative is to arrange a 'bungy cord' tie-down system which will simply stretch if any component of the clew pennant goes. Another point to watch carefully is that the reefed part of the mainsail doesn't get pinched by the reefing pennants. This can quickly cause serious chafe.

Leading halyard and reefing controls aft is gaining popularity and there are a variety of ways of doing this. Many people have tried a one-line system. The reefing line starts at the outer pennant position on the boom, goes up through the reefing clew and back to a sheave at the end of the boom and through the inside, before re-emerging at the gooseneck, going up to the reefing tack eye before finally coming down to a block at the mast foot and leading aft. The strains on this line are quite considerable and friction usually makes it slow hard work to pull in this large amount of line. A couple of British production boats, namely the Freedom 40 and Southerly range have successfully arranged this system. Expensive roller-bearing blocks can make all the difference and if these are shackled to both the clew and tack fittings, further reductions of friction can be achieved. A simple two line system can operate without a great deal of adaption from standard spars and their fittings. Having tried both I prefer to have the two-line set-up. Against it is the fact you have to have two lines for each reefing sequence, therefore with three reef positions you must have six lines, stoppers et al. However, the friction is minimalised, so the job is much easier for a weaker crew. With this arrangement the ropes split into shorter lengths which is more practical when they need replacement or end-for-ending as reefing lines tend to. Many prefer to have a mainsail with two generous slab reefs and when a further reduction is required change over to a very strong trysail.

During its period of popularity, mainsail roller reefing developed into quite an efficient and quick method of reefing. Eric Hiscock always swore by it and even after trying a modern slab system on his last yacht, *Wanderer V,* he still reckoned it was superior. The speed of the boom turning can make quite a difference and when the simple 'through mast' roller reefing systems came on the scene, and it became possible to roll the boom on a 1:1 ratio (as opposed to the fearfully slow geared rollers) reefing became quick and easy. Pick up any sailing book of the early to mid '70s and you'll see all the ocean racers of the day, *Prospect of Whitby, Quailo, Morning Cloud* etc, all demonstrated that roller reefing can produce a well-set mainsail.

Our Rival 34 *Euge* was fitted with a through-mast roller reefing mainsail and I first thought it would need changing to slab reefing. However, I tried it out, the system worked very well indeed, I never bothered to change it and it never gave us trouble. What *was* against it was that it took twice as long to reduce sail as slab reefing would have done and I always had to go forward to reef, whereas slab can be led into the cockpit.

The late Angus Primrose converted his through the mast reefing gear to be operated from the cockpit by fitting a drum in place of the normal permanent winch handle on the front of the mast and having a twin endless line leading to the deck and then aft to a Lewmar

'Sidewinder' drum winch next to the halyard which had also been led aft. This system worked very well indeed.

## Trysails

When a mainsail is deeply reefed in bad weather, the strain on the leech is enormous as a result of leverage exerted by the mainsheet, and although tightening the topping lift can take some of the weight off, many a mainsail has been ripped in half in such circumstances. Another disquieting factor in heavy weather is the boom thrashing around. If it can be lashed into its gallows or on the deck life will be much happier. It is also asking a great deal of a mainsail to be the sail for everything from a flat calm to a howling gale. A mainsail heavy enough to withstand several bad gales will be useless in light airs and unwieldly the whole time. Dr Ronnie Andrews, a circumnavigator and past Commodore of the Royal Cruising Club, is one of many highly experienced yachtsmen who believe a trysail is the answer for heavy going.

Traditionally, a trysail was always approximately one third of the mainsail's area, but Dr Andrews prefers it to be a little bigger, nearer 40 percent. To be practical to use in bad conditions the sail must have its own independent track. Trying to reach a normal slide gate six or seven feet above the deck with a heavy trysail in gale conditions is out of the question. A track can be screwed to a wooden mast or rivetted to an extruded aluminium one but never use self-tapping screws to hold it to aluminium as these can shake loose in bad weather which weakens the track and makes getting the sail down very difficult indeed. By having its own track coming down to the deck, the trysail can be left bent on, in its bag, during passages, simplifying setting it. It shouldn't be sheeted on the centreline (the sail will 'cup' and lose efficiency) and twin sheets should be led through blocks aft on each side and taken to spinnaker winches. If you don't have these winches, three-part blocks and tackles can be used, but with these the crew must watch out when tacking.

A trysail should be heavily made (10oz minimum for yachts displacing less than 10 tons) and triple stitched with a wire tack pennant that raises it above the stowed mainsail head to avoid chafe. When we had a trysail made for our 35ft (10.66m) catamaran *Foreigner* I stipulated a row of reef points in this already tiny sail. Our friends, and even the sailmaker, thought we were over-doing it, but in a subsequent severe Atlantic gale we were thankful – under whole trysail she was surfing almost out of control. When it was reefed the catamaran became quite docile in comparison.

All your eggs in one basket and the sort of design feature to steer clear of no matter how strong it appears   *(Yachting Monthly)*

### A Running Rig

For decades the hallmark of a long distance cruising yacht was a pair of running booms attached aloft and coming down to either rail. The tradewind running rig of twin boomed-out headsails evolved as much because it is a fairly trouble- and chafe-free set up for running downwind as the fact you could take the sheets back to the helm and most yachts would thus self-steer. For the pioneers of ocean cruising with limited crew this was a major breakthrough. Anyone who has used self-steering gear after experience of watch on/watch off hand steering will understand the significant impact this rig had. It nevertheless had disadvantages. It was expensive in sails and special equipment and inflexible in terms of sail area in fluctuating conditions (and even tradewinds can come and go all the time). The configuration also makes most boats roll dreadfully. Hiscock said that *W anderer III* could roll from 32 degrees one way to 32 degrees the other in a snappy two seconds! All the same, before the days of self-steering gears these disadvantages were easily ignored for the joy of a free helmsman. Few are fitted today but their broad principle can form the basis of a modern running rig.

The first thing to bear in mind is that tradewinds are not the constant-direction, constant-strength dream that many writers have you believe. Even in well-established tradewind belts the wind veers and backs constantly, and can blow anything from a meek Force 2-3 to a thundering Force 7. The demands of a running rig are that it is free from chafe, maintains good balance and it is easy to trim when the wind veers (ideally it should be unnecessary to gybe it). As well as this the sail area should be flexible. This is quite a tall order, but far from insurmountable. It should not be necessary to have any specially-made sails, but twin booms, expensive and space-taking as they are, make life so much easier. Unfortunately, more than anything else the suitability of a running rig is in direct proportion to the amount of money spent on it. There are a number of methods and variations on them, so I shall start with the poor man's version.

Assuming that the yacht isn't a schooner (unless the modern variant with twin equal-height masts), the following will work on most rigs. For running, a mizzen can be forgotten unless you are in very light airs or hand steering. The *very* poor man's running rig is simple but works well and we crossed the Atlantic with it. A single running boom is a must however poor you are. If your first tradewind passage is the Canaries to West Indies trip and you don't have a running boom, cut down a small tree in Madeira (*madeira* is Portuguese for wood and the island is covered in forests).

It is also important to have plenty of anti-chafe protection on the shrouds. This needn't be permanent but before making a long downwind passage it will pay to cover the shrouds in split cheap plastic hose, taped on at six-inch intervals (any greater distance and the weight of sail against the hose can pull it off). Also, spreader tips and roots must be copiously bandaged with strips of canvas and/or foam taped in place. Alternatively, the old-fashioned method of baggy-wrinkle is surprisingly efficient. Assuming the trip is mostly downwind, it doesn't really matter about the windage, as long as the whole lot is removed when you get into port.

In light airs the poor man's running rig uses the mainsail eased out a fair way, but vanged down heavily so that the sail doesn't press against any part of the rigging. The largest headsail is then boomed out opposite this (goosewinged) and the next largest headsail fairly well sheeted on the same side as the main, hanked, if possible, on a twin forestay (running is one of the few times twin forestays are efficient).

The first sail to come down as the wind increases is the mainsail. This is not a simple job running downwind and we have found the best way to do so is by sheeting it flat amidships with somebody on the helm before lowering. The sail is then stowed and covered. Because the smaller jib is no longer being 'fed' by the genoa it will need a wider sheeting angle, so the sheet should be led through a block on the end of the eased out main boom (which normally needs lowering on its topping lift), taking care not to let the stowed sail or its cover chafe against a shroud.

Dependent on sail wardrobe these two headsails can be changed as the wind increases. The main disadvantage (and it really is a drag at 3 am or after the fifth squall of an afternoon) is that the rig cannot be sailed by the lee and is best from a run through to broad reach . When a squall comes through or the wind changes direction and one needs to gybe, the whole lot has to be reversed which can be quite a procedure. I vividly remember one watch during a particularly squally afternoon when after three complete gybes with all the work that required swapping sails and booms over, I decided that when the next squall came through with its 60 degree windshift, I'd keep the wind over the stern by altering course and wait for the hour it generally took for the squall to lose its force. As the big black cloud approached and wind increased we were soon hurtling along at great speed, now uncomfortably across the wave train and rolling more. We made great progress towards Brazil (we were aiming for the Caribbean) for an hour. Then another hour. Finally, after three hours the wind looked as if it had changed for good so I reluctantly gybed over, mentally working out how much distance we'd lost. Twenty minutes later the wind had swung back to its original direction and the whole lot had to be gybed back.

A roller-reefing genoa is a great thing to have as part of a tradewind rig, because you can exactly tailor your downwind sail area for the right speed and the reefing control line quite literally becomes a throttle cable in boisterous running conditions. Our Rival 34 *Euge* made a very respectable passage time on our second Canaries-West Indies transatlantic crossing by judicial use of the roller furling genoa in this way. The only running boom was standard IOR size (when attached to the mast and held horizontal it extended a foot or so in front of the forestay) and was left permanently attached to the roller genoa. Even when the sail was rolled right up – all except that last foot

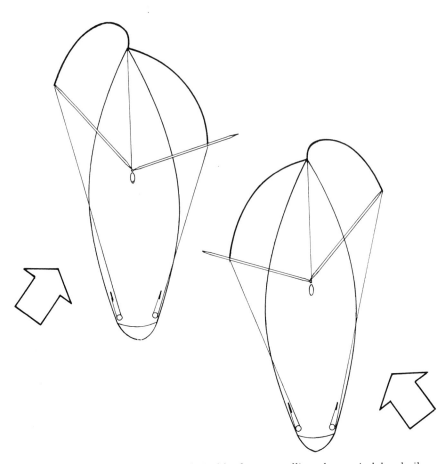

**Fig 7** Extra-long poles are very desirable for controlling downwind headsails, enabling the wind to veer through 75-80 degrees without the need for much deckwork

– the boom was left attached and ready to go. The storm jib was set on its inner cutter headstay and boomed out with a temporary boom concocted of awning battens, dinghy oars and even the deck scrubber all lashed firmly together. It was a rough crossing with the wind rarely dropping much below Force 7 and for the greater part of it we ran under storm jib with a couple of feet of genoa unrolled opposite it. This rig was a hassle when it needed to be gybed, but because of the roller we were able to keep set exactly the right amount of sail, and we adjusted it several times each hour as the conditions fluctuated. The result was an 18½-day crossing for the 2,700 miles which on a 24ft 10in (7.56m) waterline we are very proud of.

For running downwind it isn't necessary to have a perfectly shaped headsail as it is on the wind. So a useful set up is to have a very simple roller furling gear, rather like the old Wykeham-Martin, where the sail, set loose-luffed, rolls around itself (in the olden days, the luff was lashed to a light chain to give a thick edge to roll around). It is possible to make this roller drum yourself from plywood with two bought swivels. Hoisted at the beginning of long downwind passages, the sail is used only for running or reaching in combination with and opposite your normal roller-reefing genoa, which it should more or less match in area. The ability to have two infinitely-adjustable roller jibs would be a Godsend on a long downwind passage and would increase efficiency by enabling the watchkeeper to have exactly the right amount of sail out the whole time. Another system can be used when your standard roller reefing extrusion has two luff grooves. Using a similar sized sail hoisted in this groove, it would be possible to have twins which rolled on one furling line. If the wind came round on to the quarter and you could no longer hold one of them poled to weather, the sail would be eased to leeward and both used two-ply until the wind hauled back aft again.

As mentioned above, two running booms make life much easier if they are approximately 1.3 – 1.5 x J (telescopic ideally) it is possible to rig them with outhauls and the jibs can be used with the wind on either quarter (see Fig 7), which really then gives you as flexible a rig as a squaresail and needs no gybing – a significant step. So the Rolls Royce of running rigs would be twin roller-reefing headsails of the same shape and area with over-length running booms to enable you to sail with the wind from one quarter right through to the other quarter without gybing, or even leaving the cockpit.

A sail that is also as adaptable as the square sail going downwind is the spinnaker, especially if it's used with twin booms. The spinnaker used to be regarded only as a racing sail, but now that a variety of bell-mouthed 'throttling' devices have become available, it makes a very logical downwind cruising sail. It is inadvisable with a small crew however unless it has a 'throttler' of some sort. As a long-distance running sail its weakness is that it can't be reefed, so you must be very careful not to get caught out in a tropical squall with it up, and you must be able to resort to another running rig in conditions when the spinnaker can't be used. Another disadvantage is that even with twin booms and a throttler, it is not a sail that you can comfortably leave up overnight with a short crew.

Chafe on the halyard must be watched carefully if you use a spinnaker over long distances. Have a few extra feet of halyard so from time to time the top end can be trimmed back. Also, adjust the position of the 'nip' over the block each 24 hours and use a very large diameter block always. The choice of spinnaker for cruising is critical, because you are only likely to have one which must be used in a variety of conditions. There are two broad cuts, tri-radial and radial head. The tri-radial is designed more for reaching than running. On a run it can be twitchy and need a lot of tending. The radial head is around 20 percent cheaper, and is more stable running. Don't go for too heavy a cloth (no more than 1.5oz US for less than 40ft LOA), because in light airs the extra weight will make the sail hard to fill and it will oscillate, possibly causing a wrap up. When using a spinnaker *never* put a figure-of-eight knot in either the halyard or sheets and guys. Racing men follow this rule so the sail can be jettisoned if it is holding them up at a leeward mark. For the cruising man there is a weightier reason – so the sail can be immediately dumped in a man-overboard emergency.

A final option is cruising chutes. They were heavily promoted in the late '70s & early '80s as the cruising man's answer to the reaching spinnaker. About one-third smaller than the spinnaker, and supposedly needing no pole, they were bought by the hundred and the majority of yachtsmen were disappointed. Rather like the mizzen staysail, the band of both wind direction and strength they can be used in simply doesn't justify their existence and to use safely they need almost as much hardware as a conventional spinnaker, to which they are much inferior.

### Lazyjacks

The humble lazyjack is one of the few details that you will find aboard modern ocean racers which was also used in sailing ships 100 years ago. As we have seen, one of the biggest advantages of the junk rig is the ability of the sail to self-stow between lazyjacks when reefed or lowered. They can be fitted just as effectively to a standard Bermudian mainsail.

For the uninitiated, lazyjacks are lines that run down either side of the mainsail, from the top crosstrees to various points along the boom, so that as the mainsail is lowered it flakes itself into the cradle of lines they create, stowing itself. The reason lazyjacks are used on the big racing boats is the sheer size of their mainsails which are otherwise almost impossible to stow for the shorthanded crew. They are just as useful on smaller boats because they immediately tame the mainsail which might be a handful in strong winds. They are also invaluable to the singlehander, particularly if the mainsail halyard is led aft to the cockpit. With a downhaul line from the headboard, also led aft, the singlehander can lower his mainsail without leaving the helm. Another advantage of lazyjacks is their ability to support the reefed section of a sail suprisingly neatly, making it unnecessary to tie in the reef points.

An important point to remember when fitting lazyjacks is that they pass immediately under the mainsail and not under the boom. If they pass under the boom, the sail will collect there and look sloppy. If you have a mainsail with slides on the foot there is no problem, but if you have a grooved boom it will be necessary either to fit eyelets along the foot of the sail or screw eyes to the top of the boom. In order to make

**Fig 8** Properly set up, lazyjacks are a wonderfully simple mainsail handling aid which enables one person to handle a sail on yachts up to 70ft (21m). Either the above methods can be used, although make sure that the tails pass above the boom (inset), either as shown or through eyelets in the sail

the lazyjacks easy to adjust or dismantle, make them in separate lines which are reef knotted together as they join at the boom. Also, when you attach the blocks at the spreaders, position them 6-9in (12-18mm) away from the mast so that the down part doesn't tap against the mast in the wind. This also takes the upper parts of the lazyjack lines away from the sail, so there is less chance of snagging.

When fitting the slightly more complicated system of lazyjacks in Fig 8, it's well worth mocking them up first in thin orange line that will stand out against the sky. By plenty of adjustment and standing back you'll be able to get it looking right with all the downhauls parallel etc before cutting and splicing (remember to add a couple of inches at each end for the splice). For boats up to 35ft, 4mm line is quite strong enough, but be certain to use pre-stretched otherwise parts under greater load will distort first and reduce the effectiveness of the lazy-jacks.

When sailing they cause no detectable chafe to the sail as long as the lines have plastic pipe sheaths where they pass under the mainsail.

Mast steps must have anti-snag lines above the first spreaders. The owner of this boat clearly has no concept of performance sapping windage; all the paraphenalia aloft on this ketch is the equivalent area of dragging half a sheet of plywood to windward, which in a leeshore situation might be a critical factor *(Geoff Pack)*

When the sail is about to be lowered, be sure to keep the lines taut for a neat stow.

## Mast-steps

Mast-steps are being increasingly used and the benefits are numerous. One of the most significant is the ability of one person to go aloft without having to be hoisted. As I am well built, my wife isn't able to haul me up in a bosun's chair so she used to have to go aloft and detested every last second of it and many couples must be in the same position. We made sure our next boat had steps and now if I am going aloft for any length of time I wear a bosun's chair and climb up the mast with Lou Lou taking up the slack in the halyard as I go. On reaching the position I want to work, she makes off the halyard and I sit back in the bosun's chair comfortably working with both hands.

There is a case for mast-steps extending only to the crosstrees, thereby cutting down the number of holes drilled in the mast, cost, weight aloft and windage. You can use them there for reef eyeball navigation. Certainly steps are the best encouragement to go up the mast and make regular rigging checks, which prevents future problems. They also keep you fit! The need to go aloft at sea is thankfully rare, but if you fit mast-steps the job is a thousand times easier. The best type are those with a stirrup support above the footplate, otherwise they are dangerous to use at sea. An essential addition when you fit mast-steps is to make up a cradle of very thin lines above the crosstrees to prevent halyards getting hooked around the steps (see photo). We learned this one when the mainsail halyard looped right around the front of the mast and caught a step on the opposite side. It was a good job we had mast-steps, I'd have never untangled it otherwise . . .

# Part Three
# PREPARATIONS

# 10
## Water Supply

### Capacity

Ultimately water is the sole commodity required for survival, both in terms of last ditch survival and for everyday cruising survival. The quantity of fresh water you have available is a surprisingly good gauge of your standard of living and enjoyment. Anyone who has ever tried cleaning a scrambled egg pan with cold salt water needs no reminding of the joy of washing up in fresh and the ability to shower regularly and have clean hair rather than a matted salt-encrusted mop definitely adds a few notches to the pleasure scale.

Of course some washing can be done ashore, but it can be slightly degrading to sit by the watertap on the jetty doing your laundry and certainly in some places the locals are not keen on it. So while one of the attractions of the ocean cruising lifestyle is the ability to trim down normal requirements and strip away the comforts you've always been accustomed to, it is wise not to be too stingy with water provision.

The multihull designer John Shuttleworth changed my thinking about water capacity and usage. When I sailed with him on his Spectrum 42 catamaran, I noticed that her central beam was hollow and could take a staggering 400 gallons (1,818 lit) of water. Under no circumstances whatsoever does the yacht ever put to sea with any water in that tank (she has normal tanks for 100 gallons [454 lit] anyway), but when she arrives in port after a passage with the prospect of a couple of weeks stay, she goes alongside and fills up the big tank. They say goodbye to their boot-top line, but who cares in harbour? In this way her crew can happily shower, wash-up and do what they like with fresh water until it's time to go when the normal tanks are topped up (gravity fed) and the remainder is jettisoned before putting to sea again. It seems such a sensible idea. Water is such a luxury aboard and yet it is normally completely free.

The practicalities are not always so simple as space is always at a premium, especially on a monohull. However if you look upon high water capacity as being a harbour-only luxury (at sea you must impose the normal restrictions) it opens up several options. The very ends of boats are the last place you should put water tanks because they will make her pitch terribly, and yet it doesn't matter one jot as long as those tanks are empty when you're at sea. It is the same about the boat's trim, it doesn't matter if she's down on her marks a bit in harbour, or indeed where her centre of gravity is. The dark corners of the lazarette and fo'c's'le are not normally the most convenient places to have general stowage. Is it possible to re-arrange the existing junk stored there and then construct and glassfibre-in a big tank in these places? Or what about having big flexible sausage tanks loosely set up over the coachroof in harbour? As soon as you go to sea they would be emptied, rolled up and stowed away but in harbour they would provide a generous supply of water, which could gravity feed into your main tank fillers and therefore need no extra plumbing. A company like Vetus supply a 61in x 30in (156cm x 76cm) tank which holds 58 gallons (263 lit). Two of these would look no different to an inflatable dinghy stowed on the coachroof but the convenience they would create aboard would be worth it.

### Water Catchment

In many of the West Indian islands there is no central water supply – the islanders rely solely on what they can catch from their (often corrugated tin) roofs which is then directed into a big concrete tank under the house. They call it 'skyjuice'. The houses are not particularly big, but their roofs provide sufficient water all year round to supply such water wasters as regularly-flushed toilets. For them, the trick is large tankage, it can rain hard for a couple of days and their gutters work overtime diverting the water into huge tanks which could keep them going for months afterwards without a single rainfall.

Unfortunately a yacht could never emulate this, but thought given to water catchment may save you a lot of trouble and make you more independent of the shore. On the other side of the coin, there are many regions of the world where water is very precious and you'll need to catch your own supply as the locals won't let you have any of theirs.

I have tried many different systems over the years – collecting water is a bit like catching fish, the satisfaction far outweighs the value of the end-product – and in the end it became something of a hobby. The aims are that the system be fruitful, reasonably self-tending and that you remain dry whilst doing it. At sea, where there is likely to be some spray flying about, a bucket lashed under the boom gooseneck takes some beating, but it fails miserably on the convenience and keeping dry stakes. An easy modification though is to lash a large funnel under the gooseneck with plastic pipe from its snout leading direct into the water tank filler cap. In harbour, an awning (the universal design is described in the preparation section on page 182) can collect good quantities of water – in a reasonable shower we can get 15 gallons (68 lit) an hour and in a decent downpour two or three times that amount. If the ridge topping lift is taken aft to a cleat on the backstay, you stand a reasonable chance of keeping dry while setting this one up.

If your water filler cap is situated on or near the deck edge and you have continuous toerails, one easy way to collect water from your deck is to make a small dam (a wedged piece of wood with some rags will normally suffice) on the downhill side of the filler so a puddle is formed over the filler and eventually the water pours into the tanks.

For our next boat I plan to install the Pack Mk9 system. In fact it's not original, I've seen it used on several ocean cruising boats before. The deck has just one drain each side at the lowest point. This water runs through a pipe inside the hull with a two-way diverter valve fitted. The water can go to a skin fitting and drain overboard, or the valve can be switched to direct it into the main water tank.

The weakness of the system is that the decks must be kept clean and this isn't always possible. What we plan to do then is have a standard awning which, if the decks are dirty, will be used as normal for water collection. If the decks are nice and clean though, we'll let the rain rinse them for a few minutes before switching over and using the entire deck area for water collection – very efficient indeed. The Mk 10 version will no doubt have the switchover valve right next to my bunk, so there is no need to get out of bed at night when I hear the rain start!

## Methods of Water Supply

A feature becoming more common aboard yachts is pressurized water and it is a pleasant convenience. However, you pay the price not only for initial installation and continuing spares but also electricity used and more importantly wasted water. Although I have argued the case for having plenty of water it still shouldn't be wasted and run out of the sink unused and this is unavoidable with a pressure system, especially if you have hot water where gallons of cold water are lost waiting for it to run hot. If you have a really large water capacity this is not so important, but you will increase your average water consumption by between 33% and 50% by employing a pressure system as opposed to a hand or foot pump.

If you prefer to have electric pumps, try to standardise if at all possible so a range of spare motors, valves, diaphragms, bearings and even bodies can be used for all your pumps. The best system I saw was on a charterboat where a mini 'pump room' housed the identical PAR pumps for water pressure, two shower sumps, a refrigerator sump,

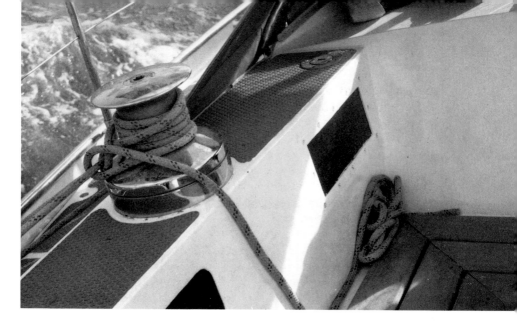

This clear inspection hatch is for a small cockpit coaming water tank which provides daily usage and, using gravity cuts out the need for a pressurized water system. Note also the tugman's hitch used on the sheet winch, which will not jam and obviates the need for cleats. The shrewd and experienced ocean cruising man spends time thinking about what he doesn't need, not what he does    (*Geoff Pack*)

and two independent bilge pumps. Each pump was bolted to a small piece of ply which in turn fitted into slides and the electric cables had crimped bayonet terminals. The skipper always had one spare pump (on its plywood base) refitted and ready to go. Whenever there was a pump failure, and there were many, it was a two minute job to disconnect the pipes and electric cables, slide it out and replace it with the newly rebuilt pump. Speed was of essence to him (charter guests don't like standing in showers half washed waiting for the water to come back) but the system relied on a single range of spares and like most of us charter skippers he knew the pumps inside out.

A water pressure system must be backed up with a hand or foot pump as well. Another modification that we found prolonged the working life of the pumps and motors was fitting an accumulator chamber. This simple device keeps the system under pneumatic pressure, which not only halves the work of the pump, but allows it to run fully and properly when required rather than the wearing sporadic action when a tap is only turned partly on or when there is a slight leak (or the valves release the pressure back into the tank).

Without doubt the most successful, convenient and efficient water system I've ever seen on a boat was on François and Pascal Grinberg's 43ft (13.1m) cutter *Scherzo*. It combines the convenience of a pressure water system with the simplicity and economy of conventional pumped water. They have two generous water tanks in the bilge and from these water is pumped (with a high capacity bilge pump) into two 5-gallon (22-lit) tanks, one in each cockpit coaming. There are

Fig 9 If the tank is situated next to a bulkhead, this system of gauging (seen on a French Amel design) is both simple and accurate

conventional domestic faucets at the galley sink and in the heads compartment and water to these is gravity-supplied from the cockpit coamings. In other words, they have the convenience of being able to turn a tap to get water, but the pressure is minimal so little is wasted, and there is no noisy pump or electricity used. Finally, the best thing of all is that they are able to very accurately log their water consumption on passage by noting down each time the cockpit coaming tanks are re-filled. The system is pure genius.

Gauging water isn't all that easy, although neither is it particularly necessary except on a very long passage. Commercial water gauges sold at chandlers do not work on tanks that are anything but rectangular boxes and such tanks are few and far between on yachts. It is desirable to have your water split up into three or more tanks, independently tapped from each other. A mental note of which tanks you've used and which are full is usually quite sufficient to keep track of consumption. A system superb for its simplicity is fitted on the French Amel range of yachts, and can be adapted into certain other boats (see Fig 9). It is calibrated by pouring in five gallons at a time and marking the scale. Although its accuracy is circumspect at sea, it is nevertheless an easy method of gauging water if you are in a dry area and are concerned about consumption.

Even if you are unable to increase your in-port water supply, the boat's water capacity in general is a point of heated discussion. Everyone knows that it's best to have as much as possible, but how much? Both our ocean cruising boats had 45 gallons (204 lit) total capacity and we managed quite adequately. As long as we were able to catch water regularly this small amount was no special inconvenience.

# 11
# *Electrics*

For years, the traditional opinion of electrics and small boats has been that the two were uneasy bedfellows and to be kept apart as far as possible. The opinion still lingers, but so much has changed over the last twenty years that it would be backward indeed to consider a boat totally without electricity. But all things in moderation.

If there is one philosophy that we've seen work time and time again for most aspects of ocean cruising it is the KISS principle – Keep It Simple, Stupid. Generally speaking the most successful cruising boats and people are the ones who have trimmed their lives down to basic necessities which they find are quite adequate and give them time to enjoy themselves rather than waste pointless hours doing frustrating repair work. This philosophy couldn't be more appropriate than when applied to electricity on boats. A house is connected up to the National Grid and we are all encouraged to use lots of power. To generate smallish quantities of electricity on a boat is not a problem with wind generators and solar panels, but as soon as your demands increase you can very quickly become a slave to electricity generation with a noisy and smelly engine or generator running for many hours a day ruining everyone's peace.

Some yachtsmen can't cope without huge quantities of power and we have seen many a boat more resembling a small power station than an offshore liveaboard cruising yacht. Their owners believe that a boat should be no different from a house with electric toasters, microwave ovens, TV and video sets etc. If I've seen one sweaty, bad-tempered and foul-mouthed yachting consumer hiking some broken electrical fitting around uncomprehending shops in distant ports I've seen dozens. Their lifestyle and happiness fall apart as soon as some part of the electric system does. If you feel you, or any of your crew, can't live without many of the domestic appliances and conveniences you have at home, you should seriously re-consider the concept of worldwide cruising.

It is a false impression that such creature comforts will make life aboard that much easier and therefore prolong the cruise. Quite the contrary, they will surely add to the frustrations and costs and spoil the prospect of a free and simple existence. Some electricity will of course be necessary and in the following pages we will look at the best ways of supplying it.

## *Battery Capacity and Storage*

To be self-reliant, an ocean cruiser needs large capacities for everything, including electrical power. Calculate your amperage requirements over a 24 hour period (amps = watts x volts) and then treble it. If you use up an average of 25ah over 24 hours, supposedly a 75ah battery is sufficient. This is not so because a battery is rarely charged right up and letting it get nearly flat on a regular basis is a quick death to any battery. It also means that you *must* charge the batteries daily and this isn't always possible.

The other thing to remember is that batteries can only accept approximately 25–30 percent of their remaining capacity in charging input, so extra charging is not an answer if you are in danger of force-feeding the batteries which permanently damages them. A parallel can be made with water capacity here. One of the frustrations of having a very efficient water catchment system is when the tanks fill in a matter of an hour or two, then overflow for the remaining three hours of the downpour. The same goes for electricity. From time to time you have the ability to collect a lot of 'free' electrical charge, maybe a couple of days of motoring in a calm, or leaving the boat for a month or two with a solar panel or shorepower attached. With small capacity the batteries are charged up in no time and the rest is completely wasted – with big capacity you make the best of it. So within weight and expense limits, it is difficult to imagine having too much battery capacity, and if you can afford three or even four 90–100ah batteries your life will be happier for it.

Positioning the batteries deserves some thought. If they are low down they contribute to the boat's centre of gravity. But then if they are too low in the bilge they may be underwater if the boat is badly flooded and this might just be the time their loss could be disastrous, if lights are needed to find a leak, the engine needs starting or a Mayday signal has to be transmitted. The engine starting battery also needs to be close to the engine for minimum starter cable runs. However it shouldn't be so close as to be affected by engine heat, so don't have batteries in the engine room.

The batteries must be in leak-proof boxes and well strapped down in case of a knockdown. If you have the opportunity to build the battery compartment make it bigger all round than your existing batteries so that in future when they need replacement, you don't have to search for identically sized units. Wooden shims or wedges will hold the batteries in place. The locker or compartment for the batteries must not be shared by any other equipment unless the battery box has a fastened lid, otherwise there is a danger that something like a spanner or length of wire could short across both terminals and cause a fire.

If, as I prefer, you have an engine room extractor fan to improve the general running of the engine and cut down fuel consumption, then to have an offshoot of this sucking the air out of the battery compartment too, there is no chance of a build up of gases.

Batteries should be maintained and checked frequently. They must therefore be easily accessible, so you are encouraged to check them on a regular basis.

## Battery Charging

Every boat's electrical consumption will be different but I will outline how our electrical system worked on *Euge* to demonstrate that there is no need for over-complication. The boat was a standard Rival 34 sloop fitted with the normal selection of domestic and navigation light fittings, plus an electronic log, a stereo cassette, an echo sounder, RDF and VHF running off a twin 90ah marine battery installation. Sole charging was from a 35amp engine alternator whose regulator we adapted to bypass (Fig 11) and give boost charging (more of that later). There was a normal battery switch which enabled us to use either or both of the batteries, and the whole system was monitored by a 10-15v voltmeter and a cheap ammeter. In other words the electrical system, except for the regulator bypass, was totally standard and as you would expect to find on 95 percent of production boats her size.

Two of us lived aboard and our electrical demands were modest. We used electric lighting always, the stereo was playing for much of the time, but we didn't use navigation lights as long as there was a watchkeeper (unless shipping was around) and we used the VHF selectively. The routine was simple, we only used one of the two batteries at any one time, the other being left fully charged up. Every two weeks or so we would switch to the other battery. In this way we always had one battery ready to start the engine (even though it could be hand-started) and over a year both batteries were used regularly and equally. At sea, the batteries would be charged (with the switch on 'Both') during the daily 4-5pm 'happy hour' (when bodies, dishes and boat were cleaned with thoroughness and abandon) and in port three quarters of an hour a day on boost-charge was quite sufficient.

This system worked well but was dependent on the engine's good running which fortunately was kind to us. With the exception of the lights and log, we relied on none of this equipment and had a hurricane lamp and Walkers Patent Trailing Log as back ups. The only way I felt the system could have been improved was with the addition of either a solar panel or wind generator (or in an ideal world, both).

If however I were to have a slightly larger boat and to add a couple of heavy drain items such as a SatNav or ham radio I would upgrade the system slightly. This I would do by adding a second, identical, alternator (with the option of bypass regulator although not use it normally) to the engine and this would be used solely for an independently circuited engine starting battery which could be a relatively small capacity car battery. By doing this I would have both belt and braces, a twin system where if any component were to fail (except the engine) there would always be a way of getting the engine started and charging the batteries (if needs be with jump cables). This would enable the small starter battery to be very close to the engine for short cables and above the level of any flood in an emergency.

The ocean cruising lifestyle revolves around self-sufficiency – one should never have all one's eggs in one basket and this is particularly pertinent to electrics, unless nothing essential is reliant on the system. Two independent banks of batteries reduce many potential problems. Also it is much better to have extra sources of auxiliary charging if the engine will not work.

## Solar Panels

Solar panels have improved markedly over the last ten years with companies like PAG in Britain producing a variety of very durable units that you can jump up and down on. Much to contrary belief, they *do* operate with shadows running across them, but obviously not quite as efficiently. The beauty of the solar panel is that it is passive, it has no moving parts, and now that they are producing really strong panels it is difficult to find fault with them. They just keep pumping in a little bit of power all day, every day.

Two 2ft x 1ft 6in (58cm x 44cm) solar panels will produce approximately· 15 ah charge per day in a sunny climate and a lean electricity using crew could just about live on that. The big advantage is that if your batteries go flat for any reason in mid-ocean, you stand a chance of not only saving your batteries (a few weeks flat would kill them otherwise), but also having a small amount of power for basics such as compass light and nav lights from time to time.

Solar panels are not cheap (although their price has been steadily decreasing) for the amount of charge they contribute, but if you look at that 15ah per day charging contribution and compare it to the cost of engine charging (both fuel and servicing) for the same input, the panels would pay for themselves after two years, and thereafter electricity is free. A solar panel is one of those items that pays hands down in the long run if you can afford the initial investment and a yachtsman heading into a sunny clime would be foolish not to fit one.

Finding the right place to install them used to be tricky, as they needed a flat place where the sun shone but no one trod. Now that the panels are stronger, can be fitted on a cambered deck and come in a variety of sizes and shapes, there is more choice. It is possible to bolt them on the coachroof, outboard of the handrail or over opening

**Figs 10a & 10b** With a little ingenuity solar panels can be fitted in a number of ways aboard a yacht which, by adjustment every hour or two, increase their output markedly hatches (obviously, you sacrifice light to the cabin by doing this), but not on the foredeck because of cable runs (with such low voltage the length of cable must be kept as short as possible). Although they can be bolted on to an area of the deck and left, solar panels work better angled directly at the sun's rays so if the installation is adjustable, so much the better. In this way they need tending every few hours, but the charging input is considerably improved. Fig 10a & 10b show a variety of ideas to make the best from your solar panel.

## Wind Generators

There are two broad catagories of windmill generators – big and small. The most common are small commercially-available ones such as the Ampair and Rutland Windcharger, which use a fairly small propeller and can sometimes be adapted to tow an impeller at sea. The other versions, available and more popular in America, are the large-diameter (6-9ft [1.8-2.7m] prop span) windmills that are only used in port and normally hoisted in the yacht's foretriangle, although I have seen one permanently facing forward attached to the mizzen mast of a ketch.

The Ampair and Rutland Windchargers are the only two small commercial versions made in Britain that are sufficiently durable and reliable for full time use, although there are several others on the market. When the wind is really blowing the power input of these models is up to 8-10 amps and unlike solar panels they work for 24 hours a day. In 20 knots of wind, the input is nearer 4-5 amps. However one should always remember that many anchorages are desirable because they are sheltered from the wind. Also that when running downwind on a tradewind route, the apparent wind is reduced and these units then don't put in as much power as you might expect. All the same, François and Pascal Grinberg on *Scherzo* found that their single Rutland is sufficient for all their needs, including running a 12v Danfoss refrigeration system, while they lived aboard in the temperate climes of Northern Europe.

The large windmill generators, with 6-9ft (1.8-2.7m) propeller diameter can pump in a really significant charge, up to 35 amps. These large wind generators vary in sophistication. Some are available with a centrifugal hub that alters the pitch of the windmill blades in different wind strengths, ensuring consistency of power input. The better ones have a specially-made alternator with permanent magnets as opposed to more normal electromagnetic fields which take power from the battery when the wind drops. The alternators are normally large diameter to increase the speed of the rotor around the fixed stator so the windmill can pump out amps at low speeds. It is not out of the question to make one of these big windmill chargers yourself, but the hardest part would be matching propeller revolutions with a low-speed alternator.

The noise of wind generators can be offputting. The smaller variety tend to drum and vibrate (particularly if you have a light craft such as a multihull) and the big variety, turning at lower speeds, make a constant swishing sound. In the light of their power contribution, it seems a small price to pay and after a while I'm told you stop noticing the noise. The danger of windmills mustn't be underestimated. Under no circumstances must their propellers be allowed to operate within arms reach of anyone on deck. Indeed when the wind starts to blow hard one must lower the large variety on to the deck, taking great care when manually turning the windvane across the wind to depower the blade.

## Propshaft Generators

The propshaft generator has mixed blessings. It tends to be used on larger boats with props big enough to drive them and the requirement for the sort of power they can produce. It has been scientifically proven that a turning propeller creates more drag than a fixed one, so the boat is going to be slightly slower when you let her prop drag. The noise of the propshaft turning the whole time can be irritating down below, especially as it will have to turn the gearbox in neutral (which creates extra wear on the cutless bearing and gearbox mechanism and is a questionable undertaking with hydraulic transmission).

In its favour, a propshaft generator can pump in a lot of power, up to 35amps, at good sailing speed, and can be quite cheap to rig up using a car alternator. It also works when you are motoring, although you must be careful not to cook the batteries. However, they don't work on propellers less than 18-20in (45cm), unless there is a clutch mechanism fitted between the shaft and gearbox.

The normal set up is a wheel on the propshaft, belted to an alternator. The ratio of wheel diameter to alternator is critical and depends on three things:-

1 Speed of propshaft rotation at around 5 knots. This can usually be physically counted (over 10 secs). It varies considerably, but a figure of 200 rpm is about average.
2 The lowest operating revs of the alternator you use. This is generally in the 1,100 to 1,250rpm range (but check it).
3 The upper operating revs of the alternator. They are normally between 7,000 and 11,000. You won't be able to count your propshaft's revs under full engine power, but it's easy enough to calculate knowing your engine's rpm and the gearbox reduction ratio. An engine running flat out at 2,800rpm through a 2.5:1 reduction ratio

will be turning the propshaft at 1,120rpm. After the step–up ratio of the propshaft alternator is allowed for, this must fall within the alternator's working range.

It can be seen then that in the above case a 6:1 ratio wheel attached to the propshaft in the above circumstances would drive the alternator at 1,200rpm sailing at 5 knots when charge would be minimal, but when the yacht is motoring fast the alternator would still be within its limits turning at nearly 6,800 revs – and putting out a great deal of power, especially bearing in mind that the engine's own alternator will be pumping in the amps.

## Water Generators

Utilising your existing propshaft with a cheap alternator is one thing, but spending good money on special charging equipment that can only be used while the yacht is under way seems to me slightly cock-eyed in the light of how little time a yacht spends at sea.

There have been several water generators on the market, looking rather like small outboard motors strapped on the stern. They can contribute up to 10amps, but as far as I'm aware none have lasted in the harsh marine environment perched over the stern of a boat, even when they could stand up to sailing speeds of six knots or more. Dodge Morgan had two aboard his *American Promise* and both lasted a matter of days. If you have money to spare, until a really reliable water generator is brought out, I think it would be much better to spend it on an extra solar panel that works in harbour and at sea.

## Wiring a Regulator Bypass

This is an incredibly simple operation and the difference it makes to engine charging hours is remarkable. Why then don't we hear of it being used on ordinary boats? Quite simply, it is not foolproof and automatic, and if you are stupid enough to forget that this bypass is operating, at best you will ruin your batteries and at worst your boat will be on fire. Never forget this, and if you're an absent-minded person, do not consider making this adaption.

A regulator is a small, usually sealed, device sometimes incorporated on the back of the alternator, sometimes fixed to a nearby bulkhead. It senses the battery's state of charge and adjusts the field current into the alternator appropriately. The result is that as the battery 'fills up' the alternator gradually tapers away the charging current it supplies to the battery and thereby protects it from over-charging. The frustrating thing is that these devices tend to work conservatively and even when the battery is only half charged, an

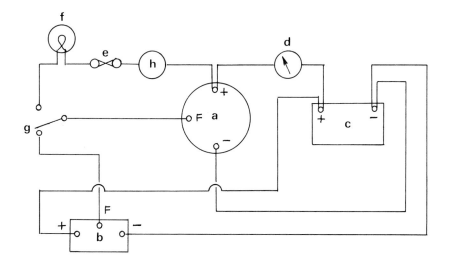

**Fig 11** The wiring diagram for bypassing an alternator regulator and thereby significantly increasing your battery charging ability. The system works well and is used extensively, but it is very dangerous if forgotten. (**a**) alternator (**b**) regulator (**c**) battery (**d**) ammeter (**e**) 10A fuse (**f**) conspicuously-positioned bright red bulb (**g**) three-way switch (**h**) optional potentiometer

alternator will only be putting in a small proportion of its charge, never anywhere near its full output capacity. As a result, the batteries are never really fully charged unless you've been motoring for a few days.

When it comes to battery charging in harbour, when you want the engine to be running for the shortest time possible it can be pretty maddening to watch the ammeter reading that the 55amp alternator is putting in only 10amps after an hour or so, when you know you've taken about 40-50 amp/hr out of the battery in the last couple of days.

Figure 11 shows the wiring diagram needed to bypass the regulator and feed the battery's full field current into the alternator, which in turn will pump out its maximum capacity. There are two ways of arranging this bypass. In both, the original regulator facility is still maintained, so if you want to motor for any length of time, it is quite possible to let the system be automatically regulated as normal. Method A is to have a three way switch, the middle position being no field current at all in which case the alternator will spin freely and produce no charge. The other two switch positions are for normal regulated field current and for 'boost' unregulated field current when the alternator pumps out full charge. It is advisable to have a bright red light in the unregulated circuit so you are always aware that the batteries are on boost charge. The second method is slightly more sophisticated and also uses a three way switch but instead of having full field current being fed to the alternator, the current can be manually regulated by a potentiometer, so by watching the ammeter and turning the 'pot' you can decide for yourself how much field current goes in and therefore how much charge is produced by the alternator. Although the cost of a potentiometer system is slightly higher, this method is best because you can manually taper the charge into the battery as it fills up with charge and avoid damage.

Bypassing the regulator does not damage the alternator at all – its maximum output is designed to be well within its temperature bounds and anyway the alternator will probably only be charging like this for a maximum of an hour or two at a time. Anyone can make this simple adaption easily for the cost of a three-pole switch, a light fitting and some wire but it is absolutely essential to remember these rules:-

1 Always have a prominent bright red light to constantly remind you that you are using the boost charge facility (this will also remind you to turn off when the engine has stopped otherwise the current will flow back from the batteries into the alternator, with possible damage).
2 Watch the voltmeter like a hawk, and switch over to normal regulated field current as soon as the voltmeter is reading 14.3v.
3 To reduce the possibility of 'force-feeding' the battery and causing it damage, make sure that this charging current is being distributed into all the banks of batteries (remembering that a battery, or a bank, can only withstand 25% of its remaining capacity in charging rate).

This system has a further long term advantage. Diesel engines thrive on hard and constant work and it is very bad for them to run for long periods under little or no load. Unfortunately, this is exactly what the ocean cruising yachtsman does when he runs the engine just for charging in port. By fitting and using a regulator bypass, the engine is having to work harder to pull the alternator around pumping out its maximum capacity, which helps the engine to some extent.

## Shore Power

Hooking up to a shore supply when available is quite a temptation. All of a sudden you don't have to worry about your power consumption, you can charge your batteries full to the brim and all manner of convenient domestic appliances can be used. The trouble is that shore power spoils you, and ridiculous as it seems, it is almost like a vice. After you've been living with it for a while it becomes quite hard to cut that umbilical cord. Once you've got used to a few of those conveniences, useless as they are without mains supply, cruising can start turning into a constant search for a shore power supply which will limit your options. Your costs will escalate because you will always have to be at a marina or dock which will cost more on top of the charges for the electricity. 'Alongside living' puts a new complexion on cruising. You can't go for a swim whenever you feel like it, you have no privacy and you become more vulnerable to bugs, rats, thieves and drunks.

Despite this there are occasions when an ocean cruiser can take advantage of a shoreside mains supply, especially if you are wintering over in a port in cold weather and can use a mains heater to keep you warm. Mains supplies vary throughout the world, although generally there are more 230v countries than 110v. The most practical shore-power rig is simply a long electric cable whose plastic insulation is flawless and undamaged. We nearly always end up buying (or borrowing) a suitable plug and if the supply is 110v we don't use it, because a step-up transformer doesn't justify its cost, weight or bulk aboard for such infrequent occasions. We carry aboard an electric drill, jigsaw, a domestic battery charger and a 2kw blower heater.

If you find yourself thinking of ways of plumbing in a shorepower circuit and appliances to your boat or becoming hooked to the joys of a mains supply while you're away, think seriously about your cruising lifestyle, because it's the best sign, deep down, that you really want to be living ashore.

# 12
# The Engine

Do you need an engine? Our first year or two of ocean cruising was conducted, to all intents and purposes, without an auxiliary for our large and unwieldly catamaran – for purely financial reasons (although I kidded myself I had a streak of purism). It put a completely different complexion on our cruising standards. On one side our level of seamanship was undoubtedly higher and we developed an ability to quickly assess situations ahead, to see if a harbour, bay or anchorage could be sailed out of, or was suited to us.

On the negative side, we were always a long way behind all our cruising friends, because although the cat could sprint over open distances quickly, we would always be caught becalmed under a headland or in the lee of an island. We once spent 26 frustrating hours trying to make up the lee of St. Vincent in the Windward Islands while our friends motored, charged their batteries up, and did the trip in three or four hours.

On another occasion, trying to leave Bayona in Northern Spain, where long periods without a breath of wind and hazy visability are common, we went out and spent two consecutive days drifting off the entrance trying to get away, drifting into the harbour and anchoring each night. All the other cruising yachts turned on their diesels and 30 miles down the coast found a good wind, eventually arriving in Madeira a week ahead of us. Sod's Law being so prominent in sailing, we would always turn up within sight of a port an hour or two before dusk and get becalmed. With an engine we'd have been safely at anchor within an hour, eating supper surrounded by our friends. As it was we generally spent several hours helplessly running the gamut of shipping leaving and entering the port, took the risk of entering an unknown place in the dark and finally dropped our anchor at 0100, tired and impatient.

As we have seen in other respects people's second or third boats are much more revealing than their first and you very rarely find anyone going on to a second engineless boat. The only exception I know are Lin and Larry Pardey, but then they've been preaching the joys of cruising without an engine for so long now, I'm sure that whatever their private thoughts they would never be taken seriously again if they fitted one.

A properly installed modern auxiliary diesel engine is compact, economic to run and highly reliable and to cruise without one is like shooting yourself in the foot. If you have purist ideas, there is nothing to stop you cruising as if you have no engine and manoeuvring under sail as much as you wish, but the day a strong current is taking you straight toward a coral reef, the ability to fire up the diesel is a fail-safe insurance policy.

## Engine Choice

The type and size of engine in a yacht would strongly influence my decision to buy her, largely because of this safety factor.

To give an example, we were anchored in *Euge* in St George's Harbour, Bermuda when a deep and spiteful depression brought a fierce south easterly gale. The following night, the British barque *Marques* was lost 70 miles north west of the islands. Our anchorage suddenly became a lee shore with a three-quarter mile fetch across the harbour for the wind and seas to build up and all the yachts were jumping and leaping at their cables. Several crews were stranded ashore, unable to launch their dinghies. We were anchored near the shore and had a dozen yachts upwind of us, one or two of which were starting to drag. By 11 o'clock at night the wind was up to 50 knots and we felt decidedly vulnerable with only 50 yards (45m) between us and a particularly unyielding concrete quay. Though we had confidence in our ground tackle, it only needed one of the yachts upwind to drag on to us. Then we would have been in serious trouble and didn't even know if the engine would be able to get us out of the situation if we dragged. In the height of the storm we decided that we were relying too much on luck so must move, awkward and wet as it would be. We got some encouragement by motoring up to the anchor. Not sure quite how much power our 25hp Volvo would have if a squall came through, we reefed the mainsail right down and made it ready to hoist within seconds if needed. To our amazement and with spray driving right over the boat as she plunged into the seas, the diesel could just about get us to windward and to safety. We re-anchored with lots of scope and swinging room and were able to sleep the rest of the night, while other yachts close inshore hung on, praying nothing would give.

Although some people say that there should be approximately one engine horsepower per foot of overall length, displacement is a more important criterion than size. As a guide you should have between 4 and 5hp per ton for the engine to have the power to cope occasionally with conditions like those described above.

It is a gross oversimplification, but serves our needs, that there are broadly three types of diesel engine. The early-style slow-revving, high compression 'thumpers' like the Sabbs and Listers have been used for decades in everything from fishing boats to concrete mixers and threaten to be with us for ever. They run slowly, steadily, and can be rebuilt time and time again. They generally only have two or three cylinders and it is normally possible to hand start them. They are also very heavy, tend to be tall, noisy and in many cases will rattle your teeth out. They are expensive to buy initially, but their simplicity leads to low maintainance and if you are planning to go away for a long time and are looking for sheer durability, the initial investment will pay off in the long run. The middle range of engines rev up to around 2,200rpm, generally have more cylinders and although they are more compact than the 'thumpers' are still fairly bulky. The new breed of modern diesels are high-revving, up to 3,500rpm and are often taken from industrial and even automotive uses. They are half the weight of a 'thumper', half the size, and run like sewing machines. They also last a fraction of the time, sometimes only 2,000 running hours.

For tropic cruising, despite its extra complication, a freshwater cooled engine is more desirable than raw water cooling because with the higher ambient seawater temperatures there is a danger of salt encrustation in the engine cooling, bores and chambers and gradual overheating. To clean them out is a major job and not undertaken lightly. On a freshwater cooled system don't forget to use antifreeze, because although you're not likely to be cruising in areas where it needs to stop the water freezing, this fluid also acts as a rust inhibitor. Your cooling system must also have plenty of pencil zincs to avoid electrolysis which should be pulled and checked frequently.

Most engine manufacturers seem to be fairly reliable but the availability of spare parts overseas is vital. Perkins (or Westerbeke – the same thing) are by far the best because they are used in tractors and industrial plants the world over. Much the same applies to Yanmar and Ford. The Danish Bukh engines have a great reputaton for reliability and smoothness but the company stopped building engines in 1986 and no one took them over. Although they guaranteed to maintain spare part stocks for 10 years afterwards, it means that their already fairly limited worldwide spares network is not going to get any better. Old fashioned slow-running engines like the Sabbs and Listers don't seem to need as many spares which is fortunate because availability is not generally good. There are snags with Volvo, despite the fact that they've cornered a big chunk of the sailing boat market. For years their engines have undergone frequent minor changes with the result that stockists rarely have the part you want no matter how basic. Not only are spares difficult to get, they are very expensive. This is a great shame because the design of Volvos is good and with their 2000 series (18–43hp) all the servicing points of the motor are easily accessible on the front of the engine block and the engine can also be hand-started.

## Starters

The ability to hand start a diesel is highly desirable as there will always be times when batteries are low.

Lucas Marine in England produce what they call a 'spring starter' for diesel engines. It looks a little like a starter motor and turns the flywheel in the same way as an electric starter motor. One operates it by winding a handle on the side fifteen times winding up very strong springs. A release lever is then thrown and the engine started. They sell a lot of them for starting emergency generators in places like hospitals. They seem like a sailor's dream until you learn their price, which in 1987 was over £550. A sum like this could be better invested in other items of equipment, or perhaps a spare starter motor and portable generator like a Honda or Mase.

If your batteries are very low there are a few dodges to get the engine going and one of these is bump-starting under sail by putting the engine into reverse gear. This only works if there is plenty of wind enabling you to sail fast and if you have decompression levers. If you do not have decompression levers, one desperate method worth trying is to insert a knife blade between the rocker and exhaust valve stems to decompress artificially. Then your battery may just have enough power to get the engine turning over before you slide out the blade.

## Maintenance

Good access to the engine is absolutely imperative or you will always be tempted to put off vital maintenance jobs. If your chosen boat doesn't have this, come up with ways to improve it even if it means that some of the sound deadening has to be permanently removed – better a noisy engine than an unserviced silent one. Bigger hatches can sometimes be cut from the yacht's quarter area. Certain ancilliary items like fuel filters, battery and even alternator can be re-sited slightly to improve access. If the panelling is large or complicated, cut smaller access hatches in them to allow you to make the basic checks – engine and gearbox dipsticks and fanbelt tensions. A perspex inspection window next to the water filter bowl could be useful.

One of the most common jobs is changing lubricating oil and yet it is nearly always difficult to do. Think about this problem before you sail. The ideal is if you can get under the engine and reach the sump plug, but this is rare and it is even less likely that you can fit a container under there as well to catch the oil. Several engines, including Perkins and Bukh, include an oil sump pump as standard equipment and as long as this is situated in a convenient place all well and good. If not, re-route it to somewhere you can sit comfortably (because thickish oil

An engine installed with this standard of accessibility is likely to be cared for and serviced much more often than one shoe-horned under the cockpit *(Yachting Monthly)*

doesn't like to be dragged up thin pipes so it's quite a physical job) and where a reasonably-sized receptacle can be placed underneath to catch the old oil. The portable pumps available nearly always leak, but it is possible to buy good-quality hand sump pumps and this is a good investment for future happiness. Working in the confines of an engine compartment is *never* fun in the tropics.

The majority of problems with diesel engines come from dirty fuel, so make certain you have at least three big filters (one of them with a water separator bowl) and plenty of paper replacements. If your fuel comes aboard initially through a fine gauze conical funnel (mentioned in the fuel section) and then passes through three more filters before it gets to the injection pump, many potential problems will be avoided.

Though dirt in the fuel will stop a diesel, it is unlikely to hurt the engine much, but if water is allowed to get in it can do a great deal of permanent damage. A teaspoonful of water reaching the injection pump can wreck it in a matter of seconds. It may be just as bad if the pump survives and feeds water to the injectors, for they will be ruined too. If you can, fit Racor water filters with drainable glass bowls, regarded as the Rolls Royce of diesel water filtration systems.

A safety feature beautiful in its simplicity, fitted to most French boats, is the fire-extinguisher hole. In the event of an engine-room fire the worst thing you can do is pull away the casing to aim the fire extinguisher because this will feed the fire with air and aggravate it. The fire extinguisher hole is an approximately 1½in (40mm) diameter hole cut in the engine casing with a plastic plug. In the event of a fire, the plug is pulled out and the extinguisher let off through the hole into the engine compartment. It is simple and highly effective.

Designers seem to take pride in the way they can shoehorn an engine into a tiny space then wrap it up in sound-deadening foam so that it can neither be seen nor heard. As well as fuel, engines need air to run on, in fact for every gallon of fuel consumed the average diesel also consumes 12,500 gallons (56,826 lit) of air! Make sure there are plenty of locations for the air to enter, otherwise the engine will lose power, use excessive fuel and run hotter, causing more wear and shorten its life.

One of the best pieces of preventive maintenance for an engine is to paint it, the engine room and the sump brilliant white. Not only will a clean engine run cooler, but you will immediately know if there are any oil or fuel leaks, especially if you also install some bright engine room lights. Once you have got the engine and engine room clean, a wipe over with paraffin cloth from time to time is no chore. Also, unless you want quite revolting bilges and even perished rubber bilgepump parts, the engine should have its own bilge sump to catch any stray diesel or oil.

Don't leave the country without an engine workshop manual, and also a diagrammatical spare parts list with all the appropriate numbers. Not only does this list bridge most language difficulties, it also makes ordering spares from a faraway spares stockist one hundred percent more efficient.

## Engine Monitoring

In the interests of economy more engine manufacturers have stopped supplying proper monitoring gauges and simply fit warning lights instead. A serious cruising yachtsman needs to know exactly how his engine is running and this can only be done by inspection of proper gauges. With practice they help you diagnose problems and quite often nip them in the bud – more than can be said of a light which will only tell you after the problem has occurred. The system should also be backed up with a loud alarm for oil pressure and temperature.

Engine hours should be logged, if you want to take care and maintenance seriously. Note down engine running hours, any servicing done or adjustments made. Engine hour meters are easy to fit, but you can just as easily write down the times the engine is running.

## Fuel

Carry as much fuel as you can without sacrificing other vital storage space or overloading. There are often spaces under the cockpit or in the bottom of deep cockpit lockers where extra fuel tanks can be fitted. Filling up with fuel can be quite a chore alongside commercial wharfs or rough little quays and the less times you have to do it the better. As well as carrying as much fuel as possible, don't be wasteful with it. A motoring range of 400 miles (approximately 25-35 galls [113-159 lit]) is the bare minimum and as long as you don't squander fuel this will generally see you through parts of the world where fuel facilities are scarce. When there isn't a fuelling berth it is often possible to get a lorry tanker load delivered to a quayside to be split up amongst several yachties. Always have a 5-gallon (22 lit) container of diesel on board, not only as spare, but also because you might have to buy small quantities and 'jug-it' back to the boat.

The fuel filler design and location can be a source of continuing aggravation and if you have any doubts change yours now. In some places they are used to giving commercial vessels several tons of fuel in a short space of time and the attendant will pass you down a massive pipe out of which will spurt diesel in huge quantities. Before you go alongside, even if you learn nothing else of the local language, find out how to say 'slow down' and 'stop'.

If at all possible, have a 2½-3in (76mm) fuel filler pipe fitted and back it up with a 1in (25mm) breather pipe leading from the tank so there are no risks of blow backs. The breather pipe must exit next to the filler so you can tell when the tank is full. No matter how much care you take there are nearly always spillages when a tank is being filled, so the fuel filler pipe should be out on deck, preferably near the scuppers, and well away from any untreated teak.

Rule No 1 for reliable diesel engines is to feed them only clean fuel. To this end, either buy or have made a really good gauzed funnel that is always put in the filler hole before you take on fuel. It is amazing the selection of grit, muck and dead insects (plus water) that you buy along with your diesel in most foreign ports. This funnel alone will cut out 50% of potential engine problems.

You will need to know how much fuel you have aboard, but don't bother with commercially-made fuel gauges. They are never accurate with yacht tanks which are always irregularly shaped. A sight gauge, which you callibrate by filling the tank in five gallon increments is by far the simplest, most accurate and reliable system and it can be fitted to any nearby bulkhead.

## *Propellers*

Sailing performance must be good if you are to keep a happy crew and this is a strong argument for fitting a folding prop. Over long distances the small contribution it makes to the boat's speed is amplified and an ocean crossing could be made several days shorter as a result. However, a folding propeller's weakness is its inability to create much power going astern. This may not seem much of a problem until you go aground, when a fixed propeller (preferably three-bladed) will stand a better chance of getting you off before much damage is done. This safety factor alone makes the drag of a three-bladed propeller worth putting up with for the rest of the time.

# 13
# Navigation Aids and Communications

### Electronic Navigation

In the last ten years micro-chip technology has revolutionised the button-pressing element of yachting and while it is a sad state of affairs that more and more people are starting to sail and buying aids such as Decca without bothering to learn the basics of navigation, it is easy to see why when the electronic wizardry we all use ashore, is so very reliable. For the experienced yachtsman who does realise that none of these systems is infallible, such aids can undoubtedly be of great value as long as they are kept in perspective.

One of the most common navigation aids is the radio direction finder. Obviously, out on the ocean its value is nil, but on the approach of land it can be very handy to home in on an RDF station, even though it is rare to have a cross beacon to fix your position and judge your distance off. The 'homing-in' ability of an RDF can be most re-assuring for your first few landfalls, when you may not have been too confident of your astro navigation. Outside Northern Europe and America the RDF coverage is not good, although most of the principal Atlantic islands have one or two aero beacons. The Caribbean has several RDF beacons but their reliability is questionable and anyway 99 percent of navigation there is done with eyeballs. In the Pacific, particularly the more interesting cruising areas, coverage is poor and your RDF will have very little, if any, use.

Satellite navigation systems have made a big impact, opening up places like the Tuamotu Archipelago where many fine seamen have lost their craft to erratic currents in the past. The battery drain of Sat-Navs is fairly high, so in order to save power and keep their hand in, many yachtsmen use traditional astronavigation during passages where precision position plotting isn't essential. They only turn on the SatNav when close to land. An astounding thing about satellite navigators which you must remember is that, paradoxical as it may seem, their very accuracy can make them dangerous! Many charts, especially in the Pacific, were made before such pin point fixing was possible, so land masses and islands are often not in exactly the right place. Atolls are regularly misplaced by up to five miles, and reefs can often be a mile or two from their charted positions. Your very accurate

SatNav will tell exactly where you are on the surface of the globe, but plotted on to the chart may put you in quite the wrong place, and you may be about to plough up a reef when the SatNav has put you off the harbour entrance. It comes back to the fact that all equipment is no more than an aid and should never take the place of good honest seamanship, and a keen pair of eyes.

My own initial scepticism about SatNav was dispelled by a quite intrepid and highly experienced cruising couple, Tom and Nancy Zydler. They've cruised the high latitudes of Spitsbergen in the north and Cape Horn in the south and rarely have I met anyone with such depth of experience. Their 37ft (11.27m) yawl *Mollymawk* was a pure seaman's boat – massively strong, utterly reliable, exuding efficiency and simplicity everywhere. They didn't even have an engine but handled the boat impeccably. I didn't expect their instrumentation to extend beyond a Walker towing log but on going below I was amazed to see a SatNav over the chart table. Tom couldn't praise it highly enough and said that it had changed the face of their sea-time because not being absolutely certain where you are, particularly in the proximity of land, causes a lot of worry. Now SatNav has taken that worry away entirely leaving them to enjoy themselves more and to concentrate on the seamanlike operation of their boat. They were

If possible keep the electrics and electronics down to good-quality basics, although don't install them as on this boat where a wet navigator's arm will soon drip on them, especially if the yacht's heel means he leans on them  *(Yachting Monthly)*

realistic about its shortfalls. It was likely to need sending back to the manufacturers annually for some repair or other (in which case they could carry on cruising without it) and they needed to buy a solar panel and run their little petrol generator more often. This was a small price though for the peace of mind it gave them.

## Other Instrumentation

A variety of precise wind and water instrumentation has been developed by the racing field. Their accuracy is generally very good but though they may impress your friends they really have little use. Basics are undoubtedly handy – the echo sounder and speedlog – but none of the other modern instrumentation is really necessary for ocean cruising, nor will it contribute much to the seamanlike running of a yacht at sea. At the height of an Indian Ocean gale it might be able to tell you that it is blowing exactly 52 knots, at 78 degrees off the bow and the boat is making 1.78 knots VMG to windward, but your real priorities must be in the strength and quality of your rigging, the integrity of openings and hatches and the reliability of your bilge pumps. Again, the KISS principle holds true. A 9in (22m) length of broken cassette tape tied to the shroud provides a much more accurate and sensitive indication of wind in very light going than masthead instruments gyrating around with the boat rolling. As a matter of totally irrelevant fact, if you use eight or ten of these a year a standard C120 cassette will last you for over 90 years!

In short, instrumentation must come a long way down the priorities list and only be fitted when essentials are well catered for and there is a first class complement of basic seamanlike equipment aboard, like anchors, good rig and sails, and high capacity pumps. All on-board electronic aids should be regarded as just that – aids. If you have to rely on them in any way you should not be going to sea.

## Radio Communications

Good receivers are fairly cheap and even to set yourself up with an amateur radio transmitter is not particularly expensive. Some people argue that the element of safety that transceivers introduce to an ocean crossing backfires when, for whatever reason, you can't maintain a regular scheduled call and people and authorities immediately start worrying, possibly unnecessarily. Certainly the large majority of ocean passages take place quietly without any radio communication and while this gives a certain peace of mind to the skipper and crew, those at home would far prefer an occasional reminder that you are still afloat.

To the uninitiated radio frequencies and terminology can be very confusing with short waves, medium waves, AM, FM, long waves, medium frequency (MF), high frequency (HF) and of course VHF. It is much easier to forget all that (with the exception of VHF which most people understand anyway) and think in terms of kilohertz only.

Basically there are two broad divisions – AM and FM. FM is the same as VHF and only used for small distances, usually less than 75 miles. Yachtsmen will be using AM solely and the bigger the frequency number the further away it can be heard. Something like BBC Radio One which broadcasts in the UK on 1,053kHz can be heard for a few hundred miles. The kHz radio frequency scale goes right up to 29,999 and that can be heard worldwide on the right equipment. As you run up the scale so certain sections are allocated for general broadcasting use, for amateur (ham) radio and for marine communications.

## Receivers

These have several uses, probably the most important one for ocean yachtsmen being the ability to pick up time signals either from BBC World Service or the US WWV stations. Whilst modern quartz timepieces are highly accurate, it is nevertheless necessary to check them frequently if you want good astronavigation positions.

WWV broadcast continuous times signals on 2,500, 5,000, 10,000 and 15,000 kHz. World Service broadcast on dozens of different frequencies all over the world from around 3,915 kHz up to 21,710 kHz and these ranges are embraced in most 'short wave' portable radio sets available from High Street shops. Don't buy a set that can only be powered by dry cell batteries – you'll find that if you start listening to something like BBC World Service regularly, you'll use dozens of batteries and although they're not usually hard to find, they can be very expensive. Transformers which plug into car cigarette lighter sockets and which step down the voltage from 12 to 4.5/6/9v can be bought, although rarely abroad, so if you intend to listen to the radio regularly, get one before you go.

Technology and models are changing very rapidly but one of the best general receivers for yachts is the Sony ICF 2001 which will pick up all AM radio frequencies from 150kHz through to 29,999 kHz. In other words, as well as serving as a normal 'kitchen' radio, it will also pick up all the marine frequencies such as 2,182 kHz and the US high seas weather forecasts such as Manahawkin (New Jersey) on 4,385.3 kHz (SSB). It also embraces all the ham radio bands so that although you obviously can't talk to others using ham, you can listen in. This can become quite a hobby and very informative at times. The Sony is supplied with an invaluable Wave Handbook, which catalogues all the radio stations throughout the world with their transmission times, languages, areas and frequencies. I spent many a night watch fiddling with the radio listening to Radio Australia for a while, then Voice of America, and so on. The Sony is very sensitive to moisture, so be certain to look after it carefully.

During our years overseas we became quite hooked to BBC World Service and particularly at sea we looked forward to hearing our favourite programmes. The BBC publishes a monthly magazine catalogue of programmes and frequencies called *London Calling* which is very useful. We subscribed to it for several years. They send it out airmail six weeks in advance of the month it covers, so it stands a chance of reaching you before going out of date wherever you are. Subscription is £9 annually, and details can be had from BBC London Calling, P.O. Box 76, Bush House, Strand, London WC2B 4PH.

## Singleside Band Radio Transmitters

A single sideband radio transmitter, operating between 2,000kHz – 22,000kHz enables you to contact shoreside marine operators and other ships over a range of up to 6,000 miles. This enables you in theory to make telephone calls through coastal stations such as Portishead and WOM in Fort Lauderdale whilst you are sailing in the Atlantic. In practice it is a difficult operation that you don't do unless absolutely necessary. Commercial and naval ships are duty bound to listen in to 2,182 kHz which has a range of up to around 150 miles and is the international distress frequency, so this is a safety factor.

For all these advantages, the SSB/MF-HF radio is designed for big ships and is not a very practical or popular radio transmitter for yachts. Although one quite often comes across yachts fitted with them, their crews say they are rarely if ever used. They are also usually between two and three times the price of an amateur radio set.

## Amateur Ham Radio

Ham radios are highly popular on ocean cruising boats and for very good reasons. There are dozens of regular 'nets' organised – these are simply a regular time and radio frequency that a number of yachtsmen call in on. There is for example the Atlantic crossing 'net' which is co-ordinated by amateur radio enthusiasts in England but which yachts sailing in the Atlantic tune in to every day. Those on passage usually call in their position and the weather and will have a chat to the co-ordinator or maybe some friends who are also crossing over. It becomes a friendly daily chat session where people chip in with a bit of help and advice (I remember one person having trouble with their Aries self-steering which they subsequently rectified by someone else's helpful tip) and as a cruising grapevine it is great to learn the whereabouts of friends.

There are many smaller networks such as the Caribbean Net where perhaps just a dozen hams participate, and of course private ones where you arrange to speak with a particular set of friends maybe once a week. The friendliness of it is of course very pleasant, but ham radio can provide very practical information too. A friend of ours was in Barbados and needed to slip his boat fairly urgently. Rather than sail up through the islands trying to find a slipway that would take him straight away for a reasonable price he was able to talk to his friends on the Caribbean net who were anchored in the islands with slipways. By the next day he knew the best place to haul, asked his ham friend there to book it, and he sailed there direct. I could quote many other instances.

Many is the time I've tried contacting passing ships through the international distress frequency of 2,182kHz and not picked up any ship within hundreds of miles. The one thing about ham radio is that there is *always* somebody listening out for an interesting chat. They may not be able to help directly, but in an emergency they could instigate help. There have been several instances of yachtsmen in serious medical trouble being able to contact doctors indirectly through a ham, who in turn have been able to diagnose the problem and advise treatment.

Another practical use for ham is talking to friends back at home. Nobody is allowed to use ham without a licence, but an easy arrangement is to strike up a radio contact with a ham radio operator who lives near family or friends at home. Although passing messages to third parties is against the strict laws controlling ham radio, you can talk to your contact weekly and the folks back home will know you are safe and well.

Ham does have its disadvantages. For a start you need to be officially licenced and this requires taking an examination proving your capability to use the radio properly and within the rules. This exam is not difficult, but it is not so easy as the VHF operators exam which is very easy. If you plan to have a ham set aboard, make sure you take an evening class for the operators exam the winter before you leave.

The other disadvantage with ham radios is the heavy current drain while you are transmitting – commonly up to 60amps. This is only intermittently whilst you are actually speaking, but is the reason why many yachtsmen do considerably more listening than transmitting.

We listened in to the ham nets very regularly on the Sony ICF 2001 and found them most informative. The chit chat would often give you information on the best place to buy fuel, or perhaps customs officers to avoid and we were often able to find out where friends were and so on. The biggest contribution it made though was when we crossed the Atlantic from the Canaries to West Indies. By listening to the daily weather reports of the 14 or 15 yachts already set off we were able to wait in the Canaries until we were absolutely sure that the tradewinds had set in for that year, then head off ourselves. By plotting the other yachts' positions and their weather we were able to head just far enough south for the best winds. When we were actually out on the crossing it was somehow comforting knowing there were others nearby rolling as much as us, or when a gale came through, having a worse time of it than us. Listening in to the Atlantic ham net became one of the high points of the daily routine – our only frustration was that we were unable to talk back as we would dearly have liked to on occasions.

## VHF

This is nearly universal among ocean cruising boats nowadays. Many people use it purely as a telephone to talk to friends in port or report their departure or arrival to the habour master.

We find that the VHF's greatest value is at sea when we are able to talk to passing ships. On our catamaran *Foreigner* we had no radio at all, and after we'd been at sea for a couple of weeks, longed to have a chat with someone else. *Euge* was fitted with VHF and it was always a pleasure to talk to the crews of tankers, liners and coasters. In the Bay of Biscay on one occasion we found ourselves feeling rather like a tiddler when we struck up a conversation with the *QE2*!

We were never too proud to ask for a weather report or Sat Nav position just to confirm our astro either. By talking to ships that we were on collision courses with we were able to exchange gentlemanly suggestions which took any possible danger or aggravation away from the situation. On one occasion in a gale we asked a ship heading straight at us to alter course, because for us to have done so would have been dangerous in the circumstances. As it turned out, in the white and broken water of the gale he hadn't seen us either visually or on radar and was only too happy to take avoiding action.

## Flags

Code flags are another tradition that many long distance yachsmen feel almost duty-bound to continue, neatly furled and pigeon-holed in a special locker. If you're an especially keen flag lover and like to dress the ship overall from time to time, and have the space to stow them well-ventilated, carrying code flags can be gratifying. However, if you believe they have any practical value in this day and age think again and put the not-inconsiderable sum they cost towards a VHF.

# 14
# Ground Tackle and Self Steering

There is no logical reason for dealing with these two subjects in the same chapter except that they are two aspects of an ocean cruising boat that should be spared no expense because one or the other should be looking after you all the time. While a standard-sized anchor with either chain or rope rode will suffice most of the time, there comes a time on all ocean cruises when the anchor becomes the lifeline, the insurance policy and sometimes the life insurance.

## Anchors and Rodes

The size and extent of ground tackle is one of the few things that most long distance yachtsmen agree about – the gear must be big but at the same time fairly easy to handle. There is no point in having a big anchor and chain ready to go out as you drag backwards across an anchorage if you have no roller for it, or the pulpit is too cluttered to allow it to be passed through.

The late Bob Griffiths of *Awahnee,* a man of huge cruising experience in high latitudes, had some interesting theories on anchoring. He believed that the correct anchor and rode for specific bottoms was more important than sheer anchor size and he carried no fewer than 10 anchors on his 53ft (16.15m) cutter, and none of them over 45 lb (20kg) so they remained manageable. This may seem over the top, but he says those anchors have saved his boat on numerous occasions. He also said that if he had to choose one anchor it would be the CQR and this is an opinion echoed by the majority. Three quarters of all yachts are fitted with them. Unfortunately, the CQR is expensive and has a large number of cheap imitators, generically known as plough anchors. The latter are nowhere near the calibre or construction of the genuine Simpson Lawrence CQR.

The Danforth or Meon anchor comes next in the popularity stakes, although I've damaged two of these in the past by bending their shanks. The Bruce anchor arrived amid a storm of publicity in the '70s, but is an anchor that people either seem to love or hate. The fact that there is never a happy medium for me casts this anchor in doubt when so much depends on it.

Although the traditional fisherman anchor is still available in large sizes, the above three patent anchors today dominate the scene.

When choosing or upgrading your ground tackle remember that in many places there simply aren't protected anchoring areas or harbours to go to and you might have to put up with conditions like this   *(Mark Fishwick)*

Although various sailing books quote anchors like the Northill and Herreschoff, they are not universally available.

In mooring terms, an ocean cruiser needs adaptability – sometimes she will not only need to anchor but maybe a long line will have to be taken to a far harbour wall, or tied to a coral head or mangrove swamp. To carry ten anchors is overkill (bear in mind Griffiths cruised in some wild and windy places) but an ocean cruiser should have a bare minimum of three good anchors – two similar sized bowers, preferably of different type, and a good-sized kedge. The most practical system of rodes is to have 180ft (55m) of chain on your favourite bower. This gives ample scope for the majority of anchorages, with a bit of spare to ease out in rougher conditions. In a separate chain locker should be 90ft (27.4m) of the same sized chain (both lengths having a good eye welded in each end) used with the second bower. This can be added to, if necessary, by a 400ft (121m) length of polypropylene. A further 250ft (76m) of nylon should be used with the kedge, with 20ft (6.1m) of chain also attached. The kedge has to have this long length of nylon line for when it is used either in a running moor or stern to a beach. At sea these two long ropes can be used as drogues if necessary.

With this set up it is possible in very bad conditions to have two big anchors out and a third line taken to a fixed point ashore or on the seabed. (We also carry an old spare 10ft length of chain with big eyes at either end which can be used when mooring lines pass over a rough concrete jetty edge, or when a line needs to be made fast to coral). A system we've used with some success in bad conditions is to shackle the kedge and chain to the shackle of the main anchor then lower the two in tandem.

We've found that this ground tackle rig has been totally practical and adapts to most conditions, although it should be said the strongest conditions we have tested it in are 50 knots in moderately exposed anchorages with generally good holding.

A chain claw is a useful piece of equipment to have aboard your boat. Most of the time it is shackled to a 6ft (1.8m) length of nylon led over the bow roller and used as a snubber on the main cable and to stop the chain graunching in the roller and keeping everyone awake. You can still hear if the anchor drags. Its secondary use is by attaching to a long length of rope which is led aft to a sheet winch. If the anchor is fouled, or the windlass inoperative, it's possible to get the anchor up using this rig.

## Self Steering

The self-steering system of a long distance cruising yacht is the single most important piece of gear she carries and yet it never fails to amaze me how little thought some first-time ocean cruising crews put into this essential aid. Hand steering is quite feasible for a day or two, but if your self-steering gear fails half way through a three or four week passage, you'll never again underestimate its significance to small boat sailing. It has been described on countless occasions in the past as a non-eating crewmember who doesn't answer back and doesn't suffer from the cold, wet or lack of sleep. The increase in rest and therefore watch-keeping efficiency, navigational accuracy and general on board contentedness means that the self-steering gear should be selected with great thought and it is one of the few areas where money should be no object. It will pay you back a hundred times over.

The sometimes perplexing question is whether to go for a wind-vane gear or one of the many modern electronic autopilots available today. To differentiate, I shall call all wind-vane mechanical gears 'self-steering gears' and the electric/electronic devices 'autopilots'. The autopilot is not only cheap in comparison to a self-steering gear, it is also very neat, light, and uses surprisingly little power. It is also very easy to set up and get going quickly. However, I can't urge you strongly enough that as a primary gear, don't rely on any sort of autopilot. Most long distance sailors agree that none of the modern range of electronic autopilots is yet anywhere near durable enough to

The Aries wind vane gears are the single most popular type of self-steering found aboard ocean cruising boats; the newish Lift-Up model benefits over the old gear by dismantling easily for stowage, repair and maintenance

rely on for ocean crossings.

Every year long distance race fleets set off on OSTAR, AZAB, Round Britain and so on and time and time again the biggest cause of problems are autopilots. Some long-distance yachtsmen are forced, through the size and shape of their yachts, to have just autopilots but they generally have two or three back-ups and have many a tale of having to hand-steer. A self-steering gear may be heavy and unsightly, and perhaps difficult to mount on some boats, but it's the only way to go if you don't want to be let down sooner or later.

Originally coming on the scene in the early '60s, the self-steering gear rather went out of favour 15 years later when autopilots became cheap and reliable and were used extensively for coastal weekend and holiday sailing, for which they are very effective. Without a mass market, self-steering gears rather went through the doldrums and although one or two new ones came and went, only the enduring models survived – the Aries, Navik, and Hydrovane. To many people's disappointment, the Haslar (whose creator, Blondie Hasler, developed and popularised self-steering gears) ceased production. In the last five years there has been renewed interest in windvane self-steering gears and two interesting new ones have become available.

Using the same servo pendulum principle, the ever-popular Aries was recently updated and made de-mountable. This is a definite advantage over the old style gear which, made in aluminium and stainless, freezes together and needs to be removed with a cold-chisel unless you dismantle and clean it regularly. In America, the Monitor is an all-stainless model similar to the Aries and is used a great deal for ocean cruising. The greatest new product in self-steering gears however is the Australian Fleming. It first became known when many of the first BOC Around Alone fleet fitted them at their Australian stop-over, having become disillusioned with the variety of gears they were already using. The Fleming became the darling of the fleet, and this was in evidence on the second BOC race when approximately one third of the entrants had fitted them, the other two-thirds being equally split between Aries and Monitors.

The neat and well-engineered Hydrovane has enjoyed success for many years and been used extensively. Its principle advantage is that the horizontally-pivoting vane mechanically operates a servo rudder and this means that the yacht's main rudder can be locked, which not only saves on wear and tear but also obviates the need for steering lines coming from the gear to the cockpit – sometimes a nuisance with centre-cockpit wheel steered boats and always a source of chafe. It also means that the yacht has a second rudder if you have problems with the first.

While autopilots are not to be recommended as a primary method of steering, they are nevertheless useful on occasions, because wind-vane self-steering gear is not infallible and refuses to operate well in certain conditions. Properly set up and kept well away from any moisture or water (ie either covered or rigged to operate the steering or rudder stock from within the cabin) an autopilot can be used in very light airs, especially with the wind astern, or when you are motoring for any length of time. We had an Autohelm on our Rival 34 to back up an Aries, and made a little watertight bonnet to protect it from the rain and dew. We only used the Autohelm in very light conditions, but it was kept bone dry and served well for a year. We like to think that the bonnet prolonged its life, but whether or not it did we'll never know.

# 15
# *The Ocean Cruiser's Dinghy*

Never underestimate the constant use and hard work your dinghy will receive once you are living aboard. It is a workhorse, often left banging around with a dozen others at a concrete quayside, regularly dragged up and down beaches over sand, stones and coral, often overloaded, and rarely out of service for long enough to be maintained properly. Durability is therefore essential, but it must also be light enough to be easily manhandled, and preferably need little routine maintenance. The other major feature that marries a dinghy and yacht, is the ability to stow it conveniently aboard.

Amongst the dinghy's essential functions will be to ferry you between yacht and shore and as a cargo carrier, loaded down with water containers and provisions. A good one can be used for exploring further afield or as a base to go diving from. In some cases it may be the ship's lifeboat too. It must certainly be seaworthy enough to get you out to the yacht when the weather has deteriorated while you have been ashore and to take out an extra anchor when conditions are bad, or even in a surf with the yacht piled up ashore.

To satisfy all these criteria, it becomes fairly obvious that there is no perfect solution. As ever it boils down to a compromise and the chief debate is between the inflatable and rigid dinghy.

## Inflatables

Approximately half of ocean cruising boats have inflatable tenders. Their major advantage is the ability to stow them on a boat where it isn't possible to have a rigid dinghy. The inflatable is also very light (so you can carry it up a rough beach), it carries loads well and doesn't knock against the topsides or under the counter. The great buoyancy of an inflatable is also a big plus when it comes to carrying the full crew complement or lots of stores. If you are concerned about overnight theft, it is a simple and easy matter to haul it up on deck out of reach. Inflatables cannot be rowed into a strong wind or sea but powered by a small outboard are highly seaworthy and even when half full of water can still make progress when a rigid dinghy has long since given up for fear of being overwhelmed. The inflatable is much better as a diving and snorkelling base.

Against the inflatable is its poor rowing performance, high windage

**Fig 12** A wire bridle encased in plastic tubing should be fitted as a matter of course to inflatable tenders to ease their normally-inefficient painter fittings and provide a secure point to padlock a security painter

and light weight. This means that if you want to get the best out of it, you're tied to having an outboard engine which further increases the considerably higher initial cost of buying an inflatable. An inflatable will require more maintenance than an average rigid dinghy and doesn't stand much abuse. It will need patching from time to time, and must be washed out regularly to avoid abrasion from sand. Cleaning weed and scum off the bottom is another chore, though this can be avoided by always turning it upside down at night. An irritating aspect of using an inflatable is that one nearly always gets wet, either from spray over the bow or from puddles collecting around your feet.

A final disadvantage of inflatables is their attraction to thieves. In many places an Avon or Zodiac is almost as good as cash. Make sure you sketch the bottom of your dinghy and keep a record of the 'geography' of its patches for evidence of identification.

Inflatables can also be customised and improved for a lot of work. Never rely on a bow eye or fitting; it is much better to wrap a rope (or wire encased in plastic) right the way around the dinghy (see Fig 12) or if the dinghy has a wooden transom take the wires to eye fittings in the transom. Floorboards are something of a hassle to fit when you're cruising from day to day, but if you're stopped in a place for any length of time, they will help maintain dry feet, make the dinghy row and motor more efficiently, and keep shopping bags dry. If your inflatable dinghy has a transom, it is worth cutting a sculling notch into it, just in case you are unlucky enough to lose an oar (at times like this one generally picks up the technique of sculling very quickly . . .).

### Rigid Dinghies

A rigid dinghy will generally cost only a fraction of an inflatable. It can also be rowed efficiently without too much effort, which further cuts your running costs and keeps you fit. A rigid dinghy will also last longer than its inflatable cousin. Many can be rigged for sailing adding to your enjoyment of an anchorage, though in practice few are used this way unless there are children aboard. I doubt we'd bother taking one along again, it simply isn't used enough to justify the cost, weight and space of the rig unless you can find one exceptionally simple to set.

The main problem with rigid dinghies is finding suitable deck space for them on a boat less than 38ft (11.6m) or so. If you go for a smaller dinghy that fits it becomes a nuisance having to make two or three trips ashore each time because you can't fit everyone in, and it is useless for exploring. Rigid dinghies also invariably weigh two or three times more than an inflatable and this weight is carried high up on deck which is not good for the centre of gravity. Another point against a rigid dinghy is its seemingly magnetic attraction to your topsides at times. No matter how well you protect its gunwhale with fendering sooner or later it starts to bump.

On both *Foreigner* and *Euge* we used rigid GRP dinghies and as long as deck space allows will continue doing so in future. They were always very cheap, never costing more than £100, generally tatty, and for this reason we had less worry about them being stolen. They were never locked up. Maintenance was straightforward – we kept them clean, never let them leak, and made certain the fender was always well attached. Otherwise they received no attention in terms of painting or varnishing but being fibreglass they lasted well and stood up to terrible punishment.

A pair of long oars is essential for easy propulsion, used in galvanised (never plastic) rowlocks which must be secured with lanyards as· the right sized galvanised rowlocks are irreplacable overseas. The oars must have good protection from the rowlocks or they will get chewed up rapidly with the amount of use they receive. The best way of doing this is by splitting a 9in (22cm) length of appropriate-diameter plastic pipe, 'gluing' it in place with silicone and working a turk's head over each end.

The dinghy we had on *Euge* was the best small tender I've ever come across and is still being made by A P Marine Products, High Bullen, Torrington, Devon. At 7ft 6in (2.28m), its great advantage was light weight (75lb/34kg)) but high strength. This is achieved by the simple process of incorporating ridges and angles throughout the GRP mouldings, creating stiffness but at the same time allowing a light lay-up (see Fig 13).

If a rigid dinghy doesn't quite fit on deck, it can often be adapted with a recess, either in the bow transom or stern, to fit around the mast (see Fig 14).

The best fender material is a thick rope wired on with copper loops. These need replacing from time to time, but the materials are easy to find anywhere. The dinghy bumping problem is often best solved by attaching the end of the painter to an eye in the transom and shackling the spinnaker halyard in the resulting vee to hoist the dinghy out of the

**Fig 13** When choosing a dinghy, the first priorities are strength and lightness. The builder can achieve this effectively by utilising many curves and ridges within the moulding

**Fig 14** If a rigid dinghy doesn't quite fit on the coachroof, glass in a plywood recess in the transom to fit around the yacht's mast

water. As long as there isn't too much swell or a very strong wind, the dinghy will lie quietly against the guardrails at deck level until needed again.

Most cruising people would choose a rigid dinghy if it were possible to stow one of 10ft (3.05m) or more on deck. As it is, they are deterred by the fact they can fit only an 8-footer (2.43m) on deck, which with more than two people is crowded and doesn't have much freeboard. One solution is a nesting dinghy, the stern portion of which disconnects and stows in the forward part. In this way, it is possible to have an excellent 10 or 12 foot rowing and sailing dinghy that has the buoyancy and much of the seaworthiness of an inflatable and comes close to an ideal compromise. The snag is that these are not built commercially so you would have to make your own. This subject will be enlarged on later in this chapter.

## Outboard Engines

Modern outboard engines (and I stress, *modern*) are very good indeed and the best thing you can do to an outboard is to use it regularly as an ocean cruising yachtsman is likely to. The variety of little 2hp or so 'egg-whisk' engines such as the Suzuki, Yamaha or Mariner are so cheap, light, reliable, economic and even quiet that it's hard to resist having one aboard if your dinghy is less than 9-10ft (2.74-3.04m). Many has been the time I've regretted not having one when there was a long row to pick up water or dive on a wreck.

On the other hand, rowing helps you keep fit and rowing past a neighbour's boat provides ample time to chat whereas an outboard buzzing away at the stern puts paid to any social contact. The Hiscocks gave up their outboard for just this reason. All the same, having an outboard is much like having an auxiliary engine – you can be a purist, but choose to use it at will.

Speed is a matter of personal preference. Some people like to flash around an anchorage quickly on the plane and we have come across cruising boats with 20hp outboards for skiing. They rarely made many friends in the anchorage. For most cruising folk, time is the one thing they have in abundance and two minutes getting ashore in a dinghy propelled with an egg-whisk is no sacrifice, even if a 9.9hp could get them to the dock in 15 seconds. The smaller motor uses a fraction of the fuel and can be passed up on deck with one hand.

Like popular inflatables, outboards of all varieties are like a little cachet of money attached to the back of your dinghy and must be well protected from the thief. Make sure that it is securely locked to the tender and the dinghy is well locked to mothership or shore. If the dinghy isn't locked as well, an outboard thief will take this too (no matter how disreputable) and break the outboard off at his leisure, abandoning the damaged dinghy thereafter.

In terms of spares availability the widest-used outboard worldwide is the Mariner which is a close relation to the Yamaha. These two are used in many Third World areas on dug-outs and trading craft. If you have a larger dinghy, or want the ability to plane in a smaller one, arguably the best outboard ever built was the Johnson/Evinrude 6hp which thrives on regular use, quickly recovers from a total immersion, and is very reliable indeed.

**Fig 15** Frenchman George Nacam specially adapted his Zodiac inflatable for a sail-home 'life-dinghy'. The result had lower overall windage (which combined with greater surface area made it more resistant to capsize), better·shape and buoyancy forward for breaking waves, higher freeboard, and considerably improved space for occupants than conventional liferafts. With a simple rig and large rudder it had the capability to sail towards shore or shipping lanes

## The Dinghy as a Liferaft

Conventional inflatable liferaft design is often criticised for its lack of development, its poor durability, its capacity to capsize easily, its discomfort and the heavy ongoing expense of servicing it. For all this, it takes some nerve to dispense with it and go your own way by adapting your dinghy for a lifeboat role.

The ability to sail towards shipping lanes or shore would have saved hundreds of lives in the past and I believe that most of us would prefer the ability to help ourselves in this way to just sitting in a liferaft praying for someone to see us. The boost to morale a moving liferaft would have is important to the success of such an emergency. Many ideas have been suggested in sailing magazines and the Tinker range of inflatables are a laudable step towards the goal of self-preservation. However, Tinker dinghies are very expensive and with even half that amount of money available one could produce an exceptionally good alternative.

One is aiming to achieve many things with a 'life-dinghy', and not necessarily in this order:

1 It must be seaworthy, unsinkable and be 'rightable' after a capsize.
2 It must have room (and buoyancy) enough for the full complement of crew.
3 It must have some form of propulsion, preferably a small sail.
4 It must have good shelter for the crew.
5 Ideally, it should be arranged so that the crew are not sitting in puddles.
6 At least one person should be able to sleep with some comfort.
7 It must be ready to use at a moment's notice.

A 10ft+ (3.04m) inflatable fitted with some kind of sailing rig is an obvious choice and wouldn't need a great deal by way of adaption to make it into an excellent life-dinghy. Fig 15 shows an idea suggested by Frenchman George Nacam a few years ago.

Fig 16 is my own interpretation of what a 'life-dinghy' should look like and is the basis for the design I intend having on our next boat.

**Fig 16** The author's design for a 'life-dinghy', not to scale. The after 3ft (91cm) section (**b**), decked-in and foam filled, nestles within the principal 7ft 9in (2.36m) dinghy (**a**), with permanent lanyards so they cannot become separated. When set up, the two mating surfaces have moulded corrugations for a mechanical join and stainless catches at gunwhale and chine connect them. The foredeck and raised floor provide buoyancy, the latter having a well so occupants are not constantly sitting in water. The two roll bar tubes, made in moulded GRP, live in the dinghy normally and are hinged. They provide the basis for an awning, a mast-step and – more importantly – aid self-righting

# 16
## Spare Parts and Tools

The extent and range of your spare parts determines your level of self-sufficiency and therefore to some extent the success of your cruise. A comprehensive parts list should be made as soon as possible, something best done aboard, systematically working your way through the yacht. It will pay later, because trying to find a Baby Blake bowl gasket, Stanley knife blades, or stainless steel washers may be very difficult when you're off the beaten track.

Sod's Law decrees that you will often nevertheless not have the particular spare you need, but a plentiful supply of good glues, sealants, rigging wire, miscellaneous plastic piping, studding, seizing wire, nuts, bolts and screws, timber and scrap stainless will enable you to improvise. We took an old lorry inner tube, which cut up did service in all manner of applications from water tank inspection lid gasket to bungy cord for the tiller.

The spares locker should be stocked gradually a long time from the planned departure day, because you get the best bargains by buying out of season (we were able to purchase two years' supply of antifouling at 25%, discount), and you also allow yourself time to track down the difficult items. A friend of ours started his collection 18 months before he planned to leave, and each week would go into the chandlers and buy a shackle or rigging clamp. In this way he collected an impressive spares locker but didn't notice the cost in the same way as buying a dozen heavy stainless shackles, half a dozen cans of antifouling, a spare halyard, assorted stainless bolts and a couple of tubes of sealant, which in one go would cost a small fortune.

The question that soon arises over spares is how much of your capital do you invest in them? Getting even the most basic parts whilst you're overseas is usually difficult and for marine equipment in non-yachting centres, normally impossible. The cost of having them sent out from home can often be two or three times the price of the part itself, irritating to say the least when you could have bought it easily and comparatively cheaply a few months beforehand. It's comforting to go away with a big bank balance, but a yacht used 365 days a year needs continual looking after and spares of everything will be needed. Balancing these two factors is quite critical as an imbalance either way could pave the path to failure later on.

Spend some time tracking down plenty of different marine

chandlery catalogues (especially the mail-order chandleries) and technical brochures for any slightly complicated equipment you have on board. Thus equipped you'll have all that is necessary when it comes to needing precise measurements or specifications, and part order numbers which are often essential to purchasing the correct item.

A sail repair kit comprising plenty of patching material (a sailmaker will usually quite happily give you offcuts from his rubbish bin), polyester yarn and a good sailmakers' palm is essential. Another useful addition to this kit is thirty or forty feet of one inch (25mm) wide webbing tape – it is cheap, pliable, strong and can be used in many applications when a sail (particularly the corners) needs strengthening or reinforcing. Also carry one or two appropriate Norseman terminals so that any part of the standing rigging can be repaired if, as is likely, the damage occurs at the old terminal. Because modern blocks are so expensive we bought a dozen single and double ash blocks very cheaply from Thomas Foulkes in London. Varnished and fitted with strops, they were forever useful, especially when running in the trades when all sorts of extra blocks and leads are required.

You should understand the basic workings of your engine before you leave and to some extent this will reflect in the spares you carry for it. You can't have enough water pump kits (impellors, O-rings and gaskets) and make sure to have three or four of each type of belt used. For servicing, lube oil can be bought in most places so don't bother cluttering up the boat with it, but filters and elements are not so easy, so buy plenty and keep them wrapped in plastic. If you are reliant on the engine for sole battery charging, and money allows, buy a second identical alternator, and a spare regulator for both. Take plenty of V-belts, any specific hoses, a spare thermostat and plenty of hose clamps. A complete head gasket kit is expensive but worth having, though you'll need to borrow a torque wrench to use it.

Most people take far too many tools, most of which are heavy, and without exception rust terribly. Many jobs can be done with just pliers, three or four different screwdrivers, a hammer and a molewrench, all stowed conveniently but a long way from the compass. Go right through the working parts of the boat and see if any specialist tools are needed. The stern tube will probably need a large spanner. Winches generally need Allen keys, as do for example Aries windvane gears. We bought three of each of the Allen keys required for the Aries on the assumption we would be working on it hanging over the stern and therefore run the risk of losing them into the water, and sure enough on our return had only one set left. The heads might require imperial spanners while the engine needs metric. However, instead of having a complete imperial set for the head, just bring the specific one or two that it requires. Feeler gauges will be needed for the dinghy outboard spark plug or if, after a period of time, the engine needs a bit of re-alignment. If you're stuck, remember Knox-Johnston's trick of taking an inch of pages in a book, then working out the measurements by numbers of pages – it is surprisingly accurate.

A hacksaw with plenty of spare blades will get plenty of use, and a tenon saw with its teeth protected in an oil-impregnated and grooved batten of wood held on with elastic bands. Obviously the right tools make a job much simpler but unless you plan to earn your living with them later on, approach tool choice with the attitude of how little you need ather than how much.

Take a 12v soldering iron (they're not expensive) because crimped electrical connectors are not reliable and will need replacing from time to time. A simple multimeter will make it much easier to trace and repair faulty electrics. Another unwitting victim of Sod's Law and an item to take plenty of is light bulbs and fuses. You can guarantee that when you want them overseas, their fluorescents will always be an inch too long and the monofilament bulbs screw-fit rather than bayonet.

# 17
# Preparing for Heavy Weather

Preparing a modern boat for heavy weather is very much easier than in days of old when they were utilising much weaker materials, such as glass for windows, canvas for sails and hemp for cordage. But although the modern boat is built using inherently stronger and more durable materials throughout, in these days of commercialism there's a better chance she will have been built down to a price with carefully calculated strength limits so that flaws show up as a result.

Preparation for heavy weather must be put into perspective. Over the course of several years' cruising, the number of days a yacht spends at sea weathering gales is surprisingly few, so it is counter-productive to make it absolutely perfect for these few periods, if that makes the boat so uncomfortable and difficult to live in the rest of the time that the cruise is jeopardised by a discontented crew. Awkwardly-placed companionways and tiny or even non-existent cockpits rank along with turtle decks, watertight bulkheads and miniscule ports in making a boat highly seaworthy and impossible to enjoy. All the same, a yacht crossing an ocean must be capable of withstanding *any* weather that is thrown at her and a skipper/owner needs no reminding that the whole responsibility of this lays on his shoulders.

## Openings

As long as it avoids land, a bottle with a good cork will survive anything at sea and yachts have often been compared to this theory. For the construction of the 'bottle' you can only trust on the integrity of the men who built your yacht – suffice it to say that it is rare that one hears of the hulls or decks of modern, quality yachts being stove in by seas, or indeed keels falling off. If you have any doubts, employ a yacht surveyor and carry out any recommendations he makes. The 'good cork' part of the equation – a yacht's ports, hatches and openings – will also depend on her builder but they can be improved or upgraded if there are any question marks. Look very closely and critically at every opening in your deck, cockpit and coachroof.

**The Companionway** The normal design of washboard caters for convenience during weekend sailing, but not for heavy weather. All the washboards have to be in place and the hatch slid shut to hold them in. A great number of the problems experienced by yachts in the 1979 Fastnet Race stemmed from just this arrangement. The crews in the cabin didn't want to be locked below, so the top washboard was left out meaning that the lower ones could not be secured, and neither could the hatch itself. When the yachts rolled their washboards were lost, the hatch could not be held closed and then they were unable to run downwind with such a large area vulnerable to the seas which seriously jeopardised their heavy-weather tactics. The majority of production yacht builders have totally ignored this problem, but the ocean sailor must fit stout individual barrel bolts on each washboard and a method of securing the hatch that can be operated from both the cockpit and inside the cabin. The washboards themselves must be strong (minimum 1in [25mm] thick per 2sq ft [.185m$^2$] of area) and ideally a bit bigger than the companionway hole they are covering.

Well-tapered companionway entrance slides make using the washboards more convenient, but in extreme conditions those washboards don't have to slide up far before they fall out (assuming they are not secured with bolts), so they are not nearly as seamanlike as parallel sided ones. If your companionway entrance is not vertical but cants forward slightly, the moment it rains you must put in all the washboards. Irrespective of heavy weather, this is pretty annoying and if you can avoid it, either by extending the sprayhood aft or perhaps making up a battened fabric cover (Fig 17), do so for your

**Fig 17** Wooden washboards are cumbersome in normal sailing conditions. A simple fabric cover, larger than the opening and supported by battens, will save a lot of aggravation when rain or spray is flying about. A small amount of lead wrapped over the lower batten holds it closed sanity, especially as the engine and electrics are often just below the companionway entrance.

***Ports/Windows*** Nowadays the strength of acrylic windows is such that they are unlikely to give way but the weakpoint is the extruded aluminium frame. The subject of storm shutters is frequently raised. They were used a lot 30 years ago when a broken porthole was not uncommon. Now it would be overzealous to have either wooden or polycarbonate storm shutters for every port on a yacht, unless she had really large windows all round, in which case permanent polycarbonate shutters should be fitted (see below). But it's certainly worth the small effort and expense of pre-fabricating one storm shutter, shown in Fig 19, which should be big enough for the largest opening and stowed in an easily accessible place.

Although some people consider it amateurish, a through-bolted acrylic window a few inches bigger all round than the opening is about the strongest arrangement it is possible to have. If you use a material like polycarbonate for the window, it is likely to be stronger than the fibreglass coachroof surrounding it. If you have conventional framed windows which are a little too large for your peace of mind, it is worth considering fitting permanent polycarbonate shutters (Fig 18) which don't detract too much from the appearance.

Under no circumstances have an opening porthole in the hull topsides of a seagoing yacht. They are strictly for big ships. The

**Fig 18** If you are nervous about the size or integrity of your windows and ports, a simple remedy is to bolt polycarbonate or acrylic sheets over them; give the cover a generous overlap and use as few bolts as possible, with large washers on the outside chance of someone leaving the port open, or of the fastening or hinge giving way as the yacht falls heavily on her side is too great a risk to take.

*Hatches* Reports of modern aluminium hatches failing are almost unheard of, although from time to time they are ripped off when not properly dogged down tight. If one did go, you would have a large and vulnerable opening. A precaution for such an emergency is to choose a stout piece of plywood already in use, like a section of lifting bunk top, and try it out for size over your large hatch openings. If it is more or less the right size, make a wooden strongback as in Fig 19 (window shutters) and drill appropriate holes in the plywood to take the bolts. In this way the only addition is a strongback kept ready with bolts attached.

Cockpit locker lids are undoubtedly the most vulnerable opening on deck and many experienced voyagers prefer a cockpit designed without lockers or lids, the stowage area below being accessible either from the accommodation or a well-sealed lazarette. In bad weather a cockpit can be swept by seas and there is invariably a good volume of water sloshing around the sole. For this reason, removable cockpit floors should never be used because all of them leak sooner or later. Many boatbuilders don't anticipate the vulnerability of cockpit lockers for letting in large amounts of water in heavy weather, and not only are the openings getting bigger each year, but the hinges are nearly always tiny. The ability to dog the cockpit locker lids down tight is of paramount importance. A lost cockpit locker lid could quite easily lead to the loss of the yacht in extreme conditions.

**Fig 19** A plywood storm shutter, as large as the biggest port with a wing-nutted internal strongback, should be located where easily accessible in an emergency

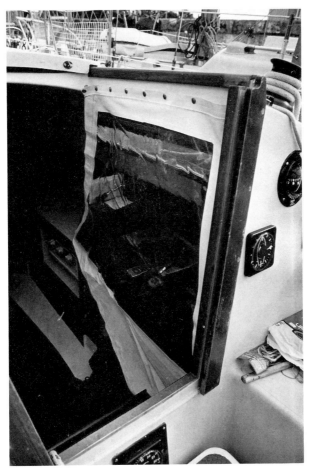

A fine miasma of spray always finds its way below at sea and a feature such as this will protect the navigation station, especially if you have no sprayhood    *(Geoff Pack)*

### Preparing Below Decks for Bad Weather

High fiddle rails, deep sinks, smallish lockers and removable struts to hold in books will make life easier in normally boisterous seagoing conditions. To prepare better than this for heavy weather is difficult, because try as you may items will start flying about. Always carry a bag of rags to stuff into lockers where breakables such as jam pots and crockery are stowed, and don't throw away old socks – they are ideal to put over bottles to stop them rattling.

There is some discussion about fitting barrel bolts to all underbunk lockers so that in the event of a capsize the contents are held in place. Having experienced a knockdown in a North Atlantic gale on *Euge* I don't believe that normal catches would withstand the combination of weight and centrifugal forces imposed on them in a knockdown, but the chances of this happening are very rare and chaos will be inevitable however well you prepare for the possibility.

Three items *must* be firmly harnessed. The batteries must have either webbing straps holding them firmly in place or a wooden crossbar bridge bolted or lashed down. The gas bottles must also be firmly lashed down because should the working one be thrown on its side or inverted, liquid gas can flow through the regulator. This can cause a seventy-fold increase in pressure on the low-pressure side of the appliance. The cooker must also be firmly attached to the gimbals because many will only swing to 90 degrees before dropping off their gimbals and flying free. As well as having captive gimbals, the cooker must also have a mechanical restraint that prevents it swinging too far and pulling off the gas pipe. A gas bottle should always be turned off in heavy weather (if at no other time) but if this has been forgotten a lot of gas can come through a fractured pipe before somebody can get to the bottle to switch off, and obvious dangers aside, this could make the cabin uninhabitable until the fumes are cleared.

## Heavy Weather on Deck

The sort of strains that are imposed on deck equipment in heavy weather were demonstrated to me in the above-mentioned knockdown we experienced in *Euge*. Our two amidships stanchions, which were heavy-duty stainless steel, were bent down to about 45 degrees with the other stanchions distorted less (but with two cracked bases) *on water pressure alone*. Knowing the force required subsequently to straighten them out gave me considerably more respect for the sea than I'd had previously.

Deck-mounted liferafts are vulnerable and must have very firm wooden or stainless chocks backed up by strong *independently mounted* eyebolts for lashing down. A far better arrangement is to have the liferaft in a locker, or mounted in the cockpit where it has some protection.

Spray dodgers, if fitted, can be guaranteed to self-destruct unless there is a quick way as heavy weather approaches of either unlacing them altogether or just disconnecting the lower tie downs, rolling them up and lashing them to the upper guardrail wire. They should be made with at least a 4in (10cm) ventilation gap between them and the deck so that even in moderately rough conditions when the yacht's rail is immersed they don't trap water and become damaged. An alternative to lacing is to attach their lower edge with Velcro, which will pull free if the sea gets behind them.

Spray hoods are rather difficult because in bad weather they really ought to be folded flat on the deck and lashed down to avoid damage. Yet it is in these very conditions that they give sterling service. Our answer is to make it very flexible, by using a long length of bungy cord as a restraint aft (see Fig 2, page 91). In this way even when it was clouted by big seas it gave way and was never damaged.

In really severe conditions a boom needs to be restrained in some way. For centuries seamen have used gallows in various shapes and forms and many yachtsmen swear by them. Others consider them heavy, cumbersome and old fashioned. Gallows advocates maintain that as well as supporting the boom, they are also a stout grab pillar when you are entering or leaving the cockpit, form the frame for a cockpit-only sailing awning, and can't be beaten as a comfortable support for taking a sextant sight. A very simple alternative for supporting the boom in heavy weather is a shaped wooden chock bolted in place at the point where the lowered boom touches the side-deck or cockpit coaming. A simple lashing then holds the boom firmly.

A lot of heavy weather preparation comes back to the Keep It Simple philosophy. Study the ergonomics of the tasks you may have to perform and make sure that nothing is too complex or too awkward or far away to get at.

In heavy weather ergonomics mean safety. If a self-steering gear has to be adjusted by going aft or even leaving the cockpit, a crew member is being put into unnecessary danger each time an adjustment is made. A headsail roller reefing winch on the sidedeck near the rail on the lee side could result in the watchkeeper overbalancing and going over the side. Faults that are minor irritants most of the time become danger black spots in a storm and should be eliminated.

Harness attachment points must also be laid out with ergonomics in mind. You shouldn't need to reach a long way for the next attachment place, neither should it be necessary to cross the deck without being attached before reaching the next point. The use of harnesses as a matter of course is a good habit and ease of use makes that habit easier to pick up. The cockpit must have a strong harness attachment point and this is best positioned within reach of the companionway, so in coming on deck or going below when balance can easily be lost if the boat lurches, a person can remain clipped on throughout. This was another cause of men lost overboard in the 1979 Fastnet Race.

Although a harness should keep you attached to the boat if you go overboard, getting back on can be very hard indeed so look for ways of rigging the harness to keep you inboard. A catamaran's wide beam solves this problem because the wire jackstays run up the middle of the yacht, harnessed to this it is not possible to stray near the gunwhales and go overboard. If the coachroof is not too cluttered the same system can be used on a monohull as long as the harness lanyards are kept short enough. When fitting jackstays make sure they are fairly tight, otherwise when you roll going downwind the wire will scrape and clatter on the deck causing chafe and irritating those below.

# 18
# *Preparing for Hot Climates*

## *Ventilation*

The comfort of life aboard in a hot or tropic climate is in direct proportion to the shade you create and the extent and quality of ventilation. We've met dozens of poor yachties getting even poorer in air-conditioned bars ashore because life was untenable aboard.

Good ventilation has to be thought out for the many circumstances a yacht will find herself in – at sea with water flying around, lying head to wind at anchor, laying alongside a jetty, and when it is pouring with rain.

There are many tricks to ventilation, but probably the most important single factor to remember is the means for air to evacuate easily, thus providing through ventilation which is the aim. A locker with a single vent is only marginally better ventilated than one with no vent at all. One vent hole should be drilled or cut low down in the locker and another high up, so as air warms up it is able to rise, escape and draw in fresh air through the lower vent. A similar thing applies to areas like the after double quarter berth often fitted into modern production boats. There is usually a single small hatch or port overhead but, if an opening porthole were fitted into the transom near the occupants feet, or into the cockpit side, air could flow right through and transform the cabin. Louvred cabin doors are very good in this respect.

Dorade boxes with cowls are generally good although the amount of air coming down through them is not great. They can be improved by making the modification in Fig 20. Dorades come into their own at sea and when it's raining, when they are often the only method of ventilation. The more you have fitted the happier you'll be in these circumstances. Unless you have plenty of time to make them in wood, the best way is to use an ice-cream container as a female mould and laminate as many as you require from it in GRP. Rather than make a traditional wooden baffle, cut out a 3in (76mm) aperture in the deck and epoxy-in a short length of plastic guttering pipe. Make sure that they can drain on either tack. Some people (including me) have fitted dorades to a cambered coachroof and only made drains at the lowest point. As soon as you heel the other way, water collects until it drains through the aperture into the cabin (and hopefully on to the person who made them).

**Fig 20** Dorade vents are essential for ventilation when spray or rain don't allow the hatches to be left open. A second cowl fitting directly over the vent hole can be used to improve flow when it is unlikely to rain. With an acrylic top they let in a little more light below

A yacht spends the majority of time in port laying head to wind on her anchor and in these circumstances opening deck hatches are by far the best method of ventilation, especially if they're hinged on their after edge. A boat under 35ft really needs one over the foc'sle and another over the saloon, and thus equipped she meets 80 percent of ventilation requirements. On boats over this size, two opening hatches are generally required for the saloon. A small hatch over the heads/shower compartment is desirable. As long as the furniture isn't too ornate and the loo roll covered up, this hatch can be left open in the rain or at sea providing ventilation when all other hatches have to be dogged tight.

It is an advantage to have a hatch over the berths. If this is left open at night you wake the moment it starts to rain and close it, but you will never wake up let alone get out of bed to close hatches elsewhere when it starts raining at night. This arrangement also has the automatic effect of making sure none of the over-berth hatches are allowed to leak.

Opening portholes or windows in the coachroof sides are very handy when the yacht is laying across the wind, and also at sea when the leeward ones can normally be left open. They don't contribute to ventilation when the yacht is lying head to wind. Unfortunately it is rare to find opening ports that are stout enough to be trusted in very heavy weather and stand up to being opened and closed regularly without developing leaks. The leaking problem is made worse by the

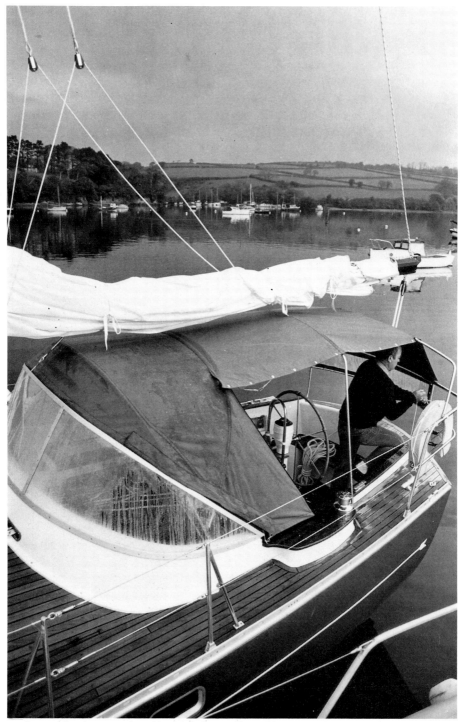

A combination sprayhood/awning is excellent if kept simple; this one will require sidescreens if the sun is to be kept out of the cockpit   *(Yachting Monthly)*

**Fig 21** It must be possible to close a hatch without touching the windscoop. With eyes on each corner, this design (using aluminium extrusion) can be reversed to let in air from the bow or stern and still be left rigged in a shower

fact that most coachroof sides are angled so the windows often collect puddles.

Windscoops can be a Godsend in certain circumstances and it is well worth making one before you leave. If your boat has a centre cockpit and wheelhouse it tends to act as a wind break, so little air gets into the after hatch and a scoop will be necessary. A scoop will catch the lightest zephyrs and funnel them into your cabin. Fig 21 shows a set up for a scoop that can be used with the wind in any direction.

Finally, depending on where you plan to cruise, it may be worth considering fitting a couple of electric fans for when conditions are muggy. Make sure they have continuously-rated electric motors and can withstand being left on for a few hours at a time. The protective grills usually rust afloat unless you buy some spray lacquer and liberally coat them with it before you start.

### Awnings

Until you have experienced living in a very hot or tropic climate you may be inclined to put an awning low on your priority list. Don't !

This particular piece of equipment ranks in the top three essentials for living aboard a yacht in hot weather.

There are two types of cover to consider – a proper awning extending from the mast right aft and a small cockpit cover used when sailing. The cooling effect a full size awning has on the cabin accommodation is very noticeable. Often we return from a trip ashore longing to get back aboard a cool, shaded and well ventilated boat.

What is needed is an awning that is easy to set so you don't hesitate to rig it, and one that allows the crew to move around freely without negotiating a cat's cradle of lines, and without being bent double. In many tropical regions the climate features occasional heavy downpours between bursts of scorching sun and the type of awning described below (see Fig 22) copes with both conditions and allows life to carry on comfortably throughout.

**Fig 22** Supported by the spinnaker pole forward, and a special stout after pole, this design of cover is very popular in the tropics. The side curtains can be rolled up and if the centre lifting point is lowered during rain and the drain fitting piped direct to the water filler, it makes an efficient water catcher. Don't use DIY eyelet kits – they rarely last. Better is to sew in doubled-up 1in (30mm) webbing tape (inset) for all canvaswork purposes

This cover is common in the Caribbean and among ocean cruising fraternities. It features a reasonably flat top with vertical side curtains reaching almost to the guardwires, which keep out the rain and sun and provide some privacy. The curtains can be rolled up out of the way to cut down windage. The flat top has an attachment point in its centre where a halyard or topping lift can be shackled on and hauled tight to create a watershed for rain, also stretching the whole cover for a tight, neat appearance. By installing a plastic skin fitting in the cover near the middle water can be collected when it rains by lowering the topping lift. If a short length of hosepipe is directed into the water tank filler you can, after five minutes' free flow for cleansing, collect quite a lot of water. The awning for *Euge* collected 15 gallons (68 lit) an hour in steady rain and two or three times that much in a good downpour.

The design of the cover requires the running/spinnaker pole to be threaded through a sleeve forward and a separate, equally stout, pole aft. Twin or divided backstays simplify the setting by fully supporting this after pole. If you have a single backstay you'll need some extra lines to brace each end of the pole. When the awning is taken down, the after pole is unlashed from the backstay and the cover rolled around it working forward. As the after pole will be shorter than the forward one, the ends of the resultant sausage can be folded back and the whole stowed either in a large cockpit locker, on the coachroof or behind a berth.

Using a handcrank sewing machine it took Lou Lou a weekend (approximately 12 hours' work) to make the awning with three or four hours' help from me marking and cutting out, plus splicing up all the lanyards. We used 18sq yd (15m²) of acrylic material which, although more expensive than plasticised fabric, is longer lasting, better looking, largely unaffected by ultra violet rays and more pleasant to work with and stow. One simple discovery revolutionised the cover and its fastenings – using 1in (25mm) webbing, available from chandlers, for the longitudinal strengthening (they take the strain off the cloth itself) and also in short length to substitute for brass eyelets which are rarely strong enough in the DIY kits available. These 'tabs' are simply 8in (20cm) lengths cut with a hot knife (we used an old kitchen knife heated red-hot over the cooker flame), doubled on themselves and sewn with a square and cross pattern on to the cover, preferably in the direction of the strain. These enable the cover to be set up very tightly and have never let us down, as eyelets have on numerous occasions.

Tautness is the secret of success of the cover, especially on the fore and aft ridges between top and side. If these are allowed to slacken, the cover not only looks sloppy but will oscillate and flap in a breeze and collect water in puddles rather than in your tank. This ridge line should extend from the yacht's maximum beam at the cover's forward end to the same aft. Resist the temptation to drape the awning over ropes stretched from shrouds to backstays because, accounting for inevitable stretch and the fact the shrouds are normally set inboard, the whole thing ends up looking like the conventional boom-over cover, and collects puddles easily.

One problem with the flat-topped awning is dealing with the boom and topping lift. Solutions vary from boat to boat, but one answer is a boom gallows or crutch and another is to use a short wire strop taluritted to the backstay and clipped on to the boom end. We just left the boom resting on the sidedeck which looks a bit French but doesn't get in the way. Another system is a sewn tab under the cover's central lift point and the boom supported on a short rope strop from this – the topping lift being attached to the cover directly above it. For simplicity's sake it's better not to divide the cover aft to accommodate the topping lift and boom although with Velcro-fastened flaps a watertight join can be achieved.

**Fig 23** When sailing in very hot climates, some kind of a sailing awning can be a blessing. This design, made simply with plastic piping, suffices and is considerably cheaper than a custom Bimini top

Equipped with such a cover it should be quite possible to sit in the cockpit dry on rainy days, or if not then certainly to have the companionway hatch open to promote ventilation.

A cockpit-only sailing cover used in moderate conditions is very pleasant to have and provides essential shade for the watchkeeper over the hottest three or four hours of the day. Rigging such a cover is not easy though unless you have boom gallows forward of the cockpit, because while a pole can always be attached to the backstay or mizzen rigging, finding a place for the forward attachment is not so easy without lines running in all directions – which you can do without when under sail. Also, the mainsheet nearly always fouls such a cover.

One arrangement that seems to work quite well has a strong strut, such as an oar, lashed to a bulkhead handrail right alongside the companionway. Jutting up and firm, this allows the forward batten of the cover to be attached, but there is still quite a lot of complication and string needed. Fig 23 shows a design that can work. Its success is dependent on the height and positioning of your stanchions.

In America they've developed the 'bimini' top, a permanently set-up cockpit cover on a stainless steel frame which is both practical and effective, although hardly improves the look of the boat.

### Sun Deterioration

It is inevitable, and largely unavoidable, that the yacht, her gear and equipment will deteriorate steadily from the strong ultra violet rays of the sun in warm latitudes.

The most vulnerable items are the sails which in a tropic climate won't last much longer than 12-18 months without becoming brittle, unless they are covered at every opportunity. If you make or adapt your mainsail cover to the design shown in Fig 24 it will be quick and easy to use so you will cover the sail as soon as it is lowered. If you expect strong winds, or leave the boat for any length of time, this cover will need copious rope lashings wrapped right around it.

Hanked-on headsails should either be taken below or left on deck in UV-resistant bags (acrylic is the best, but quite expensive). If you have a roller genoa, to take it off the headstay each time is not really practical so a 1ft (30cm) wide sacrificial acrylic strip edging to the leech and foot is essential. These acrylic strips unfortunately add quite a bit of weight to the sail in the wrong places and are rather prone to damage, so expect them to be a continuing maintenance chore.

Dark colours will absorb heat and cause quicker deterioration no matter what the object is or what it is made of. This applies to inflatable dinghies and wooden hulls as much as smaller items. It is essential to use and choose light colours. This is especially so for the deck which will otherwise make the cabin very hot. A dark colour also

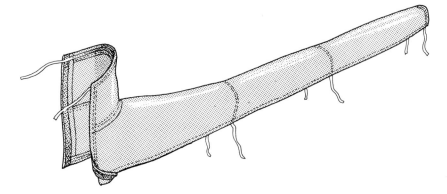

**Fig 24** A loosely-fitting sail cover that is simple to rig is one that will be used regularly. A Velcro-fastened front and just two or three tapes will suffice in the majority of conditions. When leaving the boat, or in strong winds, a rope lashed around the outside will hold it in place

makes the deck impossible to walk on in bare feet. White might seem bland to many people, but it is the most practical colour for yachts heading for hot climates.

## Barometric Pressure

One piece of traditional equipment that doesn't strictly need to be aboard an ocean cruiser is a barograph, lovely though it is. If you are given one as a parting gift, or have an ample budget, fine, but don't feel it is necessary. It is a pleasant ornament, but in the tropics barometric pressure becomes diurnal – in other words the pressure variations are exactly the same over a 24 hour cycle and the jaggedy 's' shape will be the same nearly every day of the year with only minor variations, so they are of little help. A barometer however is an essential instrument outside the tropic regions. It will suffice perfectly well and cost only a fraction of a barograph.

# 19
# *Emergencies*

It requires a huge effort of will to spend a great deal of money on safety equipment that you are probably never going to use. Yet the moment that equipment is needed any little money you saved by getting slightly cheaper goods seems blind, stupid, and most certainly a false economy. You must develop the attitude that prevention is better than cure.

I have had my fair share of emergencies, none of which I'm proud of. I've suffered the ignominy of being dismasted on three occasions, been aboard a yacht at sea with a serious fire, had a boat start to break up in mid-ocean and been driven ashore with a danger of total loss. Still I sail around thinking it'll never happen to me! Immediately afterwards, the importance of preventing anything similar happening is paramount, but quickly enough that fades away in the knowledge you came out of it alive and reasonably unscathed. This attitude alone is a bigger danger than the potential emergencies themselves and tiresome though it may be, one of the only ways to overcome it is to develop sometimes mindless routines aboard to help prevent the problems in the first place.

## Man Overboard

Being of heavy build, I sail with the knowledge that if I were to go overboard and become unconscious, the chances of getting me back aboard are infinitesimal. When Lou Lou and I started cruising we promised each other and ourselves that we would *always* wear harnesses when working on deck or when alone on watch. We splashed out on what were then the best and most expensive harnesses, the Ancra, which were high specification, easy to use and with a lanyard that could be unclipped. We quickly got into the habit of putting them on, and the ability to remove the heavy lanyard and carbineer clip meant that they were no discomfort to wear all the time at sea, even when below, as you might a belt. Combining this with plenty of convenient clip-on points and efficiently laid out jackstays, the routine soon stuck and now we both sleep well off watch in the knowledge that the other can't be lost overboard. We also have a rule that the one on-watch calls down through the companionway hatch if ever they need to go on deck. It may seem unfair to wake an off watch sleeper when you do, but it beats the shock of waking up hearing

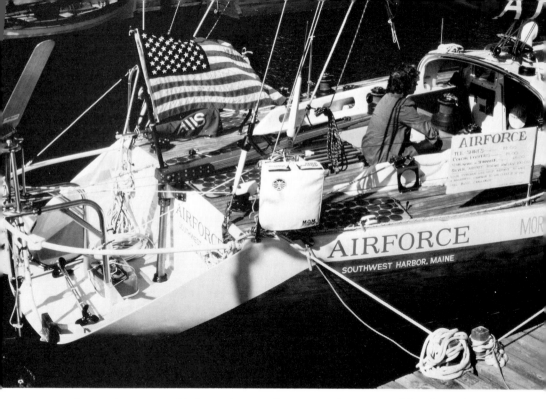

A stern 'sugar scoop' is becoming popular among the ocean cruising fraternity. It offers easy boarding and loading from a dinghy and access to the self-steering at sea but most important of all it makes recovery of a man overboard much easier    *(Geoff Pack)*

clattering on deck above you, and if you're awake you are alert if any help is needed.

This system illustrates a routine that two people, normally far from keen on anything routine, persevered hard to make a habit of. Now it is a habit, we enjoy our sailing that little more knowing the chance of long, unscheduled mid-ocean swims has been cut right down.

Keeping aboard is an obvious priority, but being prepared for a man overboard situation is just as important. Some advocate trailing one or two floating polypropylene lines astern, attached to the tiller or self-steering in the hope of the one in the water catching them and pulling the boat off course, thus alerting the off watch as she tacks or gybes. It is a good idea in theory but in practice a boat travelling at six knots covers a little over 10ft a second and unless you are trailing so much rope that you are slowed down considerably, the chances of a shocked and disorientated swimmer being able to reach and locate the rope quickly enough, are very slim indeed. Assuming they did it is unlikely they would be able to hold on even if it was knotted.

A lifebuoy with floating strobe and danbuoy attached still offers the best means of pinpointing somebody overboard and it goes without saying that this should be clear and ready to run immediately. A danbuoy tube, either incorporated into the hull or in the form of a plastic guttering pipe firmly lashed on the sidedeck near the stern can take away much of the clutter of the man-overboard equipment.

Retro-reflective tape will be the only way to spot a man overboard at night, so buy a reel of it (it is made by Scotchbrite/3M) and sew and glue it to all the life-saving equipment as well as the shoulders and cuffs of all sailing jackets (so an arm in the air might be spotted) and the shoulder straps of harnesses.

Think out how you will get someone out of the water and practise it. There are now a number of good (and bad) man overboard recovery aids on the market. Most assume that the casualty is in the water alongside and achieving this is of course the biggest hurdle. A stern boarding ladder that extends deep into the water is of great value, but this can only be used with the yacht across the seas otherwise the pitching motion makes recovery both dangerous and difficult. Perhaps the most significant contribution to safety is the advent of the 'sugar-scoop' stern arrangement which allows a crewmember to get close to the water and haul the casualty the short distance into the scoop.

## Major Leaks

That great ocean sailor Bob Griffiths had a particularly pertinent piece of advice about serious leaks. When a leak is discovered your first priority is to find it! 'To use time and energy bailing when the leak might be stopped is not good thinking' said Griffiths.

This may sound obvious in the cold light of day, but in an emergency the brain doesn't always work so clearly. We were in fairly big seas off Bermuda watching the Tall Ships Race start, with about a dozen people aboard, not all of them seafarers, when Lou Lou calmly and quietly announced to me through the corner of her mouth that the bilgewater was above the floors and we were sinking. We'd been hardened by a couple of years of chartering beforehand, and in comparison it seemed a minor problem. Not wanting to panic the landlubbers I pumped the bilge surreptitiously until it sucked dry, but five minutes later the bilge was full again. As I could pump from the helm position and everyone was distracted by the lovely ships around, nobody noticed that I had to pump all that day until we dropped anchor again in port. The problem could easily have been solved with the most elementary investigation when I would have found that the bilge water was hot! We'd been motorsailing all day and the engine cooling water was not injecting into the exhaust because the pipe had fractured and was pumping all the water into the bilge.

Most flooding emergencies can be traced to very obvious sources so before you assume that the garboard has sprung or the keel is dropping off, check that the toilet isn't overflowing, the bilge pump isn't siphoning water back in to the bilge or that a hose clamp hasn't loosened on a seacock and allowed the pipe to slip off. Before you head off, spend a couple of pounds replacing all seacock hoseclamps and put two clips where there is normally one on every fitting below the waterline. Seacocks are not infallible and next to each one the prudent sailor should have a shaped wooden cone on a rope lanyard ready to be rammed in the hole if the seacock fails in any way.

## *Flotsam*

The likelihood of serious damage from hitting flotsam is a steadily increasing one. Between 1980 and 1983 at least $50 million-worth of containers were washed overboard from cargo ships, many remaining just awash. Hitting one of these would be enough to sink most yachts, except possibly steel ones. Yachts have been lost in the last few years by hitting containers, tree-trunks and even an old freezer held afloat by its insulation material. A cargo pallet, if not piercing the hull, could damage the prop-shaft or rudder. One yacht in the English Channel had her whole propshaft ripped out and the inaccessability of the gland meant that she nearly foundered as her crew couldn't reach the leak without removing the fuel tank. The busy areas of Northern Europe are the worst affected. A ship lost overboard 2,400 drums in a Bay of Biscay storm in 1984, a situation made no better by the fact the skipper didn't report the loss for four weeks.

**Fig 25** If you are concerned about hitting flotsam, it is not out of the question to have washboards fitted across the forward bulkhead. They are unlikely to be completely watertight, but will reduce flow to managable levels

**Fig 26** Fish traps, nets and general flotsam can cause serious damage which might be impossible to repair overseas. With an unprotected propeller, a length of wire fitted between skeg and rudder will avoid many problems

A simple modification like this could save a lot of problems in the long term *(Yachting Monthly)*

**Fig 27** If your yacht has a spade rudder, a welded stainless steel deflector plate, strongly epoxied in place, will eradicate many potential problems

A watertight bulkhead forward is a good precaution, but a huge sacrifice of space in a boat of less than 40ft (12.19m). Fig 25 shows an alternative arrangement for a conventional forecabin. The plywood washboards would have to be stowed handily, maybe under the forward berths, and any other major holes in the bulkhead, for example heating or ventilation ducts would need to be stopped up. This arrangement wouldn't be entirely watertight, but might reduce the flow to a level the bilge pumps could cope with.

Smaller pieces of flotsam can also be a menace. The fishing industry throws 23,000 tons of plastic packaging into the sea annually, as well as losing more that 133,000 tons of synthetic netting and lines. A grill should be fitted over the engine seawater cooling seacock. If you have a fin and skeg design the suggestion shown in the photo on page 191 or Fig 26 will help to protect the propeller. Similarly, if you have a skegless spade rudder, the addition shown in Fig 27 can avert the possibility of a rope jamming up the rudder.

## Dismasting

To prepare a special jury rig is impractical because you can only really put something together after the accident when you know what is left of the original rig. The best preparation you can make is to have at least a dozen bull-dog grips and a handful of large diameter thimbles in the spares locker and a coil of wire that exceeds the length of your longest capshrouds. This can be ready to make up a spare shroud if necessary but will obviously come in handy to start a jury rig with the running poles.

Sailing books of yore talk of cutting away the rigging after a dismasting. It is something that has been passed down from sailing ship days and from my own experience is an action one should take only if the stump is in immediate danger of holing the yacht. There in the water is the basis of your jury rig and there is always the remote chance that it can be repaired once you get back to port. If the rig is lost in heavy weather it can make a very effective sea anchor if all the shrouds are disconnected and the forestay and/or headsail halyards left attached at the bows. On the basis of weight, space, expense and lack of use I have never carried a set of bolt-croppers on board.

The danger in a dismasting is if the jagged end of the mast punctures the hull. Although lifting the mast, with the tangle of ripped sails and spaghetti of cordage, back on board can be a Herculean effort and one that shouldn't be underestimated, it is not normally out of the question to get lines attached near to the stump and with sheet winches haul just the end up near to the deck, perhaps getting a turn of rope around a crosstree to help steady it.

## Grounding

In many emergencies, swift action can solve the problem quickly and simply before it escalates. The difficulty lies in recognising the fine line between expediency and panic. This is especially so in tackling a fire, but also when a boat hits the bottom a quick bit of action in the right quarter can sort out the problem almost before you know it's happened.

In terms of preparation for going ashore the only things you can do is to make sure that the main anchor and kedge are laid out ready to go immediately. It is an old-fashioned custom to disconnect the anchors from their cables for a long passage, dating from the days when anchors were large, unwieldly and vulnerable on the ship's cathead. There is no need to do this today and yet a surprising number do. The dinghy must be in a state of readiness (also so that it can be taken in the event of having to abandon ship). A three-bladed propeller may be a bad drag when sailing but is worth having for the power it has in reverse gear when you are trying to back off.

Heavy strandings are few and far between, but a reasonably adventurous yachtsman will have plenty of odd glancing blows and scrapes with coral and rock. If you particularly plan to sail off the beaten track a sacrificial keel shoe is worth considering. There are two varieties. For a traditional wooden boat a steel shoe can be fabricated, liberally sealed with pitch and bolted in place. As well as protecting from cosmetic damage during the occasional grounding this fixture also has the significant advantage of saving the bottom of a keel, which often doesn't get antifouled, from the danger of teredo worm.

If your boat is fibreglass and has a internal encapsulated ballast the answer is to laminate a ½in (12mm) thick GRP shoe over the bottom

18in (45cm) or so of the keel. Don't worry about the weight, it's in the perfect place ! Although the existing keel should be sanded back to the gelcoat, ultra-strong adherance isn't vital as long as the shoe, once laminated on, is screwed in position with dozens of self-tappers. Coral is hard and unyielding and with this sacrifical shoe you can do a fair amount of GRP ripping and tearing before you come anywhere near the original structure.

## Liferafts

It is not within the scope of this book to catalogue the extensive and continuing criticism of conventional liferaft design. Until we start building good dinghies that double as lifesavers the existing range of liferafts are the only choice we have.

An exception is the Tinker range of inflatable dinghies made by J. M. Henshaw in England, mentioned earlier. They are not, in my opinion, suitable as the yacht's principal tender for a number of reasons. One is that an ocean cruiser's tender is a daily workhorse and takes a great beating alongside dinghy stagings, being dragged up and down beaches and so on and there is a limit to what a sophisticated inflatable such as the Tinker can withstand without putting its liferaft role into jeopardy. I also feel that at present the liferaft conversion and sailing equipment is too complicated and fussy for the dinghy to be prepared as a liferaft for every passage. Although the Tinker Traveller is at least 25 percent more expensive than a comparable liferaft there is nevertheless a strong case for having one purely as a liferaft and, like its contempories, used for nothing else.

A modern liferaft and a personally prepared emergency pack constitute a vital combination. One is pretty much useless without the other. Every emergency pack will differ according to the sailing area and crew aboard. The one outlined below is based on my own, prepared for a one-year North Atlantic circuit cruise for two people. It caters for the principal hazards of liferaft habitation, except extreme cold, and gives a broad guide to what is necessary.

Before preparing anything, the first job is to look closely at your existing liferaft and its contents or, if you're about to buy a raft, to inspect the maker's options and plan from there. Don't be tempted to buy a 6-man liferaft when you have just two crew on the grounds there will be more room and rations. The size of liferafts and their ability to withstand capsize is directly related to the human ballast in them. A large raft with few people in will capsize much sooner and with greater frequency than a properly loaded one and the capsize factor is an important contribution to eventual survival. Conversely, do not be tempted, on considerations of expense, to buy a model that satisfies the minimum requirements. If you are buying a new raft, one desirable feature, which could make the difference between life or death, is an inflatable double floor, offered as an option on most designs. This will create a much more comfortable base to sit on but, more important, it will insulate against crucial loss of body warmth in colder waters. In the lower latitudes, it also alleviates the aggravation to body sores of fish and turtles rubbing against the bottom of the raft. To have a double floor fitted to your existing liferaft is very expensive, and will add between £70 and £120 to a new model. With a small crew, a more viable alternative is to equip everyone on board with one of the many popular survival suits used by ocean racing crews. Alternatively, have a stowed air mattress like a Li–Lo, or inflatable cushions, ready to be grabbed with the panic bag.

## Panic Bags

Liferaft manufacturers generally provide basic packs which vary considerably in contents. I will refer to these as 'raft kits'. Whichever you have, it will need to be supplemented. Avon, for example, make no apologies for the limitations of this equipment in their liferafts by stating, 'You must consider what additional emergency equipment is required for your journey and this must be stowed where it can rapidly be loaded into the liferaft.' The contents of the British RORC standard kit gives the most basic survival items (listed below) while the more

Preparation is an essential element of the cruising lifestyle and never more so when it comes to the compilation of an emergency pack    *(Geoff Pack)*

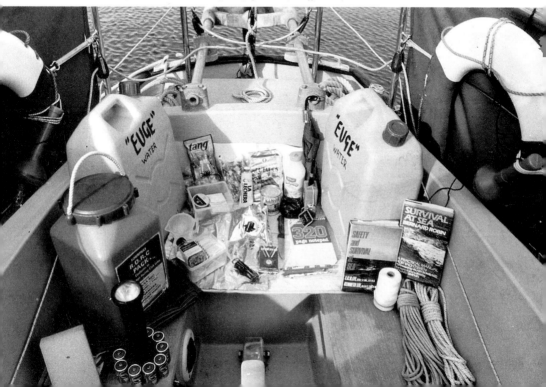

expensive emergency raft kits include a small quantity of water and a couple of parachute flares. The contents are based on an anticipated rescue time of around 36 hours.

As well as preparing an emergency pack, it's a good idea to make a list of four or five items which see everyday use aboard but must be taken into the raft in the event of the yacht foundering. Our list comprises sextant, almanac, flare pack, oilskins and extra water. Paste your list to the inside of the loo door so you read it every day.

**Water** Whilst some raft kits contain water, it is generally a very small quantity – sometimes as little as half a litre (one pint) per person, which doesn't go very far. Water must therefore be taken aboard the raft in addition to your prepared emergency pack. Twenty litre (4½ gal) containers have the advantage of high capacity but, weighing around 20 kilos (40-45lb), are heavy and unwieldy for a tired and frightened crew member, so a number of 10 litre (2 gal) containers would be better. Keep these in an accessible cockpit locker to form part of the ship's normal supply, ensuring they are refilled regularly with fresh water. Water containers should never be filled to the brim. A little air left inside creates enough buoyancy for them to float. Have bright yellow containers that, in the event of the boat going down quickly, could be pitched into the sea with a better chance of spotting them from the raft.

Looking on the bleak side, if rescue hasn't arrived before this water is finished, rain collection and its storage have to be anticipated. A rectangle of waterproof material, about 185mm x 122mm (6ft x 4ft) with many eyelets around its edge can be very useful as a shade, makeshift sail, blanket, pillow or rain catcher. As well as being able to catch water, you must have somewhere to put it, if you have been unable to get water containers on board the raft. My emergency pack includes six bags taken from the inside of wine boxes. These take up little room when stowed and give an extra 18 litres (4 gal) storage capacity. Solar stills are very useful, as Steve Callahan found during his 2½ month drift across the Atlantic after his yacht sank during the Mini-Transat. A graduated water cup is usually included in the raft kits and should be added to your bag.

**Food** Food is not included in any raft kits. Naturally as much food as possible will be taken from the stricken vessel, but the emergency pack should contain a supply of sugary foods. If adrift for any length of time, fish will provide a protein-rich diet, but its digestion requires a lot of water which might not be available. Sugary foods are not as demanding in this respect and are more suitable. The Baileys, who survived 117 days adrift in the Pacific, recommend compressed glucose and vitaminised survival biscuits.

**Shelter/Health** These items are dealt with simultaneously because they are closely related. Exposure will lead to death much faster than hunger or thirst. Protecting your body from cold in higher latitudes and the sun in hot climes should be an initial priority of liferaft occupants.

Survival suits are ideal but, if these are unavailable, oilskins should be included on the loo-door list of extra equipment. A small foldaway umberella for shade, if for any reason the liferaft canopy is damaged, could double up as a rain catcher. A pair of heavy gloves will keep hands warm in cold weather and can be used for handling fish and turtle catches.

The emergency pack should contain a first aid kit including sunblock cream, Vaseline and seasickness tablets. Most raft kits include these, but make a point of adding more. Seasickness must be guarded against in the unusual motion of a liferaft as the body loses precious fluids through vomiting. Special personal medicines for those aboard, like heart pills, must of course be taken and a supply of multi-vitamin tablets included and taken regularly.

**Signalling** Attracting attention is a high priority and you need every practical means available. The invisibility of small craft in bad weather was illustrated during the sad loss of Graham Adams' *Adfin's Rival* in the Western Approaches of the English Channel in September 1983. Although the crew were able to communicate with a nearby ship on only 1 watt VHF power, the ship could not find them. I put my faith in an EPIRB as their success record has been impressive. The best EPIRBs transmit not only on 243Mhz but also on 121.5Mhz, the civil aviation distress frequency, which all civil airlines monitor. However, for coastal waters they are not as effective and one has to rely on more basic methods. Alongside our emergency pack is strapped a comprehensively equipped RORC flare pack. Other means of signalling are a heliograph mirror, a torch (with spare batteries) and a whistle.

**Survival** Those making long passages should take special care in their preparation of survival items, although much of it is also necessary for the coastal emergency pack. Survival equipment in the RORC-standard liferaft includes a rescue quoit, sea anchor, knife, bellows, repair kit, baler, two paddles, rescue signal guide and general instructions on how to survive. The extra raft kits usually supply tin openers, plastic bags, basic fishing kit, sponges, spare torch bulb and batteries. To these should be added extra fishing equipment (if possible, take a small harpoon), extra knife, many small (30mm x 30mm/12in x 12in) plastic bags and a spare torch which uses the same batteries as the first. Plenty of extra lines and rope should be thin and strong. A Swiss Army knife is a perfectly adequate 'toolkit' on a liferaft.

Mid-ocean navigation is likely to be basic, but necessary all the same. Quartz wrist-watches should give accurate time and date, and a hand-bearing compass is a must. Sextant and almanac will enable a meridian passage to give your latitude. A timed 'equal altitudes' sight either side of noon provides longitude to quite acceptable accuracy without the need for any plotting.

Last but not least for the emergency pack is an Admiralty routeing chart. At the start of any long voyage, I always slip the appropriate month's routeing chart into the emergency pack. This is vastly superior to an ordinary chart, giving shipping lanes, currents and wind and climate data which could be vital information for survival.

*Morale* Seemingly unimportant items may contribute to morale which is a vital factor in survival. For instance a food obsession is common in those conditions. The Robinson family dreamed and planned the restaurant they would open on their return home. Similarly, the Bailey's fantasised over the preparation and consumption of various dishes and made sketches of the dreamboat they subsequently built. Therefore include pencils and notepad in your survival gear, as well as a pack of cards. Instruction books, like *Survival At Sea* by Bernard Robin (Stanley Paul) and *Safety and Survival At Sea* by E. C. B. and Kenneth Lee (Cassell) may be useful.

Having accumulated the contents of an emergency pack it is nescessary to decide how it is best stowed. With just one container, there is the chance that, if lost, all your eggs are in one basket. However, two containers are more difficult to handle in an emergency and Sod's Law guarantees that if one is lost, it will contain the most important equipment.

The emergency pack must also have some form of attachment, like a snaphook or rope tail, so that it can be positively secured to the raft while other things are being passed down from the yacht, or to prevent loss in bad weather if the raft is capsized.

Even if it takes up prime accommodation space, the emergency pack must be situated as close to the companionway as possible and not stuffed up in the quarterberth. The higher it is the better, in case flooding makes it difficult to find or remove. A good alternative with a sealed container is to stow it in a cockpit locker, ideally the one the extra water containers are in.

The emergency pack, like the liferaft itself, is something few of us are ever going to use and it's therefore easy to satisfy one's conscience by purchasing a liferaft only, and praying you never have to use it. However, the next time that you go to a boat show, visit a liferaft stand and inspect the contents of the standard raft kits and decide whether you could entrust the survival of your family or crew to them.

## Fire

There are dozens of easily combustible materials all over a boat and speaking as one who has experienced a serious fire at sea, the best possible method of dealing with it is nipping it in the bud by swift and immediate action. A fire blanket right next to the galley is the simplest first precaution, then lots of BCF/Halogen fire extinguishers, available within hand's reach all over the boat, so no-one can be trapped below without firefighting means.

The reason I suggest carrying so many fire extinguishers is because of the difficulty of having any serviced at their correct intervals, which may mean some becoming defective.

Controllable discharge fire extinguishers are a great boon for the ocean cruiser because if you handle a small galley fire, it can be out in seconds whilst the firefighter is training the remainder of the one-shot extinguisher over the side. This is frustrating and possibly dangerous because you're cutting down your fire-fighting ability should you be unfortunate enough to have another fire before you have the opportunity to replace the extinguisher.

## Intruders and Pirates

In the last few years half a dozen rather grizzly incidents have put the spotlight on this unpleasant subject and have perhaps been reported out of proportion. Rape and robbery happen anywhere and most cruising areas are no worse than anywhere else. Nobody with any sense goes looking for trouble spots in any country. Certain regions of the world though are undoubtedly dangerous, especially with drug-running being so prevalent. The South China Sea has a bad reputation as does Columbia, West Africa, the waters surrounding the Phillipines, Indonesia and to a lesser extent the Red Sea. The Bahamas is a massive drug trafficking centre, but yachting goes on quite happily as long as you don't stray into certain islands or anchorages that any local will name for you. Most potential problems can be avoided by steering clear of large cities.

Some ocean voyagers take the precaution of carrying guns but this is a step needing very careful consideration. A yacht carrying a gun will be expected to declare and surrender it in 95 percent of countries she visits. To hide the gun is taking an unacceptable risk. If it is found on a search, penalties are harsh in tiny 'banana republics' and not only will you end up in a local jail or with a high fine, but there is a good chance of having the yacht permanently confiscated. That effectively confines the use of the gun to when the yacht is at sea, yet the need for it is many times more likely to be in harbour.

My belief is that unless you are professionally trained in weapons you would be in danger of becoming a bigger liability to yourself and your crew. If you confront a pirate at sea who is pointing a gun at your gun, he'll be more used to the situation than you and staring down your barrel is likely to pull his trigger first. If you are not pointing a gun at him, there is the chance, however small, that the situation can be salvaged.

I make no apologies for putting a one-sided argument over this matter, and speak with some experience. I also baulk at the idea of everyday people incapably touting slightly rusty and ill-maintained firearms with possibly old and damp ammunition.

Lou Lou and I came close to an unpleasant incident in Castries, St. Lucia when we interrupted thieves on our boat in the early hours of the morning. Both were very well-built West Indians, one with what looked like a rifle, the other wielding a 3ft machete. We climbed over the stern of the yacht and within seconds blind fear had wiped away the effects of the evening's rum drinks. If we'd had a gun aboard we couldn't have got at it in the cabin, and knowing how much both of us were quaking at the time it was fortunate for everyone we didn't have one. Fortunately for us, they got away with virtually nothing except my spear gun which in the darkness was the rifle I thought one of them was carrying. We gave chase for long enough to get a good description of them and their boat – information the local police showed not the slightest interest in.

The interesting thing about this incident was the aftermath. Without our knowledge or anyone interviewing us, the story reached the British press. We didn't recognise the story when we finally received cuttings. It was one of four similar incidents concerning yachtsmen in the three-year period we were in the Caribbean. The other three were far more serious, but ours was ultimately embellished to the extent that I'd been stabbed and my wife raped too . . .

None of us like things that go bump in the night, even at home. It is no different on a yacht and one of the best methods of scaring away an intruder, sometimes without even getting out of the bunk, is to have the Aldis or similar lamp at your bedside. Within the confines of a cabin, this suddenly blazing out at intruders will scare the living daylights out of them and with the bright light blinding them they are likely to retreat.

# 20
# Domestic Life

## Cooking

Bottled gas has now almost entirely taken over from paraffin (or kerosene) which was always the traditional choice of galley fuel. Paraffin has advantages in that you could easily stock up for a year if you had a good sized tank, but its availability and quality have diminished significantly, converting even staunch supporters of paraffin cooking to the ease of liquid petroleum gas (LPG). Both fuels are potentially dangerous but as one person put it 'I'd rather die with one big bang from gas than be slowly burned to death with paraffin'.

No yachtsman needs reminding of the potential dangers of gas, and because it is so trouble free and easy to use it should never be taken for granted.

The availability of both propane or butane is very good world wide. The Camping Gaz brand is marketed in over a hundred countries, but the bottles do not stand up to the marine environment well and rust and pit badly when left on a boat for a long time. This puts them out of the question on safety grounds, not to mention the fact that Camping Gaz agents won't accept them back in this condition and you have to buy an expensive replacement bottle. Calor gas is a brand name well known in Great Britain but not so much elsewhere. Each country has its own brand name, but fortunately the actual contents will always be either butane or propane.

Butane is commonly used in many European countries, except Scandanavia. With the exception of Brazil, propane is by far the more popular everywhere else and yachts are best geared up for this before leaving. With a propane system, you can easily adapt to butane, but not vice versa, because propane is stored at a much higher pressure than butane and might explode in the wrong bottle. Although they are built to very high specifications, never have a blue Calor or especially Camping Gaz bottle filled with propane. Check your appliances to be sure, but most cookers and heaters will run just as well on either gas. In Britain, propane containers are the red Calor bottles and can be obtained in 3.9kg, 13kg and 19kg sizes. Before you leave, make sure on your last swap that the shop-keeper gives you brand new bottles – it'll be the last time you exchange cannisters and those ones will stay with you for the whole cruise.

The trick to having an adaptable system is to bulkhead-mount your propane regulator (37mb) with a flexible pipe leading to the bottle. In this way, if you can't get your own bottles filled, you can use local ones temporarily and only need to change the bottle connector on this pipe to run on the new bottles. After a while you build up a stock of connectors which is very handy. Always carry a spare length of approved high pressure flexible gas piping so that as your pipe gets worn out it can be replaced.

We have never had trouble finding cooking gas, although it is invariably necessary to go to the central gas plant, normally in the main port, to get bottles filled. We would generally hire a car to do this run, rowing around the anchorage first collecting everyone else's bottles and asking a share of the car hire. This normally worked out cheaper than a taxi. When you have bottles recharged, make sure that the operator doesn't over-fill them. The limit is 70 percent in hot places, 80 percent in temperate climes. This can be ascertained by weighing the bottle with bathroom scales or a spring balance and deducting the 'tare' (ie empty) weight stamped on the bottle's collar. This should be no more than the gas fill figure also stamped on the collar. We always found three of the 3.9kg bottles perfectly adequate. If your gas locker will accommodate extra, by all means have it, but four small bottles are much handier than two big ones.

A gas solenoid shut-off switch is obligatory on all American boats but don't have much to be said for them. They seize solid with rust sooner or later and are yet another drain on the battery. A much better device is something like the Gas-low which monitors gas pressure between the bottle and appliance. By turning off the bottle you can find out very quickly if you have a gas leak by seeing if the pressure is maintained. This should be done daily, no matter how good the system seems to be.

### Refrigeration

Despite everything that has been said about keeping things simple there is no doubt that a refrigerator in a tropic climate is mighty nice.

The big drawback is its huge power consumption which makes you dependent on daily engine-running schedules, with all the attendant cost and extra servicing. A custom-designed, professionally installed small fridge (not freezer) will draw a minimum of 50amp/hours *daily* in the tropics. A more typical stock model can easily consume between 120 and 145amp/hours a day. An alternative is an engine-driven compressor pump, but again you are looking towards a minimum of two or three hours engine running a day.

All the same, approximately half the ocean cruisers sailing the world today are fitted with some form of refrigeration but forget about having a freezer. The greater differential between ambient and box temperature for freezers gives them a voracious power appetite and you can easily become a slave to feeding them. Most of us have a large fridge at home loosely stuffed with a lot of food and drink that doesn't really need to be there. On board, you can get away with a small volume (1½-2cu ft) only putting in it what you need cold that day and not using it as a general store. You must also learn to open the door as few times as possible.

Yacht refrigerator efficiency is more related to its installation than its cost. The design of the box itself has to be very good indeed. British designs tend not to be reliable as there is little experience at what is needed to remain efficient in the tropics. By keeping the box small you will have more room for insulation. You can't overdo this, and if your fridge is situated in an area under or behind which there isn't much usable space, fill the entire area with two-part polyurethane foam. The absolute minimum should be six inches all round, but thinking about all the power you'll save in the long run, there's nothing stopping you putting in 12in if you can.

Refrigeration is simple to understand in principle and with some basic knowledge and a stock of spare driers the average yachtsman can troubleshoot his own system.

Most use the refrigerant Freon 12. Basically this takes a continuous circuitous route first through the high pressure side of the system, then the low pressure before arriving at the compressor pump to start the cycle again. The compressor pumps Freon into the high pressure piping. Being compressed, the gas leaves this pump heated and makes its way into a heat exchanger, known as the condensor, where that heat is extracted (either by a 12v fan or salt water piped from the engine cooling). The nature of the gas is that as it cools it condenses into liquid form. It continues its route, still cool but under a lot of pressure, through something called a drier which is like a water filter on the engine – it removes both impurities and any moisture from the Freon. After this operation, the Freon is forced through a tiny orifice (the expansion valve) and is squirted into the cold plates, or evaporators, in the actual fridge box now on the low pressure half of the system. The expansion valve matches the performance of the compressor against the efficiency of the evaporator, thereby maintaining a balance between the high and low pressure sides of the system. The sudden drop in pressure in the evaporator plates immediately changes the liquid Freon back to its natural state as gas and at the same time there is a rapid drop in its temperature. As the now very cold gas flows through the plates it absorbs any vestiges of warmth that comes from them which in turn has come from the fridge box. Finally, the gas, now warmer, continues its way to the compressor pump to re-start the cycle. A fridge is therefore just a heat pump which sucks warmth in through the evaporator and expels it through the condensor.

There are many variants, and if the components are properly matched it will usually dictate the efficiency of your system. First of all, the compressor pump can either be driven direct from the engine or from a 12v motor. There are several variations of heat exchanger. Firstly, a straightforward 12v fan can be used, although power consumption tends to be fairly high. On the bigger, engine-driven compressor models, the motor's raw cooling water can easily be tapped (before entering the engine) to take away some of the condensor heat. Friends of ours, Richard and Cathy Cottier, fitted their condensor in the yacht's main water tank (in the keel, itself naturally cooled by ambient seawater outside) and cutting out the 12v fan reduced their battery drain considerably. On the low-pressure side, the efficiency of the evaporator to absorb heat is directly proportional to the length of the piping and therefore surface area. Steve Dashew in his excellent book *Circumnavigator's Handbook* describes his 'finned evaporator' which for a small increase in cost improved his system greatly by having fins on the piping to increase the surface area.

Eutectic plates are simply a snake of evaporator piping immersed in a sealed box filled with a combination of water and an anti-freeze-like solution. Sometimes called holdover plates, they are used with engine-driven refrigeration systems when you will only be running the system for two or three hours a day. They're like a block of ice that freezes at a lower temperature than water. The refrigeration is run for a couple of hours and the eutectic plate freezes. Like a block of ice, it keeps everything cool for a period of time (hopefully 24 hours) before needing freezing down again by running the motor and refrigeration. The smaller the eutectic plate, the less time it'll keep frozen and the more often you'll have to run the engine, so the more plates you have the better. However, the compressor capacity has to be matched to the demands of the plates.

Having had an engine-driven system for two years I am inclined to vote for a modest 12v electric system. It would have to be backed up with both solar panels and wind generators because otherwise you have the engine charging for up to 40 percent longer daily than you would with an engine-driven compressor system. A combination of solar panels and a big wind generator will help 'subsidise' its power consumption and you will be able to cut down engine running times considerably. We once met an American who claimed he could 'convert wind into ice cubes' (ie run his 12v fridge off the wind generator) but I doubt this very much in the tropics.

If you decide to go ahead with refrigeration, the name that comes up time and again for efficiency, reliability and economy is Danfoss. Many other brands use Danfoss components and I've heard nothing bad about them.

One system that has been used with some success is the heat

absorption type of refrigeration. Ammonia refrigerates directly on being heated, so with a small flame to do the work, there are no moving parts, no noise and no power used (other than paraffin or gas). Companies like Electrolux produce such fridges for parts of the world short on power and at the outset they seem like the answer to the yachtsman's prayer being very economic (less than a gallon and a half of paraffin a week) and not particularly expensive. Absorption refrigeration has its problems though. It doesn't like motion of any kind, nor is it keen on vibration, so it can normally operate in harbour but not at sea. Another disadvantage is that they can be a bit smelly, and they tend to warm up the cabin, so ventilation must be especially good.

The manufacturers of this type don't like to recommend them for use on boats because of the fire risk, but some yachtsmen do use them with care.

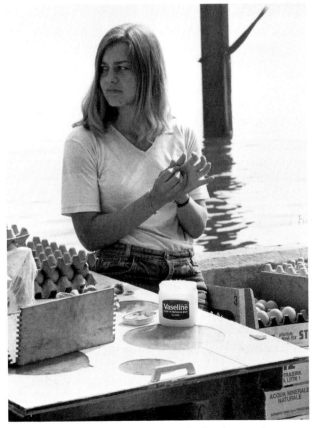

Using Vaseline is one of the more laborious methods of protecting eggs; many argue that totally fresh eggs don't need any such treatment for the few weeks' duration of a long voyage   *(Colin Jarman/Eyeline)*

## Provisioning

The mountain of tinned food tradionally associated with long voyages is the first to forget unless you are planning to make a singlehanded circumnavigation non-stop. We made this mistake first time and we've spoken to dozens of others who've regretted taking on a massive stocks of food. The boat disappears even deeper into the water, there's not a free inch of stowage space and trying to find anything entails dismantling and re-assembling a three-dimensional jigsaw puzzle. After all the longest passage is perhaps five or six weeks and you can buy most provisions at either end. There is also something unromantic about lying to an anchor in a perfect crystal clear lagoon with tree frogs chirping away ashore, the palm trees silhouetted against an impressive tropic sunset, a local rum drink in your hand and then being served Fray Bentos steak and kidney pie with Co-op tinned peas (on Special Offer at 22p). Of course it pays to carry enough food on board for emergencies. You may take a lot longer to reach port than you had bargained for, so never provision just for the days you expect to be at sea.

If you shop in port as and when you need to, you are likely to eat more fresh food and enjoy local delicacies. There seems no point in stocking up with cases of tinned fruit such as peaches and pears if you are heading for the Med where fresh fruit is cheap and plentiful. On the other hand do make sure you take plenty of your favourite things as some of them may prove prohibitively expensive abroad, if available at all.

### Tinned Versus Dried Food

Dried food can often only be purchased in bulk at the wholesalers which can mean less variety if you have to buy it in 100 serving packs. It is light to stow but it must be kept absolutely dry and you may have to increase your water capacity to rehydrate it. It is not as easy to prepare as tinned food which can be made into a delicious meal in minutes on a stormy night just by emptying a few tins into a pot with some chopped onions and heating through. Depending on how dry your stowage, the length of time you intend keeping them and your thoroughness, tins can be protected against rust by varnishing. This is another of those traditional long voyage chores that not many people bother with now. It has been found by experience that tins will last quite long enough as they are. As long as a tin hasn't 'blown', it's amazing how well the contents are preserved in a tin whose outside looks dreadful. It is quite sufficient to rip off the labels and mark the contents on the top with indelible pen, then store them in as dry a place as you can.

If possible, try out a small quantity of everything before you buy in bulk. It will save you a lot of tasteless meals.

## Food Stowage

Fruit bruises easily and must be stowed in trays with newspaper wedged between each piece. Vegetables need light and air and a good place is in hanging nets. Another way of storing veggies is to have a big ventilated bin lashed on deck, the sort of thing bakers use to deliver loaves of bread in with a cover over it to keep out spray. If you can spare it, lettuces stow very well with their base submerged in fresh water which is changed regularly. Tomatoes should be completely wrapped when green to slow down the turning process. Lemons will keep indefinitely if wrapped in aluminium foil.

Eggs are usually recommended to be protected with vaseline, which is horribly messy and time consuming. They keep well without protection for 3-4 weeks, but you can prolong the life of half a dozen or so by putting them in a wire basket and dipping in boiling water for 30 seconds. Dried eggs are available again which are great for cakes and scrambling and help to stretch out the fresh supply a bit longer.

Butter is a problem in hot countries as even tinned butter goes rancid quickly above 70°F (21°C). Margarine is a good substitute and in the tropics they sell a peculiar tinned substance, sometimes called Glo-spread or Oleomargarine, which has been specially processed to stop it melting. It is good for cooking, but we would rather go without than spread it on bread.

Cheese keeps well if bought in its wax or covered in silver paper and stowed in the coolest place possible. Cured ham, salami, and sausages all make a pleasant change from corned beef and can be stowed strung up as in the delicatessen.

After a few weeks at sea, one is usually craving something crunchy and we have always had great success with sprouting beans. There are a great many to choose from. Mung, toh foo, and even chick peas all sprout well and mixed with a tin of sweet corn, some rice, oil and vinegar they make a refreshing change when all the lettuce has been eaten.

Do not overlook the possibility of preserving food as you go along. We have met many people who have dried their own fish by cutting it into strips, hanging out like washing until completely dry and then packing between layers of salt in air tight containers. Lou Lou has successfully bottled fruit and vegetables using a pressure cooker and kilner jars when we've arrived in a port and found a glut of some local speciality going cheap.

## *In The Galley*

Buy a good quantity of bay leaves as these help to keep weevils out of lentils, flour, rice and pasta. Dry commodities like these store best in wide mouthed plastic containers.

In deciding where you will be stowing your food, don't forget that, apart from being handy to the galley, you will want to get at it without continually disturbing the off-watch crew members or unseating the navigator. Above all make sure it is in a dry place.

Most cruising cooks rate their pressure cookers as their most important piece of equipment on board. If you take one (and they certainly save fuel) don't forget spare gaskets, relief valve rubbers and weights (these always get thrown overboard with the washing up water!).

It is a good idea to buy stainless steel replacements for all your cooking utensils as these last much longer.

A minute timer in the galley is a useful item, not just for cooking but reminding you of the noon sight and watch changes.

It may not sound very seamanlike, but it is very useful to take along a granny basket (one of those shopping bags on wheels) for carrying provisions, gas bottles etc, because the car you have always taken for granted will not be there. We had a cheap steel one but it rusted badly and next trip, shall·treat ourselves to a specially-made stainless or aluminium one with good-diameter plastic wheels.

Toiletries and cleaning materials are expensive in certain places abroad. Shampoo is a must for sea water baths as it lathers beautifully in salt water; we bought ten family-sized supermarket shampoos for this purpose. An all-purpose cleaning fluid such as Flash serves many uses aboard so will also be needed in big packs.

# 21
# *Everyday Life Afloat*

## *Future Maintenance*

Messing about with the boat can be very pleasant and there will be plenty of it with everything receiving much more wear and tear than ever before. But you don't want to become a slave to it, so it is worth taking a few precautions before you start to keep future maintenance to a minimum.

In warm, tropic waters osmosis in fibreglass hulls is much more likely, aided and abetted by the strong sunlight in the waterline region. To reduce the risk strip the antifouling off and coat the undersides with the latest two part epoxy anti-osmosis treatment. Technology is changing fast so research what is considered the best at the time you need it.

When you antifoul, one job that will save you hours and hours of toil in the future is to raise the yacht's waterline by at least six inches, preferably nine. Not only will your boat inevitably sit a little deeper in the water with all her stores and extra gear, but from time to time she'll be out of trim and raising the waterline will save a lot of scrubbing off of weed (which grows quickly in warm climates) from the first few inches of the topsides. Also, it is unavoidable that you will sometimes have to moor in dirty, oily harbours and raising the waterline saves your topsides from the resulting yellow stain that is so hard to remove.

In the interests of preserving your topsides (either gelcoat or paint), a simple fender curtain approximately one third of the boat's LOA and coming to within 6in (15cm) of the waterline will save a lot of grief when lying alongside little stone quays or oily harbour walls. When berthed for a short time anywhere where fenders have to work hard for their living or get filthy or damaged, go ashore and find a couple of old car tyres, ubiquitous in ports the world over, and use them as fenders for the duration of your stay alongside, with a fender curtain totally protecting the topsides.

Exterior varnishwork is best kept to a minimum. Sacrilege though it may seem, it may be worth getting the varnishwork on areas of a wooden boat like coachroof sides and cockpit coamings to a good standard with lots of coats, then paint over it. You then always have the ability to revert to the varnishwork when the cruise is over. Americans seem to make the best varnish and several of the Caribbean charter fleet operators, who are genuine experts on maintaining

Don't waste too much time making the yacht look prissy and immaculate; a hard-working life and many oily or weedy waterline scrubs will remove the shine

It's heartbreaking to see the state that immaculately-kept yachts sometimes get into in many commercial harbours; this happened in Tenerife, an island otherwise noted for its tourist appeal   *(Geoff Pack)*

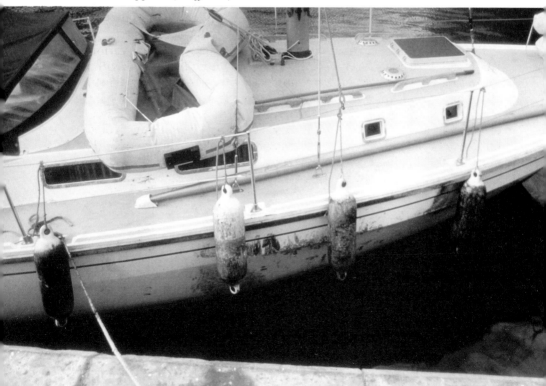

varnishwork, use the US Pettit products, the Bak-V-Spar varnish being highly recommended with UV filters. When you get to the States or Caribbean it is worth buying in a stock of this. The difference in your varnishwork will cushion the blow of its price. In the tropics varnishwork has to be recoated every 8-10 weeks for it to remain looking good. This may sound horrific, but once the brightwork was up to this standard it needed only a very light rub down before being recoated, preferably early in the morning before the sun becomes too hot and the varnish too sticky to apply.

## Photography Afloat

The environment afloat is about the worst possible for delicate camera equipment. It needs cushioning against the chance that it could fall out of a locker at sea and fly for a few feet. A smallish but robust aluminium camera box looking like a suitcase and padded inside can be purchased in any camera shop and affords good protection. Ask in camera shops for any silica-gel cachets they have spare. All camera equipment comes from the manufacturers packed with these silica-gel bags and shops often have some lying around. They are the best way of keeping moisture away from the equipment and, toasted under the grill every six months or so to dry it out, will remain effective.

There is a huge choice of highly sophisticated electronically operated cameras, but I went for the basic and hard-wearing Olympus OM-1 with Zuiko lenses, fitted with 'sacrificial' UV filters for protection against scratches. It lasted four years afloat but had to be written off after that. Make sure to take along three or four CdS batteries for the light meter. You'll never find them overseas.

Processing films abroad is a constant problem. The various laboratory processes, even with well known names like Kodak, often mean that a film bought in one country can't be processed in the next. Black and white, which anybody writing for publication will need, is almost impossible unless you are lucky enough to find a keen amateur to process for you and colour slides are equally difficult. Kodak publish a booklet listing all the Kodak offices and agents all over the world, plus all laboratories that accept Kodak, and other makes. It is available, free, from Kodak House, P O Box 66, Hemel Hempstead, Herts HP1 1JU. It may be less bother in the long run to make an arrangement with someone at home to have your films developed and send on the results.

In terms of transparency films, Agfachrome CT18 is widely available as are Kodakchrome 25 and 64 and Ectachrome ER. The longest time you can hope film to last is six months on a boat in hot weather. Keep it as cool and dry as possible and watch expiry dates carefully when you buy.

Photographic equipment and the seagoing life don't mix easily; here the author's Olympus is put to work earning its keep before it finally gave up the ghost   (*Yachting Monthly*)

## Earning Money Overseas

On first impressions this can be fraught with difficulties involving work permits and entry visas and many a cruising yachtsman has been chucked out of a country for illegally working. In reality, cruising work can be had in many places, on condition that you go out and find it – it rarely comes to you.

A high proportion of yachtsmen finance their cruising life by working along the way and some come back at the end of three or four years with more money than they set out with. The beauty of it is that the overheads of living aboard are a fraction of those doing the same job living ashore, and you have become used to living a little frugally, so you need only work for four or five months to support the next year's cruising.

The best possible way of earning money is by using a specific skill. We met two dentists in the Caribbean who'd sailed their 26ft sloop down from New York and were holed up in Bequia filling the neglected teeth of grateful yachtsmen as fast as they could. The quarter berth had become the operating table, the patient propped up with pillows and the yacht's spotlamp wedged into the bulkhead bookshelf to shine into their mouths. A diver's air bottle provided power for a drill and a fierce Jabsco water pump had been adapted to vacuum the mouth. They were making a fortune!

Competent diesel mechanics are always in demand, as are refrigeration experts, and electrical engineers who can repair radios, autopilots, or general electronics will have an easy time of it. We made a corner in sail repairs, upholstery and cover-making and our dear Reeds Sailmaker sewing machine paid for itself time and time again. However, the work will never come to you unless you gain a reputation. Our best advert was making a really good awning for ourselves so that as people went by in dinghies they'd asked where we got it. In this way we had dozens of orders, including a 700sq ft all-over awning for an 86ft ketch, which was made entirely in our 34-footer's saloon with a hand crank machine, evidence if ever it was needed that you'll do anything when you're broke. In the charter centres of the Caribbean and Mediterannean, there were always expensive crewed boats wanting a new sailcover, windscoop, or cockpit cushions.

Unfortunately this form of earning money is very popular now, but those who are really good still manage nicely. A South African friend of ours started making trendy but simple Bermuda-type shorts out of nylon spinnaker material for her husband and within a short space of time she couldn't churn them out fast enough. Another friend crochetted bikinis in the Caribbean, and with a lovely figure herself to show them off never had problems selling them at vastly inflationary prices to tourist shops. Clearly one has to aim for the richer cruising areas, especially where there are big boats, but when finances are starting to run down this must be embraced as part of the cruising plan.

Writing for magazines is a possibility if writing comes easily and you are a good photographer, but be prepared for the fact that editors receive three or four manuscripts about ocean cruising topics for every one about home waters cruising, because the blue water yachtsmen have more time to write. The trouble is that 95 percent of the readers are coastal sailors who like to dream occasionally of blue water but are generally more interested in home waters. Diary-like accounts of voyages are almost universally rejected. It is far better to take a small incident or experience and examine it, perhaps for entertainment value, or for the lesson there is to learn.

If you plan to submit articles, write to the magazines and ask for their contributor's guidelines. Most have a typed résumé which will give a clear idea on the sort of subjects they like to see, the type of illustrations they can use, and the sort of article length they prefer to accept.

Chartering is many a yachtsman's idea of a dream come true until they've tried it. If you have a boat of 45ft or more, it seems an obvious way to make money, but as a general rule it rarely pays off. Cruising boats make lousy charter boats and vice versa. Chartering has to be a business. You must have equipment and accoutrements that have no place on a long distance cruiser and you must be established with a US or European agent and have a good brochure. It is easy to see that anyone contemplating a costly holiday with all the air fares will be more easily attracted to the well presented, established boats, even if they cost more. So you won't get sent charters by the agents, who will have dozens of other yachts on their books, until you are proven with happy guests in your wake, and you can't gain that reputation until you've done some charters. Clearing this hurdle will take a couple of years rather than months, and a much better alternative is to get a job with a charter company and lay your own boat up temporarily.

A charter boat also needs paraphenalia to be attractive. It is the norm to have nine or ten sets of snorkels, flippers and masks aboard (so there is the right size for everyone), one or two windsurfers, diving equipment, plus a big and stable dinghy with powerful outboard for skiing. Charter guests straight out from a cold climate need permanent protection from the sun for the first few days, so a bimini or permanent sailing awning is required. They also generally use a great deal of water and electricity which must be replaced. Six charter guests could be going through 100 gallons of water a day.

Day charter can be lucrative in holiday areas, but recognising this authorities have imposed clampdowns and only issue licences to locals. You can certainly pick up the odd illegal day charter from time to time, but it is risky. In the Canaries, the routine among yachtsmen was to anchor off a holiday beach. Within minutes you could be sure that a tourist had swum out and was engaging you in conversation. With a little subtlety, it was not difficult to get them to come for an informal day sail with you, bringing along a few friends. However this is not something one could do regularly without risking a lot of trouble. The rules are the same the world over in all holiday areas.

## The Blue Water Bookshelf

The essence of ocean cruising is self-sufficiency and independence. It used to be said that there should be absolutely nothing aboard that the skipper or crew couldn't repair, but that may be going a bit far in these high-tech days. However, the right books to refer to may save you a lot of frustration and money. Given that you will also want to take a library to read for pleasure there will be space limitations but the following is a basic list of books I have found helpful.

*Independent Traveller's Handbook* (Heinemann). Gives endless information about travelling in general, addresses of consulates, national holidays, and dozens of useful articles on photography, dealing with locals, currency and so on.

*Yachtsman's 8-Language Dictionary* by Barbara Webb (Adlard Coles). You would have thought this book would have been invaluable for long distance sailors when in fact it is very rare indeed you can buy sailing equipment in foreign countries and therefore don't need to know what a cranse iron is in Portuguese. For Mediterranean sailing it is likely to get more use. If you're short of money, this one could be dropped from the shopping list, if not, have it just in case.

*Anchoring and Mooring Techniques Illustrated* by Alain Gree (Adlard Coles). This is a mine of excellent information, and whilst it is likely to be of more use in preparation than practice, it is nevertheless a nice one to have aboard.

*Care and Repair of Small Marine Diesels* by Chris Thompson (Adlard Coles). One of a number of good books on basic diesel maintenance.

*Complete Canvas Worker's Guide* by J. Grant (Ashford Press). As its name suggests, this book is useful if you either plan to earn some money or if you want to save money by making awnings etc yourself. It describes how to make just about everything canvas/fabric aboard from sea anchors to flags and harnesses.

*Flags of All Nations* (Brown, Son & Ferguson). This is one of a number of similar books. Make sure you have an up-to-date one as flags are constantly changing and not only is it annoying to spend a lot of time making an out-of-date one, it goes down like a lead balloon with the authorities when they see it flying proudly from your crosstrees.

*Meteorology at Sea* Ray Sanderson (Stanford). Again, one of a number of very good books available on the subject and undoubtedly helps to get the most efficient weather forecast in many regions of the world – by doing it yourself.

*Safety and Survival at Sea* by E. C. B. and Kenneth Lee (Cassell). Hardly gripping or fun reading, but an essential for the emergency pack.

*Sails* by Jeremy Howard-Williams (Adlard Coles). Universally recognised as the bible on sail handling, care and repair.

*Self Steering Without a Windvane* by Lee Woas (Adlard Coles). We carry this aboard for one reason only: if our windvane breaks down in mid ocean. On this basis alone, it is cheap insurance.

*Ships Captain's Medical Guide* (HMSO). There are several yachtsmen's first aid books around, but none have come anywhere near the standard of this work. Some of its information is inappropriate to a yacht (it was written for ships' captains) but it is nevertheless comprehensive.

Then there are the navigation books, many of which are unavoidable for safe seakeeping. These include:-

*Ocean Passages/World Cruising Routes*
Relevant *Admiralty Pilots*
*Celestial Astro for Yachtsmen*
*Sight Reduction Tables for Air Navigation, Vols 1-3*
Choice of *Almanacs*
*Admiralty List of Lights*
*List of Radio Signals*
*Admiralty Catalogue of Charts and Publications*

Traditionally, ocean cruising yachtsmen have bought *Ocean Passages for the World* which is far from suitable but the only thing available for passage routeing. Now Jimmy Cornell has produced an excellent substitute called *World Cruising Routes* (Adlard Coles) which although not totally precise in its information, is far preferable to *Ocean Passages*.

Admiralty Pilots are expensive and often inadequate for the yachtsman, but one would be foolish to sail without them. When Atlantic cruising we only used one of our eight volumes on a single occasion, and then it didn't describe the bay we were entering. Instead we always used commercial yachting pilot books and guides. For the Pacific and high latitudes, they have perhaps more use, but a stock of commercial yachting pilot books and guides for the area you are visiting will be needed. More often than not, they are not on sale anywhere but the particular area.

The *List of Lights* and *List of Radio Signals* are in theory essential. In reality the information they contain is invariably out of date for the lighthouse or RDF station you are wanting to check. It is far better to determine the local situation before leaving and *never* rely on the information in these books, but use them as a guide.

Charts. Carry a copy of the Admiralty chart catalogue. Though bulky it will enable you to order your charts from overseas and there is no cheaper place to buy good charts than England. Even so they are expensive and it is easy to get carried away and spend several hundred pounds. It is best not to plan too far ahead. If you want to circumnavigate for example, buy charts as far as Panama and if you still want to continue wait there a month or so while new charts are ordered and sent to you.

Everybody faces the same expense and often you can swap charts and pilot books with someone sailing in the opposite direction to you. Another dodge is to talk to big ships in harbour. They are very friendly and all have a cancelled chart drawer where sheets with more than six corrections are written off. Even so they may be newer than the ones you are carrying from home. From time to time the contents of this drawer are dumped, make sure you get to see it first. Alternatively, you may be allowed to take a tracing or photocopy of somebody else's charts. This is a definite risk, but if you were stuck for a particular chart it will be the lesser of two evils, and used with caution, considerably better than nothing.

## Documentation

This is more straightforward than most people think. For a British yacht all that is needed is either the old-fashioned formal Certificate of British Registry, or if your boat doesn't have this, the Small Ship's Registration (SSR) document from the Royal Yachting Association. Make sure it is made out in your name. SSR is accepted all over the world and the RYA report that they've never heard of anyone having problems with it. We have never been asked for the licence for our VHF radio, but it would do no harm to carry it just in case.

Thereafter, documentation is only individual country generated.

You will often be asked to fill in myriad forms in triplicate and produce them for whatever reason as you clear out again. As long as you have valid passports and the correct visas, nothing else is required, except sometimes your clearance from the last country. If you arrive in some West Indian islands without outward clearance from your last port it is not unknown for them to send you back for one.

It is always advisable to toe the line with beaurocracy which is worse in smaller countries. In some the customs officers, who are very often also the police, have a great deal of power and there is nothing to stop them from putting you in jail, or even confiscating the yacht if you don't do things exactly as they wish.

A small tip is to buy postage stamps and stick them on the back of your registry documents. Always have made a ship's rubber stamp, suitably grandiose, and print it all over the postage stamps. This may sound infantile, but it gives a document credence in some countries!

## Mail From Home

Mail takes on a completely new complexion when you are far from home. The arrival of letters is a great excitement, but you have to brace yourself for plenty of disappointments and lost parcels.

Giving someone a blanket instruction to forward all mail will mean spending a lot of money shipping worthless leaflets and mail-shot brochures around the world, so you must trust whoever you choose to forward your mail to open everything and be selective.

Poste restante addresses vary considerably in efficiency and are usually regarded as a final resort, unless there are good local reports of them. Normal routine is to find out through the cruising grapevine where there is a reliable address ahead and if possible send a card there asking them if they don't mind holding your mail. Few ever object and you can then phone or write home with the new forwarding address. Airmail nearly always arrives within two weeks anywhere in the world. If you can't find an address ahead, wait until you arrive in a place you plan to stay for a while and seek out a forwarding address then. Embassies, harbourmasters' offices, cafes, boatyards, hotels, and banks will all help.

Friends will always want to write to you in an exotic location, but it is better to encourage them to send to your home-base address for forwarding. Otherwise letters will forever be arriving too late to catch you before you sail on and may never catch up.

## The Home Base and Finances

The obvious person to handle your affairs is a relative. If they have your Power of Attorney this might save problems and it would be easier if you make them signatory to your bank account. However, relatives are not always available to do the job and some ocean cruising people use their banks to provide a similar service. Despite the fact that in financial terms we were lousy customers, we found our bank manager and his staff interested in our movements, which probably make a welcome break from everyday routine, and although we didn't formally use them as our homebase, they were very helpful with money matters.

Getting cash overseas can be a frustrating affair. There are no hard and fast rules as regulations and facilities change constantly. Certain credit and charge cards, especially Access, Visa, Barclaycard and American Express can be used to either obtain cash, make purchases or buy travellers' cheques in many places and this is about the most reliable system. However, in many third world locations such niceties are worthless. They are only interested in the US dollar note. It is wise to have as many different ways of obtaining money as possible and never let yourself get low on cash before sending home for more. Keep the number of transactions to a minimum and transfer money in largish chunks. Cashing money overseas is a very expensive affair whichever way you approach it. One ocean voyaging friend solves the problem by taking all his money with him. It may seem outrageous advice but he has cruised for years and used to spend many frustrating hours trying to have money forwarded from home. With his present system he has no problems, no bank statements, is never overdrawn, always knows exactly how much he has left, and gets no bank charges. He claims that before he lost more money in forwarding transactions and bank charges than ever he made in interest. The money was very well hidden (not under the bunk mattress), and although his boat has been broken into on a couple of occasions the intruders never found his cache. Those cruising on a fairly tight budget without much income going into their home account might find the simplicity of his system makes sense.

# 22
# *Common Worries*

As this is a large area of concern for the would-be round the world yachtsman, particularly if taking children, you should before leaving consider the following points:

1 Have a dental check up well in advance in case you need a course of treatment, allowing at least three months.

2 Get medical insurance cover for any foreign countries visited (in particular Canada and the States). British readers should obtain DHS leaflet SA30.

3 If you intend visiting anywhere in Europe, then ensure that you visit your local DHSS office and get form E111 completed and stamped (it lasts five years). This will allow you free medical services within the European community. Without it you have to pay. You may have to pay at the time, but should get a refund.

4 Make an appointment to see your general practitioner. Tell him of your plans and where you expect to travel and find out what innoculations you will require. This may change from time to time, but your GP will be able to advise you on this. The common innoculations are tetanus and polio, both of which may require a booster. They may also be required for cholera, typhoid, paratyphoid and yellow fever. For the latter innoculation you will have to attend a yellow fever innoculation centre – read DHSS leaflet SA35. Allow three months to cover all innoculations. Also ask your GP about the latest malaria prophylaxis.

You will need to ask your GP if there are any reasons why you should not embark on such an adventure and needless to say, do this at the earliest opportunity. For example if you suffer from some on-going problem such as kidney disease and require constant medical backup, then you should consider your decision carefully and ask the specialist at your next routine outpatients' appointment.

Having a well-controlled chronic on-going disease isn't in itself a reason not to go, but you must ensure that you have enough of the correct drugs and that someone else in the crew is briefed on your condition. Diabetics for example should be able to anticipate and avoid hypoglycaemic attacks and should have at least two emergency injections of glucagon, whose use they understand.

Everyone should know their medical history and whether they are allergic to drugs such as penicillin. If this is the case it is worth investing in an SOS talisman.

Your GP is not obliged to give a medical examination on request, but most will though they are entitled to charge for it. As you will at times be days from medical help, ask if you can have a course of a broad spectrum antibiotic for your emergency kit. He will not be obliged to prescribe but may understand your situation and give you a private prescription. Check that it is one that has not produced any side effects for you on previous occasions.

5 Take a first aid course. These are often organised during the winter months at yacht clubs and evening classes.

### First Aid Kit

This first aid kit can all be assembled over the counter from any High Street chemist such as Boots. Don't buy a prepacked kit as it will not be adequate for a long cruise and will also be expensive. The cheapest and best way to store your kit is by buying a medium or small size fisherman's kit box (£5). Remember of course to stow medicines out of the reach of children.

| Drugs and Creams | Extra Useful Equipment |
|---|---|
| Kaolin and Morph mixture | Thermometer |
| Immodium | Cotton wool |
| Aspirin | Sterile dressing pack |
| Paracetamol Elixir (for children) | Dumbell sutures |
| Stugeron | Swabs |
| Piriton/Triludan (anti-histamines) | Finger stool |
| Nurofen | Plasters |
| Otrivine eye drops | Poultice and magnesium |
| Milk of Magnesia | sulphate drawing paste |
| Xylocaine gel | Paper clips |
| Savlon or other antiseptic cream | Tubigrip sizes B and D |
| Diorolyte sachets | Splints (a suitable piece of wood) |
| (rehydration salts) | Sling |
| Aftersun | Elastocrepe bandage |
| Suntan lotion | Crepe bandage |
| *Broad spectrum anti-biotic | Splinter forceps |
| *Contraceptive pills (if required) | *Magnifying glass |

This entire medical kit could be purchased for around £40 (1987) including the fisherman's case but excluding the items marked with an asterix. With this kit you should be able to cope with 99 percent of problems yourself, at least until medical assistance is available. Also for around £5 you can purchase a first aid book of your own choice, such as the *St John Ambulance First Aid For Beginners*. For more serious problems, take along the *Ships Captain's Medical Guide*.

You should have no difficulty in staying fit as the sea is a very healthy place and sailing requires a degree of physical effort. You will probably be fitter than ever after only a few weeks at sea. Accidents however are a different matter and, as ever, prevention is better than cure. The first way to avoid accidents is to run a tight ship with well maintained equipment. Pace yourself and think carefully. Don't take short cuts, don't push yourself to exhaustion or you will become careless.

In foreign ports be careful of buying vegetables and meat and always wash them carefully. Assume tap water is not clean until proved otherwise. The sun is one of the reasons many go away in the first place, but make sure it doesn't do you permanent damage. Skin cancer is becoming more prevalent and the risk of getting it increases with more exposure to the sun; over-exposure also causes premature ageing. Wear a sun hat and always walk on the shady side of the street.

Armies recognise the importance of correct footwear and yachtsmen should too, as walking barefoot in tropical areas may easily predispose you to infection of one sort or another.

Finally, remember that AIDS is becoming increasingly prevalent worldwide and that under-developed countries have no facility for screening donor blood. Generally it is best to have any surgical or dental treatment in Europe or the States, or countries where blood is screened and intruments sterilised to a high degree. Whilst one can arrange to have known problems dealt with at home, one cannot plan for emergency surgery and the risk of flying home may exceed the danger of AIDS transfusion.

## Thieves

The value of items you have aboard is greatly increased by the fact that many of them are irreplaceable without returning home and this alone should sharpen your precautions against theft. Taking an expensive yacht into poor areas inevitably puts temptation in the way of those ashore who see a potential goldmine sitting in their midst. Simply locking up will not keep out determined, professional thieves. Their crowbars will make short work of any resistance a yacht can offer and only if you have a well-prepared steel or aluminium boat do you stand the slightest chance that they might give up.

You have certain things in your favour. Few thieves want to run the risk of confrontation. They are generally fairly hyped up and nervous themselves as they work, so will avoid bumping into someone if possible. After our confrontation with thieves we *always* left the companionway hatch wide open with one light and the stereo cassette on whenever the boat was left during an evening. The cassette player was the auto-reverse type that played alternate sides of the tape automatically, so would provide constant music until turned off. With the hatch open, light on and music playing softly it looked as though somebody was on board. It could have been coincidence, but we never had a problem afterwards. A second dinghy, perhaps a cheap inflatable, trailing astern, would complete the ruse.

Use your knowledge of your boat to trick potential thieves. Every boat has dozens of little hidden nooks and crannies, behind linings and in lockers, that could house an envelope with important papers and travellers' cheques or cash. A friend of ours kept all his cash in an old Duckham's grease tin, impeccably cleaned out on the inside and put amongst the other maintenance materials in the paint locker.

Unless a padlock is situated in a specially-designed tight corner where a thief can't get a crowbar or hacksaw at it, it will be useless and certainly won't stop anyone with the slightest determination from getting down below. A better method is doing away with padlocks altogether and having a strong stainless steel pin inside that drives

A determined thief is very hard to stop although a little pyschological as well as physical deterent can do wonders  *(Yachting Monthly)*

right up through the strengthened companionway. We made one using bungy cord as a spring and with a light control line leading back into an aft locker with camcleat it looked quite unobstrusive.

Most aluminium hatches can be ripped open within seconds. A better arrangement is to have closely-spaced steel 'prison' bars put under the deck protecting the opening. Leave the hatches undogged and in this way they won't be damaged. In a steel or aluminium boat the bars can be welded in place, but on other forms of construction they are welded to a single strap which itself is bolted right through the deck. This stands a good chance of holding if the bolts are beyond arm's reach from the hatch. The forehatch must have a removable frame of bars, as the crew are likely to use this for access. One system, suggested to me by George Taylor, is a steel foc'sle ladder which swings up under the deckhead covering the opening at the same time.

Wooden companionway washboards sitting in wooden slides can be broken into very easily by splitting the wood. If you are serious about preventing thieves, the best way is to replace these by using heavy sectioned aluminium or stainless steel U-channel bolted or welded in place. A single or perhaps two washboards can then be made by using ¼in aluminium sheet with plywood screwed on to add bulk and stiffness.

A built-in safe, particularly on a steel or aluminium boat where it can be welded in, seems like a good idea at first, but Mark and Amanda Wilson, cruising their 43ft steel cutter *Hanne IV* in Brazil, found to their cost that when a thief finds a safe he will look no further and once in the cabin out of sight will work until he opens it. Having been completely cleaned out, they now recommend hiding places instead, but don't put all your eggs in one basket or money in one place.

Dinghies, particularly those with outboards, are prime pickings and it's a sad state of affairs that in some cases the culprits have been other yachtsmen. There can be quite a trade in tenders. The transient nature of their owners means that a thief only need hide a dinghy and outboard for a few weeks until the owners have gone. If he then steals another and hides it he can often enough sell the first to the new losers. Inflatable dinghies like Avons and Zodiacs are so common, and often indistinguishable, that they are as good as currency, several hundred pounds tied only with a bowline to the harbour wall. Sometimes the best answer is to do some local enquiries and put the word about that you're prepared to buy your dinghy and/or outboard back. This may take some swallowing, but the inconvenience of losing a dinghy is great, not to mention the fact you might wait months before reaching somewhere to buy a replacement.

There are two ways around the dinghy dilemma. One is to have a dinghy that is so disreputable as to be not worth stealing or make sure the outboard is firmly locked on and the dinghy *always* attached with a stainless-steel wire painter whether it's ashore or alongside the boat.

Personal security ashore is not easy either. We were robbed in Lisbon and it all took place so quickly and smoothly we hardly knew it had happened at first. The best answer is to carry as little of value on you as possible and don't look too rich (by local standards, not yours), with a lot of jewellery, cameras and so on. Buy a good money belt, but don't take from it in conspicuous places. If you sew in an extra Velcro fastener it makes a noise, so you hear someone trying to steal from it. In dodgy surroundings we adopted the routine that Lou Lou walked in front of me carrying any valuables. If there were any problems I could see what was happening and had a start on the thief.

Finally, that great old seaman Joshua Slocum said 'it is well known that one cannot step on a tack without saying something about it'. He therefore sprinkled carpet tacks over *Spray*'s decks in the Magellan Straits when he expected trouble, and sure enough late one night he was woken by howls and splashes as natives discovered them and pounced over the side. In these days of sophisticated burglar alarms this may sound simplistic, but one person we know cut out a couple of pieces of old carpet to fit the cockpit seats and companionway entrance. She then liberally pierced them with hundreds of carpet tacks from underneath and lays them out before going to bed. She lives in fear of the night she ever starts sleep-walking, but otherwise these adaptations of Slocum's methods are worth considering. The tack-laden carpets are rolled up and put away each morning.

### Chafe

Happily, with modern materials like stainless steel, plastic pipes and synthetic ropes and sails, the chafe on an ocean cruiser is no longer the major problem it used to be.

By the end of our 11,000 mile Atlantic circuit trip in *Euge* we hadn't put a single stitch into any of her sails. Although by then they needed to be valetted with odd little bits of damage and stitching sorted out, ostensibly there was nothing wrong with them because we always watched carefully for chafe. The same applied to all her sheets and lines. We had stainless 1 x 19 standing rigging which is very smooth for a sail to rub against. Stainless standing rigging is considerably more expensive than galvanised, but for reduction in future chafe is well worth the extra. The alternative is plastic pipe sleeved over the wire before splicing, but this increases the windage by two or three times.

Spreaders should be checked for any roughness and the spreader ends well parcelled with thin strips of mattress foam, well taped up. Other than this, the key to cutting out mainsail chafe is an easily-rigged tackle as a preventer which is *always* used when sailing off the

**Fig 28** The top few sail slides on a mainsail should be bound on with narrow webbing tape, finished off by sewing along their edges

wind. Removing the topping lift when the mainsail is being used significantly reduces irritating stitching and batten–pocket damage on the leech. Always hoist and lower the mainsail when on the wind, or in such a way that it wasn't dragged up against the standing rigging. The first two or three slides at the head of the sail get more strain than the others and the best method of attachment is with narrow webbing tape wound around several times, then sewed along its edges (see Fig 28).

Headsail chafe is a completely different ballgame. The most prominent design error is to have spreaders too long and which press into the genoa when it is hauled in tight. This is prevalent on many amateur and home-build plans. There are many ways around it. Though ocean cruisers don't generally need to go to windward much, when they do it's generally in anger and for a good purpose, so don't kid yourself that the problem doesn't exist. The first test is to determine how much performance is lost if the sail is eased enough for it to stop rubbing. Check tacking angles and boatspeed with the sail in tight and eased out. If this is insignificant, the spreader tips can be well parcelled and the sail have a sacrificial patch sewn on. Under way, make sure to check it regularly as fluctuating wind strengths can cause enough stretch and contraction in the sail to start the chafing when the wind drops slightly. If the performance loss is just too much, the only alternative is to shorten them, but don't do this without consulting the designer or a naval architect.

A common problem area for genoa chafing is the pulpit. Working sails can often be set on a strop high enough to clear the pulpit, but genoas on boats less than 40ft nearly always touch the pulpit when eased out. Attack any rough stainless welding with a file and if there are any sharp protuberances or fittings for the sail to rub against, such as the terminal fittings and welded eyes for the guardrails, a piece of plastic pipe, split and sewn in place can cover many of them. If the sail or stitching starts showing any signs of wear or damage, again a sacrificial patch will be necessary.

There is nothing you can do about headsail hank wear short of using high quality fittings, such as the French Goiot brand, from the outset. If your boat has galvanised rigging, make sure that the forestay is stainless, otherwise you'll have rust problems very quickly. With a roller-furling headsail, boltrope wear can be quite a nuisance especially if the gear is getting old and the extrusions are slightly worn. Sacrificial tabling works to an extent, but one is always limited by the width of the groove. Filing the edges of the extrusions can help to a degree, but ultimately one is faced with having to replace the extrusions. Figure 29 shows a simple method of easing a chafing problem common on many gears.

Chafe on lines can be eased, but rarely totally eliminated. The bowlines on the clew of a headsail for example are susceptible to wear. Make the sheets over-length so that every couple of years, after end-for-ending, they can be trimmed slightly to lose the chafed section. The same goes for halyards, especially for the spinnaker.

**Fig 29** A common point of chafe on a roller headsail is where the luff tape enters the extrusion, especially if there is any distance between this point and the drum. Lashing the tack to the extrusion solves the problem

Chafe occurs throughout a boat and it is worthwhile buying a few feet of half-round brass or stainless strip and fitting it in potential problem areas – all around the existing mooring fairleads, on the foot of the companionway, where self-steering lines rub slightly (these are killers – moving constantly) or maybe where the wire jackstays pass around the forward corner of the coachroof. Line up the lead of the kedge warp from stern fairlead to sheet winch and see if brass or stainless strip is required where it rubs on the cockpit coaming.

A short length of chain, to wrap around harsh mooring objects or over the edge of quaysides, will save your mooring lines but so will the way you use the warps and fairleads. In wild conditions a mooring rope that is taken through a tight bend will chafe away to nothing very quickly, no matter how smooth the fairlead or how much chafing gear you parcel it with. If you are moored in bad conditions watch tight corners, both on the boat and ashore where a large radiused bollard is much more preferable to a steel eyebolt.

# 23
## The Last Six Months

I'd always imagined that the final six months of our workaday lives before cutting ties and leaving would be a matter of pleasant evenings spent drawing up provisions lists, dreamily ticking off the charts we'd need on the Admiralty chart catalogue and making sure the boat had a well stocked bosun's locker. Then as the big day approached, we'd tie up all those little jobs, stow the pile of food just delivered on the quayside, say goodbye to friends and then off into the blue yonder. Little did I know . . .

It wasn't until we were almost ready to go that I realised how much time and money could have been saved had we attacked the last six months' preparation in an orderly and logical fashion. We considered the period very carefully, but still ended up keeping everything in our heads, and tackled jobs and problems as they arose. Had we taken stock of everything that needed doing from square one and listed jobs and their priorities, our lives would have been much simpler.

Very few people are in a position to drop everything suddenly and disappear to sea for a long period, so for the majority the idea will have been nagging for many years. It's not usually until eighteen months or two years before leaving that the plans come into focus and fixing the approximate date becomes possible. From this period the commitment to the project accelerates quickly and the disposal of house or flat and contents and a large chunk of your possessions and straightforward home comforts becomes quite hard. Devotion to the dream becomes apparent during this period and it is the point that many projects founder.

You will probably have an approximate departure date in your mind, so when you get to within 8-9 months of this the first move must be to fix the initial cruise plan, stage one. Having broadly decided where you want to go, buy a set of monthly routeing charts and start juggling the stage one cruise plan with dates, to establish D day (departure day) to within one or two weeks. Give yourself two or three weeks in hand to allow for the inevitable last-minute hold-ups.

Having decided the date you can start working out the amount of money you are likely to be able to get together before leaving and link this with terminating your employment and completing other business matters. In Great Britain, if you technically emigrate before you've earned a certain sum in that financial year you may be entitled to a substantial tax rebate, so this could influence the dates you fix.

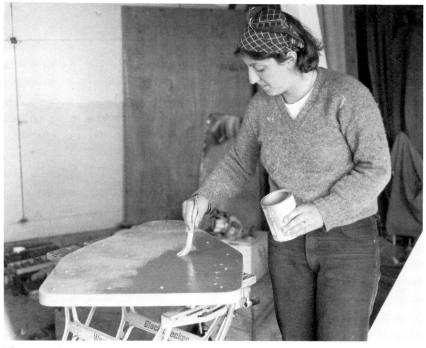

There are times when preparation seems never-ending. If time is getting tight and maybe the season's catching up on you, bear in mind that painting can be done anywhere. It's better to make off while the weather is still good with peeling paintwork than take on a bad storm in immaculate colours

Unfortunately the money side of cruising is crucial for most of us and a liberally allowed-for financial strategy covering the preparation period is imperative from an early date. This must be monitored carefully because the final six months is a highly expensive period, and before you know it things can get frighteningly out of hand, as a thousand and one small costs and expenses you never dreamed of start cropping up.

Tackle officialdom as early as possible. Find out early how you personally stand in terms of maintaining stamp payments, pension schemes, life insurances and so on while away, because when you venture into these paperwork empires with an out-of-the-ordinary request, months can pass waiting for a satisfactory answer. On our first trip we wanted to carry a Verey pistol aboard for distress signals (and neophytes that we were, for the possibility of piracy that we had been advised by 'experts' we would undoubtedly encounter). What should have been a fairly straightforward process of getting a Firearms Certificate through the local police became prolonged and complicated when a police messenger dropped our application off the motorbike on his way to the local government offices. This single incident held us up for nearly a week when we were otherwise ready to go and, had it not been for their later kindness and efficiency, could have taken much longer. We had applied for the certificate in plenty of time but had not allowed for such slip-ups.

Now aware of the extent of administrative work that will need clearing up, and with much of it in hand, it is important to review health in general. This, and innoculations are dealt with by Dr John Prosser in Chapter 22, but time is of essence, and looking on the bleak side, they may tell you something that could alter your decision to leave. First aid and a basic medical understanding are important in a yacht that could be at sea for weeks, so enrol at least two crew on a comprehensive first aid evening class. The Cruising Association at Ivory House, St Katharine Dock, London E1 organise excellent yachtsman's first aid courses. Although you need a strong stomach to look at some of the colour slides, the lectures teach you how to cope in an emergency and deal with the more common cuts, burns and ailments. Local adult education centres and yacht clubs also run similar courses so seek out the best in your area.

The days before you leave will be hectic, and you will probably spend a great deal of time achieving very little, so it is important to get as much done on the yacht as possible, a few months in advance. If her refit is incomplete, she needs modifications, engine servicing, sails checked, or any alterations, plan to complete these in plenty of time, otherwise, as the final weeks approach the jobs simply don't get done. Head the list with the jobs that affect seaworthiness. If she hasn't been painted, or items of inessential new gear haven't been fitted, don't worry. You can always stop for a quiet month or two further south and finish things off.

Get important sea trials done early as well because the last thing you'll have time to do in the last few weeks is go sailing. One of the last jobs on *Foreigner*'s refit was to build and fit new rudders, which, in itself, didn't take long. However we made the foolish mistake of leaving until late the fabrication of the new pintles and gudgeons. When we 'phoned the only galvanising plant within 75 miles, the company was closing down for a two week summer holiday the following day and could not treat our fittings. We finally managed to get them galvanised, but it wasn't without a lot of persuasion and a long fast car drive, which took the better part of a day I'd not budgeted on wasting.

About six weeks before you are due to leave, order all your charts, pilots and any other literature. This leaves it late enough to maintain relatively up-to-date charts and publications, but not too late for the chart agent to get any he doesn't hold in stock.

At this stage as the tempo begins to rise, you remember a host of little items that need seeing to, affairs that need clearing up, awkward spares to get hold of, provisions waiting to be collected, plus chasing the non-delivery of other items. A small notebook and pencil should

This kind of attitude to provisioning stems from the great days of Chichester and Knox-Johnston; good cooks will strike a careful compromise between this extreme (which only weighs the boat down and invites monotony) and fresh provisions in every port

live in your pocket so as soon as you remember something you can jot it down immediately.

To add to the confusion, you'll probably experience little nervous doubts and with long hours working and sleepless nights going over everything in your mind, the temptation to rush through everything and be away from it all finally is very strong. Despite this it pays to plan your time-table to leave the final two weeks theoretically completely clear. At the start of our first venture we still had one or two things to buy and do but on the whole we left the period free. We considered ourselves and our yacht well prepared, but nevertheless during the final two weeks we were rushed off our feet and never had a minute to spare.

Somebody had mentioned our plans to the local newspaper, which subsequently put our faces on the front page, having the effect of summoning just about everyone we'd ever known to come and visit. However, on the positive side, it was only being recognised from the newspaper at the police station that procured us our Firearms Certificate, a document which usually takes about three or four weeks to process, in less than three hours!

There is no need to over-emphasise the level of activity during the final weeks, and this can be eased considerably if you have a car available. More by accident than intention, we still owned our car during the week before we left on our first voyage due to a seasonal slump in car sales which meant we were unable to sell it and it was absolutely invaluable. The fact that I drove over 1,000 miles in short trips during our last seven days speaks for itself. Although I wouldn't advise keeping your own car until this late, if you have access to another it is well worth using it, and, in the interests of keeping to schedule, even justifiable to rent a car or van for the final week or so.

Finally, as you sail out of harbour, the months of hard work are over and you begin to unwind – and almost immediately remember the things you've forgotten, the business you've left unfinished, the chandlery you've ordered which probably arrived the day after you sailed and a host of other minor items that would be better cleared up. It is a good idea to pre-plan as an extension of your preparations, a rendezvous with an informed friend or relative about a week after you've left, and a little further down the coast, rather than heading out into deep water immediately. You can arrange with him or her over the telephone to bring any hangover mail, late deliveries or anything else you may have left behind. We did just this and sailed from the rendezvous with completely clear minds.

The overall success of a project involving tearing up so many roots and leaving home waters for a future with so many variables and unknown factors is very closely related to the integrity of the initial preparation. The Slocum Society researched, some while ago, the number of people who actively planned to go away on an extended passage within a year and later compared it to those who actually went. Of 105 people who planned to leave, only five got away. While there were individual reasons for each failure I am sure that most of them stemmed from the fact they simply were not ready, either materially or psychologically and put the trip off until next year – and the next, and the next. Without the need for the sometimes unrealistic attitude of 'get everything finished in good time', if your preparation and its priorities are assessed and planned from the very beginning there is no reason why you should not be one of the five.

# Acknowledgements

My sincerest thanks go to both J. D. Sleightholme and Andrew Bray, successive Editors of *Yachting Monthly* for not only giving me realistic encouragement to make the break and go initially, but also for their patience and great support before, during and especially after each of our ocean cruising projects (not to mention the writing and illustrating of this book). Without Des and Andrew's contribution, interest and help, our cruising life may never have got very far.

I would also like to thank John Prosser, a keen and well-travelled doctor, who put a lot of effort and the benefit of his experience into the medical section in Chapter 22. Finally, my wife Lou Lou for her constant help and contributions during the writing and editing of this book.

# Index